SOCIAL
THINGS

~

SOCIAL THINGS

~

AN INTRODUCTION TO THE SOCIOLOGICAL LIFE

~

CHARLES LEMERT

Fourth Edition

ROWMAN & LITTLEFIELD PUBLISHERS, INC.
Lanham • Boulder • New York • Toronto • Plymouth, UK

ROWMAN & LITTLEFIELD PUBLISHERS, INC.

Published in the United States of America
by Rowman & Littlefield Publishers, Inc.
A wholly owned subsidiary of The Rowman & Littlefield Publishing Group, Inc.
4501 Forbes Boulevard, Suite 200, Lanham, Maryland 20706
www.rowmanlittlefield.com

Estover Road
Plymouth PL6 7PY
United Kingdom

British Library Cataloguing in Publication Information Available

Library of Congress Cataloging-in-Publication Data

Lemert, Charles C., 1937–
    Social things : an introduction to the sociological life / Charles Lemert. — 4th
ed.
        p. cm.
    Includes bibliographical references and index.
    ISBN-13: 978-0-7425-5935-6 (pbk. : alk. paper)
    ISBN-10: 0-7425-5935-1 (pbk. : alk. paper)
    1. Sociology. 2. Sociology—History. I. Title.
HM435.L46 2008
301—dc22   2008004923

Printed in the United States of America

∞™ The paper used in this publication meets the minimum requirements
of American National Standard for Information Sciences—Permanence of
Paper for Printed Library Materials, ANSI/NISO Z39.48-1992.

For
SANG-JIN HAN

No one I know lives the sociological life more fully.

And, in memory of
CHET MEEKS (1973–2008)

He lived so well and died far too soon.

Contents

~

GLOBAL THINGS

PREFACE TO THE
FOURTH EDITION

~

One of the unsolved puzzles surrounding social things is how we who live with them come to understand them when they have changed.

Since *Social Things* was first published in 1997, it has become clear that something fundamental has changed in the more salient of the structures of social things. When the second edition appeared in 2002, it was obvious that an adequate name for those changes was globalization, which led me then to introduce a new chapter, "Global Methods." Global methods are those refinements of sociological competence whereby people now must learn how to interpret the stories they download from departed kin or friends who beckon them from far away global places to their search for a better life.

When, just a few years later, the third edition appeared in 2005, global things had become even more inescapably weird. Hence, still another new chapter was added, "Global Things Queer the Social." The sociological life must now be lived without shelter from the wider global realities that are never as straightforward as one might like. Now, still later, as the twenty-first century settles in, it is apparent that social life, once nestled more or less predictably in the hairy arms of a nation, is suspended in the uncertain virtual space between the communities and neighborhoods of the older national societies and the new global realities themselves. The palpably queer difference is in the speed with which a web of social ties can fly away as jobs disappear, civil strife and disease enter, and war and its counter measures distort the normal course of daily life.

Now, in 2008, what had begun to surface in the early years of the twenty-first century seems all the more confirmed. Just as previously it had appeared that one cannot think of social things without also trying to figure out the global situation, so now that necessity seems all but certain to be here to stay for the foreseeable future—perhaps then forever.

The thing about social things, even when they become global things, is that one never knows exactly what they will do.

However the world turns in the years ahead, the new global situation is evidently one in which we must not only learn new and effective global methods for the living of the sociological life, but we must be willing to think about and talk about aspects of social life that once were kept in private or, at least, in the dark. However shocking the new chapter 11 in the previous edition may have seemed to some, if not to others, it now is apparent that frank talk about sex of all kinds and of the pleasures and threats associated with it is but the least of the disturbing subjects that must be taken up in public life.

In 2008, the terrors of the attacks on the towers of American economic and military power on September 11, 2001 have given the word "terror" a new social meaning. Some in the North American and European communities speak of terrorism as if it were the kind of practice engaged solely by people from far away places deluded by strange religious and political ideologies. Yet, a growing number of clear thinking people have come to realize that terrorism comes in many forms—including, sad to say, the military misadventures in Iraq and Afghanistan led by the United States government. Many brave young men and women have lost their lives defending an uncertain war policy. Yet, also, many innocents in villages and cities across these two war-torn lands have been slaughtered—and slaughtered by terrible violence brought down by agents of the global powers as well as by those who operate from the caves and shadows of mountains and deserts. To learn to live the sociological life is to learn to accept things as they come down, then to imagine why they are what they are. We live now in a time when life requires us to refrain from jumping too quickly to conclusions shaped by what we once believed to be true and good.

Now, as the first decade of the twenty-first century draws to an end, one of the sacred truths of any earlier time must be open to some doubt. Everyone in her right mind wants to know and to do the good. But what the good might be for the global family of man is less certain than for centuries it once has been. What is the good of war and violence, of disease and starvation, of economic inequalities and uneconomic deterioration of the natural environment? It was once thought that these things, though admittedly evil in themselves, were necessary in the long run to assure peace, justice, and a good life for all human beings. Now, it seems more and more that violence, disease, poverty, and pollution do not yield so rapidly to good intentions, even when those intentions are backed by remarkable advances in technology and science. One day they may. But today so far they have not—and this stubborn fact of life makes living the sociological life harder still, if not so hard as to be without its powers and pleasures for those able to live it.

This edition of *Social Things* retains its original allegiance to the long-standing article of sociological faith first laid down by Emile Durkheim—that social things are facts in and of themselves and that they can be known and understood. What is added now, however, is a bit more thought on one of the obstacles to that knowledge. Sociologists, both professional and practical, have long realized that understanding social things is a practical competence, but also that it is a competence often beclouded by fear and other inflictions that cause us to ignore—or, better, to want not to know—some of the realities that beset us in the daily grind. Now, in the fact of events relatively new to human experience, we must consider more directly that the failure to know and to seek the good in social life may be due less to threats made by evil people or happenings than to, in a simple word, *incompetence*. There is no new chapter on the subject, but there are, here and there, considerations of this strange fact of social life.

Just as 9/11 has become a symbol of the new social meanings of global terror, so now the handling of the Katrina disaster in New Orleans, like the war in Iraq, may be a symbol of systematic incompetence. Yes, I realize that some reading this will read it as an outright political bias on my part. To them, I would say that *incompetence* has always been with us. Global powers have long put themselves in a weakened position by acting, or failing to act, because they believe they knew better. A very liberal government in the United States did just this in Vietnam in 1965, just as a highly cultured civilization in Germany gave itself over to Hitler's evil ways in the 1930s. There are many other cases throughout history that certify the fact that systematic incompetence is not unique to one or another type of political thinking.

I admit to a reluctance to preface a book on so wonderful and exciting a subject as that of the sociological life with such a sad note. Yet the truth is that truth, however hard to come by, can only be come upon when we face *all* possibilities. In the end, the attempt to live honestly, even without knowing all that might be known, is the important thing. If you will look about you, and look deeply into your own life, you will find, as I have, that whatever terrors there are, life is filled with possibilities, even pleasures, awaiting those who take social things on their own terms. If they are more available to those able to buy and read a book this does not mean that they are forever hidden from the whole of human community.

Charles Lemert,
New Haven, Connecticut

INTRODUCTION

~

Just around the corner from an apartment we once had in Brooklyn there was a small deli we visited for milk and the morning papers. The owner kept such long hours that we could drop in late Saturday evenings for the early sections of the Sunday *Times*. Since the sports and front pages were not available in that neighborhood until the morning, I would return for them the next morning. Being by nature always a little unsure of myself, I would on these occasions prepare in my mind a small account of why I now was taking some more paper. "It was I who last night. . . ." But before I could finish, he'd wave me home. Though he never knew my name, he knew who I was. Once I had come out in the bitter cold without my money. Again, as I fiddled through empty pockets, he sent me along with my milk for breakfast. He trusted me to pay the next time.

Then one day he was gone. Murdered for the Friday night receipts, probably for drug money. Thereafter, life was changed—grotesquely for his wife and seven children, but also for me and my wife and everyone in the neighborhood. It was not just that we suddenly felt ourselves at a risk we had ignored until then but that this kind man, nameless to most of us on the block, was lost forever. His violent disappearance made life less than it had been.

He was Abdul Kareem Alsahybi. This I learned from newspaper accounts of his murder. He had come to the United States from Yemen to build the small business that would give life and possibility to his children. It is hard work to keep a local deli going. The profits are slim, painfully won. This is why Mr. Alsahybi and others in his trade are forced to install lottery machines. On a good day, these instruments of state-sponsored gambling can bring in more than all the newspapers and sandwiches combined. These were the gains for which he died.

Had I not known him, and only read of the murder in the papers (had I, that is, even noticed the back-page story), his death would have remained in a vaguely realized state of distant occurrences. It would have remained, thus, amid the millions of events that fill and form daily life—deeds and doings we notice, if at all, as we surf the channels of world news. Whenever we stop to think about them, these events—each one a triumph or tragedy to another in the sorority of humankind—rise up real before us.

Whatever our differences from each other, all of us live in society with others. In the abstract, society is a mystery. But in the press of daily life, society is an innocent bumping against others. They, like us, rush to buy their morning papers and get the coffee they had not taken time to brew at home; or, unlike many of us, they hustle for coins to buy whatever brew will warm bones chilled by a long, unsheltered night on the pavement.

When forced to think about it, we know that others go about their lives much as we do, even those who must beg their food and warmth. Others do their own things in their own ways. Somehow, the combined force of all these comings and goings, givings and gettings, can be said to be society. Since we hardly ever notice what others are doing, it is certain that we never actually see this so-called society in action, much less think about it, without some good reason.

Yet, society gets under our skins. It is ours to use, but it is not ours alone. It is in our heads and guts, but it reaches well beyond our psychologies. It is, thus, under our individual skins, but we also expect it to be under the skins of those we encounter—tugging, hinting, proposing, judging, punishing, comforting, and, yes, even depriving and frightening us. Amazingly, these social things work, imperfectly but well enough, to keep the social whole going.

Most of the time you and I have no good and practical reason to think about so abstract a consideration as "society." Then, unexpectedly, something happens. One day, we are caught unawares by the unusual arising out of the ordinary and we are brought home to the reality of social things. When people are thus surprised, they become sociologists as best they can.

There are many different kinds of sociologies, some of them academic ones, but the most important ones are the sociologies whereby people make sense of their lives with others. Literally speaking, sociologies are nothing more than logics of social things. Though some persons are specially trained in the logic, or science, of social things, even this qualification begins where it begins for us all. Advanced education is not required for a person to recognize the truth of some things.

Most people, most of the time, have a good enough common sense of what goes on in their social worlds. If they did not, their survival would be at even greater risk than for many it already is. Mr. Alsahybi just "knew" that I was trustworthy. His trust was the elemental social glue of his business—it was the basic social logic whereby he dealt with people and inspired them to deal with him. He lived a sociological life even if he seldom had time at the end of the day to think through, much less read about, what that logic was. Everyone lives with sociologies of this kind. They might not always serve us well, as late one Friday night Mr. Alsahybi's might not have served him well when he met a man not to be trusted. Life is not perfect. It can even be deadly. But where life works, it works because most people live their sociologies. When they have the time to study the world of social things, and to work through what to think and say about them, they are able to lift their native and practical understandings of these things into the light of clear thinking, then perhaps even to change their worlds, thus to add power to the living of their lives.

The logic of social things always stumbles at first against the mysterious fact that all people, notwithstanding their varied and often separated neighborhoods or tribes, are connected to each other. Just how these connections come into being and maintain themselves is hard to say, but the saying of it, in plain or fancy words, is where the sociological life begins. Why did I feel such pain and loss at the murder of this good man? What were the social filaments that stretched from me and mine to a man from Yemen whose life was so utterly different as to be beyond my true, untutored understanding? They must have been stretched delicately by his unthinking trust of his neighbors, of people who were perhaps as strange to him as he was to them. But what of the more complicated social web in which we in the larger world, in spite of our severe differences from each other, are inexplicably suspended in uncertain, dependent reliance on each other? From the passing of coins or lives at the corner store to the mysterious whole of it all, we all live amid social things, which are, in turn, weirdly inside us as we bump about.

Individuals are who they are only partly because of what they do with what they have. They are also who they are because of what the wider social world gives or takes away. My kind neighbor in the gentle passing of his days gave his children a life, for which his was taken away. Both the giving and the taking were, at different moments, given and taken not simply by the power of his own or his murderer's individual actions. They were equally, perhaps more so, the effects of the force of social things—of the commerce in that store, of the foolishness of state politics for which lotteries have become good public business, of the trade in drugs and desperation that brought a murderer to his door, of whatever transpired in the life of an unapprehended and unknown person that caused him to kill as well as steal, and of so much more that, it would seem, no one can describe it all. Yet these social things are described—by some who are professionally trained to the task, and by most of us when we try from time to time to think, as we usually do not, about those social forces that mysteriously inspire feelings for strangers who move our hearts to the realization that, whoever we are, we are not alone.

This is a book about the sociological life. It is, to some degree, a book of stories, some of them told out of my own experience. I speak openly of my life because stories of the kind I tell are the means by which we all discover our best, if imperfect, understandings of social things. Sociologies begin as people remember and talk, putting to words the sense and logic— and on occasion, the poetry—they are able to make of what has happened.

But do not allow yourself to be fooled into thinking that personal stories are merely personal, confined somehow to small interactions of local people. If the story of a man from Yemen contains trace effects of the larger social worlds, no less is true of my story, or yours. Social things are, as I will explain, structured. In simple terms, this means that certain global forces brought Mr. Alsahybi to Brooklyn just as others brought a murderer to his door. The world being what it is, it is possible that the same economic deprivations that urged him to move from Yemen are linked at close remove to those that drive others to steal and kill for drugs. He was killed by an individual. But neither he, nor we, would encounter the individuals who trust or threaten us were it not for social forces beyond our reach, though well within the pulse of daily life.

When people feel that pulse, and stop to think, then tell others about the experience, they are led into a wider world of things in which even the smallest of local givings and takings carries the energy of the larger social forces. You may well want to suspend for a while the natural inclination to think of small and large social things as though they were of different orders. The distinctions we often make between the local and global, the personal and the larger structured world, are convenient to thought. But, in the living of lives, these things are impossible to distinguish, even when most of us find it easier to see the actions in the street below than the force of global structures that cause men and women to move about, sometimes under the cover of night, to find a way to feed their kids or their habits.

Books, even storybooks, have their logics. This one begins with the idea that a more exact name for sociology could be sociological competence. More often than not, people get by without thinking all things through. Rather, they simply tell the stories of their worlds. The power of stories to move life ahead is good evidence that, behind all the ways we screw up from time to time, there is an abiding competence—a knack for recognizing, or talking about, what is going on.

This sociological competence, even when it fails us (or we fail it), is what explains the remarkable fact that people are able, with very little instruction, to figure out how to practice their lives with others. This life is, after all, composed out of a series of habits and practices whereby, when we repeat and repeat, we often get it right. The grace of social life is that, within the limits of the law and other forms of public scrutiny, those fortunate enough to be fed and continuously sheltered with an address are free to practice their lives as they wish. Some practices—like killing for dope, even for food—are outside the rules. And, even in the course of mundane life, there is always some damn busybody ready to tell us where we went wrong. But, generally speaking, the lives we practice and play out are our attempts to contend as best we can, often quite inventively, with the pain and pleasure of the social things, great and small, with which we are presented.

Sociology is also an academic discipline. I assume that many, but not all, who read this book will read it because it has been assigned them by a schoolteacher. Others will assign it to themselves. While those subjected to formal instruction in sociology are likely to entertain the idea that sociology is a thing to be studied instead of lived, I believe that sociology is, first of all, a thing lived. This conviction does not mean that I think the formal study of the living is somehow a false copy of the real thing. The academic study of sociology is, in itself, one of the more important cultural resources in any society. Thus, this book spends an entire section telling the story of how the academic discipline arose in the late nineteenth century, and since, from the practical demands of social life. Some might call this part of the book a history. And so it is. It is the story of the men and women who, in coming to terms with the lives they led and lead, found and find a way to tell their stories of social things—and to tell them in words of broad appeal to many beyond their own family picnics and neighborhood cafes.

Similarly, the third part of the book introduces the four powerful questions that all sociologies, whether academic or practical, must try to answer. How do people deal with the overwhelming power of social structures they cannot see? How do they live as subjects amid such big and mysterious social forces? How do they measure the meaning of their lives against the array of social differences they encounter, even while rushing, coffee-less, for the last bus? And, by what methods do people figure out how to live with themselves in the face of the structured differences? These are the inquiries of the formal study of social things, just as they are questions the answers to which shape the events of the sociological life. Part four, thereby, introduces the ways that globalization challenges, changes, or otherwise affects the basic questions of the sociological life.

This, then, is, if not exactly a poem, a mystery book, a tale told of social things—a tale told in order to encourage others to tell their own from the heart of the sociological wisdom buried within anyone who carries his babies across the oceans; or, at the other extreme, within anyone who stumbles at early light into a small deli run by a kind man already smoking the first of a long day's cigarettes and trusting us not to be the one who takes it all away.

THE SOCIOLOGICAL LIFE

IMAGINING SOCIAL THINGS, COMPETENTLY

He was amazing to me, a miraculous boy. In school, I tried to write as he wrote (he won the prize in penmanship), talk as he talked (he *always* had something confident to say), and walk as he walked (he had an awkward gait but he always knew where he was going). This was David Bennett. In the 1940s in the less-than-classy western suburbs of Cincinnati there were few heroes. Our fathers had come back from the war bitter and broken, not at all brash and ready to build the American Century. We hardly knew the bravest generation. But David Bennett, he was something else. We never knew what became of his mother. In those days, little white boys born to merchants or professionals of modest success knew almost nothing about separation or divorce. When our lives were disrupted, we were taught to look away in silence, even to pretend that everything was just fine. I remember my grandfather's wake as the best family party ever. His face, made over to cover lines the pain of cancer had etched, rose just above the edge of the coffin around which we children played as we always had in his presence. We knew of death, of course, but in our polite and polished bourgeois world, divorce was unheard of. One of the guys said that David's mother was living in Kentucky somewhere. Why?

Then it happened that his father grew ill and died. David was left with Gramps and his grandmother. Many years later, when we were all in college, Gramps was much beloved by the boys in David's fraternity house. Such a character he was! But not the kind of parent-substitute a small boy dreams of. We could never play with David on Saturday mornings because, we were told, he was required to mop and wax the kitchen floor. And he was never, never allowed out after seven in the summers, and this is just the beginning of a long list of what we thought were harsh domestic rules—rules we could comprehend no better than divorce or separation.

But, remarkably, David seemed to know just how to master all that befell him. He accepted his losses and obeyed the demands of his upbringing. He had the best grades. The teachers loved him. In spite of this, he was our friend. He beat me out for the last spot on the school basketball team. So what? When I last heard of him, more years ago than I can remember, he was a successful doctor, living somewhere outside Chicago.

Some people are like that. They know just how to get by, often with a grace that cannot be taught. When I grew up a little more, I was surprised to learn that I too had some of that grace. Still later, when I was able to think about it even more, I realized that most people, even those who could never hope to go to medical school, had this surprisingly durable human quality that allowed David to overcome and thrive.

This quality—one might even call it a competence—turns out to be widely distributed among humans. Not only do most people enjoy the benefits of this competence, but it often seems to come to the fore especially when things are as bad as they can get.

Across the world from Cincinnati where David and I dealt with the losses and pains of our otherwise secure worlds, other children of our generation faced far worse terrors. Some children, like many today who suffer the violence of poverty and dangerous streets, were exposed to the brutality of political terrors they could barely understand, even when they had to. One such child of my generation grew up to write a book about his childhood in Poland under the reign of Soviet military police during the gathering storm of the Second World War.

> Since the time of our house search, Mother does not let us take off our clothes at night. We can take off our shoes, but we have to have them beside us all the time. The coats lie on chairs, so they can be put on in the wink of an eye. In principle we are not permitted to sleep. My sister and I lie side by side, and we poke each other, shake each other, or pull each other by the hair. "Hey, you, don't sleep!" "You, too, don't sleep!" But, of course, in the midst of this struggling and shoving we both fall asleep. But Mother really does not sleep. She sits at the table

and listens the whole time. The silence of our street rings in our ears. If someone's footsteps echo in the silence, Mother grows pale. A man at this hour is an enemy. An enemy is a terrifying figure. Who else would come around at this hour? Good people are afraid; they are sitting hidden in their homes.

—Ryszard Kapuściński, *Imperium* (1994)[1]

These were Polish children in the village of Pinsk, sometime in 1939. The oppressive secret police of that time had already deported their father. They were children just the same, able to play in the dark against a fear they understood well enough. Like them, millions of people lie awake at night, terrified that terrible men will come, sent by evil to visit fear on children when and where they are—once in Italy and Germany, then in Russia and China, then in Afghanistan and Iraq, then in Rwanda and Darfur, tomorrow who knows where. But many people facing such terrors get by, often with humor.

What is this quality of human resilience, this competence that sustains and enriches human life, even against the odds? It is, to be sure, not a simple thing. Certainly, it encompasses what is often called the "human spirit," just as it embraces "tough-mindedness," "street smarts," "grit," and other such attributes associated with the best, most determined, and most transcendent powers of human creatures. But it also includes, in a significant way, something you may never have thought of, or even perhaps realized existed.

Even if the world in which they live is degraded by poverty or violence, most people get by because they are endowed with sociological competence. This seemingly native, highly practical, virtually ubiquitous capacity sustains us individually, but it also contributes mightily to our ability to form and keep social relations with others. Without it, social life would be impossible. Without it, every time we entered a new and different social situation, we would be forced to learn anew what to think of it and how to behave. But, most of the time, we understand what is going on and where we fit in.

Think of the number of different situations you may have encountered just in the day you are reading this book. If you happen to be a student, it is possible that earlier this day you met in a room with others with whom you are making a class. To no one's amazement you already knew just what to do. When your teacher entered, for example, it is likely that all the students, whatever their ages and backgrounds, realized it was time, gradually, to fall silent and listen. If you happen to be a mother or a father stealing a few moments to read while the children play, it is likely that already more than once today you were required to referee some fight, kiss some bruised body part, or wipe away a tear. You may not feel entirely comfortable with how you did what you did, but it is likely you did it well enough. Most parents do this kind of thing as if by second nature.

It hardly makes a difference who you are, or what you do. Nearly all of us, most hours of most days, run into social situations filled with demands and potential risks we know, as if by instinct, how to handle. Greeting strangers, entering crowded rooms, asking the time of day, finding the right subway, ordering grease-laden burgers without fries, meeting deadlines, getting deadlines extended—all these, much more, and virtually all the little events out of which we compose the course of daily life entail sociological competence.

The sociological competence of which I speak is not, at least not initially, the trained competence of the professional sociologist. But what the professionals know and have to say depends on a competence you already possess without the benefit of special studies. Indeed, there could be, and would be, no academic discipline organized under the name "sociology" were it not the case that sociology itself is a commonly held skill of untrained people and, thus, an important feature of social life itself. This may seem a bit odd to say. The more customary attitude in our society is to think of sociology as a sometimes complicated, often jargoned, though usually interesting, field of formal study and research. It is, of course, but, before it can be this, sociology is something else.

What is this miraculously effective and possibly universal human quality? Consider again those small Polish children, or others like them elsewhere in the world. What got them through the nights was an ability to imagine the reality in which they were caught. They understood, it is clear, that they were in danger. They knew that the police had carried off their father in the night. They knew why their mother kept them dressed, why she never slept at night. Straightforward? Not quite. Remember these were children for whom the ideas of oppressive police-states, of communist or fascist ideologies and repressions, even of bad men and enforcers, were at best ill-formed. Their native sociological competence, though it served them well, could not have instructed them as to the subtleties of the wider world of totalitarian regimes—regimes that in time fell away only to be replaced by more of their awful kind. What those children, like others before and after them, understood was that there was danger around, and they were able to imagine creative ways to ward off the fear, even by so touchingly gentle a way as holding each other tight in a playful game of daring, teasing, but connecting, thus imagining the only truly safe place available—a place protected by their mother's vigil, the subject of their jokes.

How human beings form relations with each other is the central mystery of any sociology. What is now reasonably well known is that children and others perform such amazing feats of courage by means of a resilient capacity to imagine—that is, by their ability to hold in mind the wider world of others, the good alongside the evil, and thus to organize what must be done. Imagination of this sort is not dreamily removed from practical things, nor is it simply a psychological endowment. On the contrary, it thrives in the practical, and it seems to be not so much an individual instinct as a common social sense. Frightened children have it with each other. We all have it, most of the time, in our dealings with the others we come upon.

Whenever you enter a room and "just know" you don't belong there, when you see a stranger on the subway and understand intuitively that it is safe to return his not-quite-delivered smile, when you are introduced to someone elegantly dressed in a certain way and know she is not to be called by her first name even if she offers it—these are among the evidences for the sociology in each of us. They may seem to be trivial manners by contrast to the urgency of survival through dark nights. And so they are. But, however small, they are not unimportant. They may seem inconsequential just because they come to us so naturally. But think of what life would be like if we regularly encountered people who were sociologically *in*competent.

One fine evening, some time ago, I met my wife at the late train after a week away. As the station cleared, we saw a woman alone and not quite sure where she was. It was dark and late, so we offered her a ride. She gladly jumped into the back seat. Then, in the few minutes it took to get her settled, she proceeded to tell us the most intimate details of her life, including how her husband had just bilked her of millions of dollars, that various famous people she had consulted thought it was terrible, and that, by the way, "I am telling the truth." She may have been, but it was hard to believe. Though her plight may have been real, something important was missing in her dealings with us. In such situations, the normal competency rule is something like this: "Try to understand the circumstances of those to whom you tell your stories; make sure, if you can, that they want to hear what you have to say." All it would take is a few encounters like this one for most people to want to go hide, or at least to think twice about offering rides to strangers. This woman, whoever she truly was, clearly had a vivid imagination, but, it would seem, she was so upset by what had happened to her that her local sociological imagination was impaired. In those brief moments with us, she could not think of a world in which one needs an invitation before telling all to kindly strangers willing to help, but far more eager to hold each other after a week apart.

Social life, whether among passing strangers at local stations or throughout the whole of complex society, depends unforgivingly on the ability of members to understand social things competently. This competence is the key ingredient in their ability to enter imaginatively into the social realities all about. That most people can, and do, is itself a miracle of sorts. What makes this so surprising is that we all know that the competence is not something we normally think about. It is not even something we are always able to provide an account of when called upon to do so. Where exactly did you learn to avoid some strangers while welcoming others, or learn not to defer to some people while giving others full formal regard? Most of us got this competence from somewhere, and at a very young age. It is so natural that, when on those rare occasions someone asks us to discuss this skill, we are more likely to be annoyed than intrigued by the request.

Sociological competence is much like our native ability to use the language we hear as infants. All of a sudden, one day, a child begins to speak, soon in sentences, eventually without pointing, eventually in reasonably correct forms of the past and future tenses. ("Daddy, I saw some sheeps on the way home!") A child does this sometime late in the second year of life or so, and without benefit of any organized instruction in grammar. Much the same happens, though at a somewhat later age, with sociological competence. The learning may be rough, and in need of encouragement or a few gentle spankings and playground pinches or punches, but it too comes relatively easily, and quite early. Some people hate to study sociology for the same reason they hate to study grammar: "I already know this stuff. Why give it a fancy name?" This is true, of course, for a great deal of our sociological competence. Most of us know a lot already—but not everything.

What we know and how we know it is a sociological competence. The very knowledge that thoughts of scary thugs who could take away your world can be faced and gotten over is a special kind of sociological competence. But we must also be aware that there is a persistent problem with sociological *incompetence*, which is actually a more mysterious social thing than one might suppose.

All of us, some of the time, and some of us, much of the time, come up against situations we simply *cannot* understand. I could take voice lessons for the rest of my life and still would not be able to carry a tune. So severe is my musical incompetence that in church my daughter will snatch the hymnal from my hands and tell me to shut up. I love to sing but the sound I make is embarrassing. Something is wrong with the wiring that connects ear to brain to vocal chords. Others have their own flaws. They are part of life. But these are not what I mean by sociological *in*competence which, as by now you might realize, is a social thing.

Sociological incompetence requires the participation of others who may be in a position to so foul up the normal course of some aspect of social life as to injure those affected by their actions or failures to act. But those who screw social things up are not usually individuals acting on their own (though it certainly is true that some individuals are screw ups). What sociological incompetence refers to is a surprisingly normal aspect of large and complex social structures. Governments, schools, corporations, even armies can become so large and complicated that people in one part of the structure have no idea what people in another part are doing: or, more likely, they may assume that the other people are taking care of things. In the end, often, no one does the job or, worse yet, the several parts end up working at cross purposes and nothing gets done.

When late in August in 2005 Hurricane Katrina crashed down on the Gulf Coast of the United States, winds and water overwhelmed the levees meant to protect New Orleans. The city was flooded, as were many of the low-lying towns up and down the coast. Naturally, you might think that hurricanes and floods are natural events. Still, at about the same time, in the Indian Ocean, huge tidal waves destroyed as many homes as had Hurricane Katrina and killed many more people. But no one suggests that these tidal waves had been caused or could have been prevented by human intervention.

In the United States, however, nearly everyone of fair mind saw that the devastating effects of Katrina *could* have been limited, if not prevented, had the several governments responsible in the area taken the threat seriously and acted earlier than they did. For years it had been known that the water walls protecting New Orleans were not strong enough to protect against a major storm. For days it had been known that just such a storm was coming. And for hours during, as for months after, those responsible to protect the people on the Gulf Coast did, if not exactly nothing, very little—and very little of what they did was helpful to save lives that could have been saved, much less rebuild homes and neighborhoods that had been washed away. Years later much of the area remained in ruins and thousands of those who survived the storm have been, it seems, permanently displaced from their home towns and neighborhoods.

It is very hard to escape the conclusion that Hurricane Katrina, a natural event, came to be a social disaster because of the incompetence of city, state, and federal authorities who had sworn oaths to protect ordinary citizens. How does it happen that people are drawn to positions of responsibility, and then fail to do their sworn duty? Sometimes they are just plain not up to the job. But, again, sociological incompetence is a more complex and social thing than individual incompetence—even if not one entirely beyond the irresponsibility of individuals. In the case of Katrina, for many years federal officials did nothing with the technical knowledge that the levees were in need of repair; nor, at the last moment, did they heed the warnings that the coming storm required a mass evacuation of the cities and towns. State officials blamed the feds. Local officials and others went into hiding as the storm broke. People were left to fend for themselves fleeing to what safe havens they could find.

The storm was, indeed, terrifying and there is no reason that governmental officials would be any less terrified than locals whose lives and homes were at risk. But when one holds a public office, his fear is no excuse for his failures to keep the public trust. On the other hand, there is a degree of pardon to be taken from the fact that when big storms hit places where so many layers of government are responsible and a kind of structural incompetence inevitably takes over. The right hand does not know what the left is doing. Worse yet, the one, in his fear, thinks (or hopes) the other will do what is needed. In the case of Katrina a number of courageous individuals and a few nongovernmental agencies were the only ones that did anything competent—that is, did something that actually saved some lives.

You might say that sociological incompetence is a common possibility of complexly structured social things like governments, schools, prisons, hospitals, and other institutions of this sort. You might even add that they are possibilities just waiting for some damn fool to fail to do his job. When the fool is found, something deep within the social body erupts—a pus that oozes into the sewage brought up by the storm. Natural disasters happen as a matter of course. They may be provoked at a distance when human habits, like the environmental abuses warming the global climate, cripple the natural world; others like the tsunamis in the Indian Ocean just happen with no apparent human involvement. But social disasters are, always, the oozing up and out of sociological incompetence that falters before the complex demands of real and terrifying events. Incompetencies of this sort are neutral as to politics, religion, or another set of values or ideologies. They are social things—ones hard to avoid, but not at all beyond the ability of the competent to manage or prevent.

In a strange way the very existence of sociological incompetence is proof positive of the prior existence of sociological competence. We of course will never know what disasters might have come down upon us because some courageous individual or group saw the thing coming and stood in its way.

Everyone complains that the news media are always reporting the disasters. But how do you report on their preventions? Occasionally the cameras catch a hero in action—diving in to save a child, jumping out to take a blow meant for an innocent. But in these cases, the disaster is already on the verge of happening. What is hard to see are the ones that never even come close to public notice. Yet, we can be assured that the world would be more danger-ous than it already is were it not for those nameless individuals, ourselves occasionally included, who, often without knowing it, rely on their inner competence to save those near at hand.

The first accepted definition of sociology was given in 1894 by the French sociologist Emile Durkheim (1858-1917). Durkheim persuaded many who followed him that, as he put it, "social facts are things, that is, realities exter-nal to the individual."[2] *Sociology*, thereby, is the science of social things. Durkheim meant to insist, quite reasonably, that, as important as individ-uals are to what goes on around them, there are also certain things that are inherently, and without exception, social in nature. The status of these social things has ever since been a topic of debate among professional soci-ologists for the simple reason that it is obviously more difficult to define social things than it is individual ones.

When David Bennett went about being a brilliant student, a fair athlete, and a generally good guy even while being required to scrub the kitchen floor, his pals could observe what he did and how he did it. I could not tell you why he made the basketball team and I did not. But he did. His jump shot was ever so much more awkward than mine. This and many other of the uncount-able little things that made him a unique individual were plainly visible. The tougher question is, What were all the features of the complex dynamic of his family life that made him the kind of kid he was? His departed mother, his dead father, his grumpy gramps, and much else, including, even, the effects of a world war on his parents' marriage or of the conventions of postwar sub-urban culture in the United States—all these came together in such a way as to play a part in making him the unusual person he was. These influences on his behavior as an individual are social things. Without them, David would not have been who he was, and is today—out there somewhere, presumably still alive, caring for his patients, perhaps looking in on grandchildren of his own as they come up against the different social worlds.

But, even now that I am a trained and certified professional sociologist, I could only barely begin to suggest just how to go about discovering the workings of those social things. If complicated in the case of one good white boy from the American suburbs, think how much more complicated the task is when, say, someone tries to explain just what the Soviet imperium was and why it wanted to frighten little children and their mothers. This is a social thing of a very consequential kind. It is one thing to observe the facts of the deported fathers, vigilant mothers, and terrified kids. Quite another to give a coherent account of the social thing itself, of the Soviet imperium in all its vast operations upon millions of people. Yet, it can be done. As a matter of fact, that little boy who hid at night in 1939 grew up to be a world-famous writer and journalist, able in adult life to describe in compelling terms how his feelings of terror as a boy might have been produced by the social organization of the former Soviet Union. That Ryszard Kapuściński could write *Imperium* in 1993 does not mean that all, even most, children who suffered as he did in the 1930s grew up to describe the social things that had made their lives miserable. In fact, most people are unable to describe very many of the more complex social things that affect them. They could, of course, were they to undergo the training, and many do it without much education at all. But the basic fact is that most people know, more or less well, how to get by in daily life. They are sociologically competent, even when they lack the advanced sociological training to describe their competence.

About the same time in the 1930s when Ryszard Kapuściński was finding his courage as a child, there was another little boy, also in Poland, in much the same circumstance. Zygmunt Bauman (1925–) today lives in Leeds, England. He is one of the world's most brilliant and admired sociologists for his ability in many books to cut to the quick of our troubled worlds. But in the 1930s, he too was a young boy who had to face up to the threats that were tearing Polish society to pieces. First, the Soviets, then the Nazis, then again the Soviets had occupied his native land. As a young man, Bauman fought in the Free Polish Army (then aligned with the Soviets) against the occupying Nazi forces. He was in effect a freedom fighter against totalitarian threats of another kind from those Kapuściński had to contend with. Bauman today writes books like *Wasted Lives: Modernity and Its Outcasts* (2004). When he writes of wasted lives he is telling the honest story of how the proud promises of the modern world have failed so many—how war, poverty, ignorant pride, over-building, over-consumption have turned so many innocent human beings into, in effect, garbage. Some may find this strong but look about at the wasted lives you can spot in the dark alleys you hurry past, under the bridges you speed by, or in the remote refugee camps of Africa and Asia you click over as you search for a pleasing sit-com to dull the mind. Bauman and Kapuściński were in this sense both sociologists—the one in name, the other in practice. Both took the monsters of childhood by the neck, faced them down, then devoted their lives to writing of the nightmares that crop up for others as they too try to live in worlds that ought to be safer than they are.

This is the problem Emile Durkheim and most professional sociologists since his day have had to face. People know a lot about social things, but they cannot talk about them very well without some help or, perhaps, without a challenge of some kind. They, therefore, are inclined, quite naturally, to mistrust the reality of *social things*, that is, of things just as mysterious as David Bennett's seemingly weird family arrangement, or of a totalitarian state's unusually evil methods.

The challenge Durkheim took up was that of establishing sociology as a formal, academic discipline against the commonplace prejudice that other things are much more real. Psychology, economics, history, and political science have a much easier time of it because it is relatively easier to imagine what they are about—minds (or the like), markets or prices, the facts of some group or another's story, how and why people vote and govern as they do. Just why these might seem more imaginable than *social things* is itself a difficult question I will not even attempt to answer. Minds, markets, stories, and votes are hardly simple things. But, relatively speaking, they seem so to many people. By contrast, just about everyone considers social things— or, more familiarly, societies—abstract, abstruse, and fluffily vague. Most people are not wrong. Since Durkheim, and certainly before, sociologists of all kinds (including small children trying to sleep in the dark) have had to contend with this inconvenient, but most interesting, fact of social life.

Durkheim himself died before sociology became much of an organized and institutional part of the university. He died in 1917, during the First World War, when it seemed that modern Europe would collapse before the continuing inability of nations and their leaders to create a stable political environment in which their people could enjoy the benefits of the modern world.

Some years later, well after the Second World War had similarly failed to make the world a better place, another sociologist made an enduring attempt to define sociology. C. Wright Mills (1916–1962), who was born just the year before Durkheim died, defined sociology in a way that made clear what was unclear in Durkheim's definition. While Durkheim assumed that social things can be as readily imagined as other types of facts of the human condition, Mills came to the more honest, and accurate, conclusion that at least one class of social facts is normally unavailable to those not specifically trained to see them.

Imagine again those small Polish children in 1939. Too young to understand much at all about the Soviet brand of totalitarian oppression, they understood at best that something was terribly wrong, that the world somehow was filled with cruel men. Though little Ryszard grew up to understand full well who those men were and why they did what they did, as a child he could only huddle back into the trembling arms of his sister. Their attempt at a playful response, a game of a sad sort, was indeed an imaginative response to social facts they could experience but only dimly comprehend. While, it seems, these children did not come to one of the more common human conclusions in the face of such odds, they might have. It is not uncommon for terrorized children to take the terror into themselves and to conclude that, in some inexplicable way, the evil visited upon them is a result of something they did. While this is just one of several self-defeating conclusions, it is a familiar one. Adult women, boys and girls, minorities, the unjustly punished, victims of family violence, children of abusers or alcoholics, even an occasional white guy of privilege are all strongly tempted to place the blame for their misery on themselves. While there are many reasons for this (most of them psychological), the sociological explanation is that, when we live in small worlds, whether as children or adults, it is usually difficult to understand the larger social forces that affect us. The more powerful social things are, the less we are equipped to comprehend them without some extra work.

This basic fact of life lay behind C. Wright Mills's now famous definition of sociology as the work of the *sociological imagination*.[3] He meant that sociology is the activity by which persons of differing degrees of training and experience often learn eventually to create imaginative reconstructions of the larger structural forces that affect their lives. Without this sociological skill, they are left with the belief that the troubles in their lives are of their own doing, or perhaps the result of some abstract fate; but, in either case, they feel that these are matters with respect to which they should, and do, feel guilty. The sociological imagination refers to the ability of some to learn—often with good luck or coaching or perhaps with formal schooling—to realize that, just as often, one's *personal troubles* are in fact *public issues*. Those children in Poland feared, and could have blamed themselves because of, a social and political system so massive in comparison to their little home in Pinsk that they could hardly be expected to comprehend the "issue" of totalitarian rule as anything other than their personal "troubles." They were, thus, no different from anyone in another situation in space and time who suffers unwittingly because of social things beyond his or her control—no different from those who fail in schools because their schools don't teach, from those unable to support their families because there are no decent jobs, from those unable to achieve their dreams because they are arbitrarily excluded from the places where those dreams are realized, from those unable to find the relationships they desire because they are still controlled by unconscious memories of sexual abuse they suffered in a long ago they cannot, or will not, remember—no different from children who grew up to suffer abuse in the Abu Ghraibs of the world.

It is not just the victims of society who are disadvantaged in this way. Most of us, whatever our circumstances, have need of a more vividly active sociological imagination, which we sometimes develop by the example of others, by the lessons of practical life, and, even, by courses in sociology. C. Wright Mills, though he was a professional sociologist, did not intend that the sociological imagination be a competence of only the more highly educated. On the contrary, he believed that the most important value of sociology is its potential to enrich and encourage the lives of all human beings. Mills was one of the first to insist with a defiant passion that sociology is not for the professionals alone—that the sociological imagination is every bit as important to the ordinary person, for whom it can be a matter of quite serious urgency. The passion with which he held this conviction explains why he exercised so much popular influence and why, in particular, his ideas influenced the politics of the early student movement in the 1960s. Though not alone in this conviction, Mills did more than anyone to clarify and convey the extent to which sociology is first and foremost a practical skill available to all men and women, even to boys and girls. Sociology's value as an academic field of research and instruction relies on this prior fact.

TWO

PERSONAL COURAGE AND PRACTICAL SOCIOLOGIES

Quite a long time ago, in 1892, just two years before Emile Durkheim first announced his definition of scientific sociology, a young woman wrote some very true-to-life fiction. Her short story, published in a popular magazine, created quite a sensation. Though the story was offered as fiction, it was a thinly veiled account of her own nervous breakdown in 1887. One of the most chilling passages describes the room to which she was confined by her attentive husband and its effect on her—most eerily, the power the room's wallpaper design had over her.

> The paint and the paper look as if a boys' school had used it. It is stripped off—the paper—in great patches all around the head of my bed, about as far as I can reach, and in a great place on the other side of the room low down. I never saw a worse paper in my life.
>
> One of those sprawling flamboyant patterns committing every artistic sin.
>
> It is dull enough to confuse the eye in following, pronounced enough to constantly irritate and provoke study, and when you follow the lame uncertain curves for a little distance they suddenly commit suicide—plunge off at outrageous angles, destroy themselves in unheard of contradictions.
>
> The color is repellent, almost revolting; a smouldering unclean yellow, strangely faded by the slow-turning sunlight.

It is a dull yet lurid orange in some places, a sickly sulphur tint in others.

No wonder the children hated it! I should hate it myself if I had to live in this room alone.

There comes John, and I must put this away,—he hates to have me write a word.

—Charlotte Perkins Gilman, *The Yellow Wallpaper* (1892)[4]

The Yellow Wallpaper, by Charlotte Perkins Gilman (1860–1935), is today considered a classic of feminist-inspired fiction in America. Its author, then still a young woman, went on to become a world-famous writer, lecturer, political activist, and sociologist—and she understood very well the significant difference between the psychological and the sociological.

The Yellow Wallpaper is of course brutally honest psychology, so brutal that many readers in that more innocent age were outraged that anyone would write of such terrifying experiences. They feared that the story itself would drive people crazy. The literary success of *The Yellow Wallpaper* was indeed due to the coercive effect of the wallpaper, which so disturbs the young woman's deep, but least stable, feelings that she is drawn into its lurid, obnoxious patterns. This is a classic instance of projective identification; the woman sees herself in what is outside her. The wallpaper's uncertain curves commit the suicide she fears within herself.

But *The Yellow Wallpaper* is also brilliant sociology. As Durkheim might have said, had he read this story, behind the psychological are the social facts. The husband, John, who hates the woman's desire to write, is a character based on Charlotte's first husband, Walter Stetson. They had been married just three years when Charlotte suffered her collapse in 1887, two years after the birth of their daughter, Kate. Walter (or John, in the story) may have held many traditional Victorian ideas about women, but he was not a traditional husband. He was devoted to Charlotte and Kate, and gave freely of his time in childcare. (Later, when Charlotte had settled in California after divorcing Walter, it was he who raised Kate.) Just the same, out of his love for his wife, he called in the esteemed physician Dr. S. Weir Mitchell, then famous as a specialist in the illnesses of women. Mitchell customarily prescribed a severe "rest cure." Some time before, he had administered the same cure to Harriet Beecher Stowe (1811–1896), author of *Uncle Tom's Cabin* and a relative of Charlotte's. It was just this cure that caused Charlotte to be confined in the cottage with its yellow-wallpapered room and to be prohibited from doing the work she loved.[5]

Though she acknowledged the devotion of her husband and the concern of her doctor, Charlotte knew that the cure was wrong. She understood in the most practical way that rest was prescribed out of the culture of a man-centered social world that treated women as though work outside the home was against their nature. Indeed, in that day, the vast, naive majority did consider writing and other labors meant for public consumption and gain to be unhealthy pursuits for women (for, that is, married white women of the middle or upper classes). Long before she became a published writer and a sociologist, Charlotte Perkins Gilman knew this was a well-organized but foolish prejudice. She understood very well that the reality of social arrangements in her day harshly confined many women to the world of domestic life—a world of which most men (then, as now) sang lofty words of praise to family values without ever having spent themselves in the hard work it takes to keep a family well and fed.

Charlotte, however, ended up curing herself by writing, at first secretly, then in open defiance of the cure her physician had imposed. Eventually, after divorcing her husband, she became a full-time writer. Many years later, in 1898, she published *Women and Economics*, which was translated and read in most of the European languages. This book was a rigorous sociological analysis of the man-centered world (what she later called "the androcentric world" and what today is better known as "the patriarchy"). Gilman never taught sociology (though she did publish in the most elite of the field's journals). Still, she was a professional sociologist in that she lived for her sociological writings, which were taken seriously by thousands of general readers and, even, by a good number of academic sociologists (many of whom, in that day, were as prejudiced against women as was the well-meaning Dr. Mitchell). Charlotte Perkins Gilman wrote books that gave compelling intellectual account of the social worlds in which women lived in her day, and, in many places and ways, still do.

But how does such a thing happen in a person's life? What emboldens people like Charlotte Perkins Gilman to stare straight into the face of social things and to imagine, even if tentatively at first, the larger social forces that limit and constrain them? What today allows women suffering under the unnatural threats of extremist Islamic codes or the political terrors of militia in the Sudan to overcome? For Gilman, as for millions of women in other parts of the world, it must have been a particularly difficult task. Unlike women and children who are exposed to physical or sexual violence, Charlotte was treated with nothing but kindness by Walter Stetson and Dr. Mitchell. One might suppose that, had her husband and physician been overtly cruel and abusive, it would have been easier for her to have arrived at the freeing counter-diagnosis of her illness—that she was depressed, not by her desire to write, but by a society that treated women as virtual domestic servants, denying them the expression of their given talents.

It is all too easy to suppose that the power of social things to determine an individual's fate is more obvious when the person is exposed to raw brutality. Perhaps, to some extent, this is so. But it is just as clear that many of the world's brutalized are *not* in fact able to imagine a world in which, as C. Wright Mills put it, their personal troubles are actually problems created by the way the social world is structured. Many women remain in physically abusive relations with men and conclude that the trouble lies with them. So, likewise, many children—but also many elderly or poor people, and others in socially precarious lives—have no idea that it might be the arrangement of larger social forces, not their personal failures, that accounts for the terrible mistreatment and deprivations to which they are so often subjected.

False consciousness is the common name for the surprising inability of some people to use their native social competence. Some can see social things for what they truly are and, it seems, some cannot. False consciousness describes the not infrequent failure of people to use their sociological competence. It is, of course, possible to have a competence without ever using it. In principle, I could learn downhill skiing, but I have never even tried it. In principle, women in abusive relations know that something is terribly wrong, but they may never get the help and encouragement to understand that the wrong is not theirs. The reason I will not ski is that I do not want to spend my money on bone-chilling and bone-breaking thrills. This is *not* false consciousness. But the reason some women remain in abusive relationships can be.

False consciousness is an impoverishment of the sociological imagination in which people are unable to understand the social things that cause their troubles. They may even actively *mis*understand them. There are, of course, psychological resistances—for example, to remembering childhood abuses. But false consciousness, though it may well include the psychological, is the more encompassing *social* aspect of the phenomenon. False consciousness refers straightforwardly to the perverse fact that in many situations the people who suffer either blame themselves for their troubles or otherwise account for their suffering by referring to almost anything but the actual social cause. False consciousness clearly has a psychological component, yet the debilitating effects of this failure to know the reality of one's life-situation are social.

Today, in most of the sprawling urban centers the world over, there are millions of men and women unable to find and keep decent jobs. Most of them are unskilled workers who know little about the technologies that drive postindustrial manufacturing. When they fail at legitimate work because they lack the training, they usually also fail to provide for their families. With rare exception, most of them soon begin to feel ugly about themselves. The feeling that one is a worthless person is psychological, but the reality of the causes and effects of the feeling is sociological. When the economy offers fewer and fewer jobs only for the more highly skilled workers, this is a failure in the larger structure of social things that causes impossible troubles for millions of individuals. The psychology of low self-esteem takes its toll inside the feeling individual, but the ultimate tax is excised by the wider global society, which, in effect, is producing millions and millions of impoverished people. Are the poor responsible for their poverty? Perhaps some individuals are. But no self-respecting sociologist could say they all are. Poverty is a social effect, felt by millions of injured individuals who usually do not understand what has happened to them. False consciousness is not knowing the difference.

The term false consciousness was invented by Friedrich Engels (1820–1895) and developed over the years by thinkers in the tradition of Karl Marx (1818–1883), the famous nineteenth-century social critic, labor organizer, and political revolutionary. In some neighborhoods Marx is still considered a dangerous radical, as indeed he was. Just the same, his ideas remain a source of sociological inspiration, even to those made nervous by his politics. Though Marx's thinking was incomplete, or wrong, on some matters, his critique of capitalist economic systems and the way he retold the story of the modern world continue to influence how we think about social things like false consciousness.

Capitalism, Marx argued, is organized around a social contradiction. While, on the surface, it has given the world many benefits and made life better for some, behind appearances its workers, in particular, continue to suffer exploitation. In his attempt to account for this contradiction, Marx came upon a puzzle sociologists still realize is not easily solved: Why does it happen that oppressed people, who clearly possess the ability to understand their situations, so often fail to do so? Marx studied the working poor in the early years of the industrial revolution in the nineteenth century and observed that, in spite of the terrible conditions of factory workers in those days, there were surprisingly few worker revolutions. Then (as in many places today), men, women, and children worked long hours for lousy wages in dirty factories, yet their rebellions were few in proportion to the enormity of their misery. Even the uprisings that seemed to succeed, as in the revolutions of 1848, were quickly put down, making way again for dirty business as usual in the industrial system.

Marx believed that workers did not rebel against economic injustice as often as one would expect them to because their oppression was not merely physical or economic. Though Marx did not himself put it this way, he was the first to suggest that oppression is as much a sociological as it is an economic or political issue. Simply put, bad sociology gets into the heads of the abused and neglected. Marx was heading toward the idea that the workers are oppressed because, in effect, they are taught to think as their oppressors would have them think. It is a little too strong to say they are "taught," as if the bosses of capitalism daily conspire to instruct their workers. But, until a more exact term comes along, "taught" will do. Even today, professional sociologists are far from agreed as to how it works that the exploited of the world so often think in ways that cause them to be less aggressive than their circumstances would seem to demand.

Marx, however, introduced the idea that something happens in the workers' relation to the factory system and the wider society that causes them to misunderstand their plight. Hence, Marx's famously cynical view of religion as "the opiate of the people." In Marx's day (more so than today), religion was among those seemingly benign aspects of a society's culture that, he thought, actually dulled the thinking of those who suffered the most. Similarly, Marx believed that the revered patriotic ideals and political ideologies of the then new democracies were not all so wonderful as they were made to seem. The masses believed (or, at least, hoped) that, after the kings were chased from power, the new liberalism in government meant they would be better off. After studying the history of the factory system, Marx disagreed, and he had the evidence to prove his point. The workers had it too of course—on their worn and broken bodies. That they could not interpret the data of their daily suffering was (and is) compelling evidence for the phenomenon that came to be called false consciousness.

Marx's sociological view of this puzzle was this: If those who profit from the exploitation of workers can get the workers to believe that, say, it is God's will they should suffer in this life in order to get a reward in the next life, then the workers will be less likely to revolt against this world because they will be preoccupied with the next one. In a similar manner (also simply put), Marx argued that the political logic of the bosses of capitalism went something like this: If workers are taught to believe that they enter the labor market as free agents and that their freedom from slavery is a benefit bestowed by good societies and liberal governments, then they are more likely to blame themselves and not the society for their misery.

You can begin to see why there will always be some people who hate Marx and Marxism. He did not have much good to say for either capitalism or modern political ideals. Yet, while others interpret the facts differently, Marx's argument is persuasive. Still today, workers in third-world assembly plants, like those in sweatshops in New York City or large-scale farming enterprises in California, migrate great distances to find work paying wages so trifling that they cannot escape poverty. A woman from a small village in Chiapas in southernmost Mexico may travel at great risk north to find work in a *maquiladora*—one of thousands of factories along the northern border of Mexico with the United States. She will work for a pittance assembling computer parts. She will be forced to live in miserable shanty-towns with few, if any, sanitary conditions. Still, the pittance she gains is greater than any amount she could earn in the rural countryside—enough more that she will send money home to support her family. In the 2000s workers may assembly products unheard of in Marx's day, but the system still exploits them as it did those milling cotton in Lawrence, Massachusetts in the 1850s.

It is not too difficult to find evidence that those who profit from capitalist enterprises have been financial backers of schools and even churches that could hardly be said to have been devoted to encouraging the indignation of the working poor. For example, the nineteenth-century forerunners of the public schools in the United States were, in effect, vocational schools that taught basic citizenship and work skills to immigrants employed in the textile mills. Today, for another example, many politicians in Europe and the United States "teach" the doctrine that immigrant workers are "stealing" costly social services like education and health care from their host societies. Such cynical instructions seldom mention that these suddenly unwelcome guests were invited in the first place by profit-hungry capitalists eager to pay the lowest wages for hard labor. At cocktail hour in New York City drinkers will munch almonds picked by Mexican workers. Their martinis may cost $15. The almonds may be free at the bar because they were picked for next to nothing by Chicanos in California living in fear of the immigration authorities. Those who complain of these violations of immigration law never mention that somewhere in the food and drink chain capitalists paid off the politicians willing to use lofty language to degrade the dispensable and lowly. "Teaching" comes in many different forms.

False consciousness is a powerful idea that helps account for the astonishing fact that many people who suffer deprivation and abuse are taught, or otherwise seduced, to think falsely about their situation, even to conclude that their troubles result from their own failures to be a better worker or, even, a better person. Charlotte Perkins Gilman, for example, could have concluded in her youth that her sickness was caused by her own moral failure to obey her doctor's instructions, to refrain from the evil of writing, or to suppress the desire to be a person of worth in the wider world outside the home. Though such things were never said to her in so many words, this was the clear implication of the rest cure her husband and doctor insisted upon. Very often false consciousness is taught and imposed by the most indirect of means—gently, quietly, even lovingly. Had Charlotte given in to the social prejudices of her day, she would have succumbed to the false thinking that made her, like other women, doubt herself. But, in the long run, she resisted with courage, and overcame.

But still one might wonder. How does it happen that, while some people succumb to false consciousness, others are able to trust their own deeper sociological competence—thus to imagine that failures in life are as likely to come down from the organized structures of social things as they are to rise up from the individuals upon whom the failure falls? The answer seems to be that many, if not all, people are able to overcome bad situations when they begin to look critically in the right place, and the right place is usually right before their eyes. Those who do get clear about the evil power of such complex social things as the world's economic injustices, or its man-made domestic arrangements, do so by the curiously obvious method of taking stock of the practical realities of the local situations in which they live. Though the competence that inspires the sociological imagination can be the source of many compelling theories, it is, first of all, a practical and concrete knowledge. Children grow up by getting over the night terrors. Women leave circumstances in which they are thwarted. Many people overcome false consciousness. Those who do, do it by courageously opening their hearts, and eyes, to the realities before them—by feeling their weariness, then seeing the world for what it is, then slowly beginning to act differently.

This may seem to be a contradiction of a very confusing sort. If the sociological imagination is the ability to understand the power of larger social things like the economic system, then how can it be that knowledge of those larger things begins in the local and concrete? The answer, simply put, is that human beings are feelers and doers before they are thinkers. Thinking is good. But, to think the truth of social things, one must first be able to feel them working in the bumps and grinds, the bruises and blessings, of daily life—in the small things. Sociology includes, without embarrassment, the ability to think about big social things like the global systems that exploit workers, thwart women, hurt children, and impoverish millions. But, insofar as all sociologies arise from sociological competence, they arise first in the mundane goings and comings in which people are mercilessly required to solve the problems of daily life.

When, after all, does a child first understand that something is terribly wrong with the political world if it is not in the concrete fact that his father suddenly disappears and his mother stands sleepless vigil all the night? Or, when does a woman first get the idea that something is wrong with the way women are treated in society if it is not in the recognition that the men in her life, even her husband or physician, are forcing her to deny what she loves to do or be? Sociological competence ultimately comes to an awareness of the bigger social things by beginning with what is right or wrong in what is going on at home in the bedrooms or kitchens, or down the street in the cafes, shops, or crack houses. The poor first understand poverty by experiencing hunger. The homeless may eventually have a theory of homelessness, but first they know what it is like, night after night, to search for shelter or warmth, for some hard place to stretch their weary bones. Victims of violence may well come to imagine with shrewd accuracy the causal relations among economic deprivation, the trade in drugs, and gang wars; but first, you can be sure, they learn to deal with the practical realities of dodging bullets and running for cover.

The sociological imagination is capable of soaring to great heights of understanding, but it soars only after a long running start through the practical challenges of daily life. Not everyone will run this course equally well, and some never escape the deadening effects of false consciousness bred in overpoweringly bad social situations. But the many who do escape are those who, with grace and encouragement, dig deep below the surface—there to find the reserve of sociological competence which, though it serves them already in the simple things of life, is also the reservoir from which to draw understanding of the practical reality of social things.

Charlotte Perkins Gilman was a sociologist whose sociology was rooted in the earthy feel of practical consequences. Even before becoming a sociologist in the more formal sense of the word, she clearly had a vivid imagination for the practical. She was quite evidently able, even in the absence of advice on the matter, to know with sufficient confidence that the rest cure was based on the sociologically stupid ideas that women did not belong in the world of paid work and that they grew ill when they ventured too far into it. This understanding, which dawned in her yellow-papered room, was pretty good sociology for a young woman who had never been to college and who, at the time she acted upon what she believed, was beset by a depression that would never be far away the rest of her life.

It is possible to speak somewhat differently of this sociological competence that arises so marvelously even among frightened children, abandoned boys, sick women, and most of us at one time or another. It might also be described as *practical sociology*—that is, the understanding that arises from the first imaginative peeks behind the surface appearances of daily life. One might speak of practical sociology as the first and formative expression of sociological competence. A competence is always a potential until it begins, however timidly, to express itself.

Practical sociology is, thus, very much a sociology in the sense that it is a kind of knowledge that coherently accounts for the reality of a person's world, a knowledge that can indeed be distinguished from other knowledges people enjoy. And it is, most definitely, practical in the sense of being a knowledge that informs in useful, powerful ways an individual's decisions to take liberating action when she can. It is important to distinguish this sense of "practical" from the lesser, more commonplace skills that refer narrowly to the utility or applicability of a knowledge, as in knowing how to change a tire, send a text message around the world, hem a skirt, prune a tree, or fix a date. Practical sociology is useful, to be sure, but it is useful because it is also empowering in a much broader sense.

Practical sociology refers to those aspects of personal repertoire that form the basis for a person's confidence in her place, rights, and possibilities in the world. When she was still Charlotte Stetson, for example, this young woman did not know with medical certainty that her cure would come from beginning to work against her doctor's orders. What she must have possessed instead was not a knowledge well formed in her mind, available in so many words to be translated into a conscious action. What she knew, it seems, was more a social animal's instinct. She knew she had to work, to read and write, in order to be who she was in the world. This knowledge, though it was rooted in deeply private feelings, could not have been simply personal.

Charlotte Gilman's early practical sociology encompassed an informed conviction that men, even well-intentioned ones, saw the world differently (and wrongly) because of the social positions to which they were privileged and from which women were excluded. As she boldly put it in 1898 in *Women and Economics*: "We are the only animal species in which the female depends on the male for food, the only animal species in which the sex-relation is also an economic relation."[6] A decade earlier when she was suffering the illness from which she wrenched herself, she had not yet formulated so articulate a social theory of women's economic dependence on men as she later would. But it is safe to assume that the germ of that idea was present in her decision to reject the controlling affections of her husband and doctor. She was, while suffering in 1887, well disposed of a practical sociology that, while expressed in a more basic language, was already a good critique of social things pertaining to white women of her class.

The Yellow Wallpaper ends with Charlotte Perkins Gilman's fictionalized self escaping the nightmarish room, saying to, and about, her husband:

> "I've got out at last," said I, "in spite of you. . . . And I've pulled off most of the paper, so you can't put me back!"
>
> Now why should that man have fainted? But he did, and right across my path by the wall, so that I had to creep over him every time!
>
> —Gilman, *Yellow Wallpaper*[7]

These lines of fiction, written years after she was herself put up in the yellow-wallpapered room, are the sure evidence of Charlotte Gilman's practical sociology. She began to think the thoughts that led to her sociology, in the rage-filled work of pulling off the wallpaper, in the painful refusal to refrain from writing, in the gallant steps that led out of the room, the cottage, the marriage, and into the world of a new life, to a career as a writer, and eventually to her own fully thought-through sociological imagination of a better world for women. Years later, when she eventually came to her full, formal theory of the social structures of the man-made world and the limitations it imposed on women, she did because she had had the courage, even while suffering hallucinations, to open herself to her own sociological competence, then to creep and crawl toward something else.

The wider life to which Charlotte courageously crawled was a life with others, particularly with other women who had suffered as she had at the hands of the man-made world. Neither practical sociology nor the interior competence to which it gives expression is ever purely and simply personal. It is one thing to suffer alone, as Charlotte did in that terrifying room, but something entirely different, and more, to come to act, then to speak, then to understand that the isolation of personal troubles is, in larger reality, a profound and pervasive social issue. Some problems are purely personal, but fewer than we suppose. Practical sociology gives us the first inkling that we are not alone, that we are connected with others even before we recognize the lines of connection, and that we are alive to the world only when we fully grasp social realities as they are.

No one should assume that young Charlotte Stetson's struggle to get out of that room was any more painful and difficult than the struggles most people have in working themselves out from the bondage of isolation into the wider social worlds. There can be pleasure as well as pain in the solitary life. But if we live only within ourselves, we are less than fully human because humans are made for society with each other. But, again, life in society, like life alone, can be as painful as it can be filled with pleasure. The good life is not an easy ticket.

The step out from the personal into the social requires every bit as much courage as that Charlotte summoned up in order to leave the nightmare for the wide-awake social world. Not everything social works as if by magic. Charlotte's depression returned. She suffered losses of love and recognition. After many years, she committed suicide. But she became Charlotte Perkins Gilman because she found the courage within to become the practical sociologist who was able to see that it was not she alone who was sick but that the man-made world in which she was linked to countless other women was unhealthy as well. Her healing came, not as a miracle, but as a consequence of courageous action to join the society of those of like circumstances.

When first we step into its circle, society is a party of strangers. We all, whatever our circumstances, enter the social worlds about us alone. But once the first steps are taken, we discover the power of the practical sociologies we share with sisters and brothers similarly seeking the work and caretaking that make the social worlds go round.

Few of us ever are able to let our wider world know about our most formative experiences as Gilman was. But this does not mean we are less well endowed with a practical sociology. Practical knowledge of various kinds are widely shared, many of them universally. Consider, for a moment, a short list of more or less instinctive knowledges: breathing, riding a bike, performing one or another of many possible sex acts, figuring out when the next bus comes, speaking, and, say, getting a prospective love-interest to go to a concert. None of these is particularly or necessarily difficult, though some are more daunting than others. At least one of them fully qualifies as an animal instinct: breathing. Several seem to fall under the heading "needs a little coaching but, once learned, never forgotten." Bicycle riding is this, as are most sex acts.

But some practical knowledge requires more social work for its accomplishment. Consider, for example, what is involved in persuading another person to join one's privately concocted scheme, as in getting a date of any kind. Nothing is more fundamental to the social business of daily life than this. Were none of us able to get some other or others to join in our untested and usually unexamined plans, nothing social would happen. The whole world would stop. Yet, even the simplest of invitational efforts is a risk, as anyone knows who has recently thrown a failed party, much less suffered through a lunch meeting with someone who seemed a good bet but wasn't. The very idea is outrageous—proposing that some other person change her doings to meet us someplace (usually specified, but often strange to the invitee) at some time (usually precise as to beginning, but left open as to ending). Of course, when it is a date for business not itself routine, as in a date implying even the possibility of romantic activity, no matter how muffled the implication, all kinds of feelings break out as anxiety, very often in sweaty palms, garbled sentences, and any number of jitters of this kind. Yet dates of the romantic kind happen, more or less regularly, more or less according to plan. They do because in most instances most people possess and use their native competence to get them done, sweaty palms and all.

We almost never think about the knowledge requisite to the accomplishment. Unlike breathing and bike riding, but like sex and the dates on which it is performed, the accomplishment is social in nature (as distinct from being nature in the social). It is, thus, executed on the basis of one's practical knowledge of social things. How one gets another to join in varies from culture to culture. In Korea, it is an insult to beckon by pointing. Instead, with palms down, the inviter wiggles the downward-pointing fingers. Americans who are accustomed to beckoning another with a raised, inward wiggle of the index finger may find the Korean practice strange. But both work. People know when and how to use the gestures made available in their natural knowledge of local social things, just as they know how, according to local customs, to defer graciously, to ward off most potential embarrassments, to resurrect a fallen reputation, or to inflate an established one. Social facts of the practical kind have been most tellingly described by Erving Goffman (1920–1982), a sociologist who was born in rural Alberta, Canada, a few years after C. Wright Mills was born in Texas. While many professional sociologists, before and since, have rendered excellent accounts of the thousands of small interactive moments by which daily life is organized, Goffman wrote about them in such a distinctive way that his countercultural view of social things has had a lasting influence. It did not hurt that Goffman's best-known writings were published in the 1960s when people were less likely to be shocked by unusual sayings and viewings.

One of Goffman's more memorable lines was: "Universal human nature is not a very human thing." By this he meant that, when we act in obedience to the practical sociologies we possess, we act to a disconcerting degree much like all others. We become, as Goffman put it, "a kind of construct, built up not from inner psychic propensities but from moral rules that are impressed upon [us] from without."[8] In other words, when meeting the date we have enticed to join us, we may well feel utterly, embarrassingly awkward. Yet it is also normal to feel that the he or the she we are meeting will be, like the stars of stage and screen, utterly cool and calm before the prospect of an encounter charged with excitement and risk. What is moving us at the moment is a feeling, and feelings are experienced as though they were entirely private. When feelings take over, as they usually do in social transactions fraught with desire, people are inclined to lose their grip on social reality, to think they alone are bumbling fools, that no one else worries about their pimples, and other less visible blemishes.

I was once in a therapy group organized, as most are, to teach its members how to feel their deeper feelings. In the group was a woman whom I felt I hated and for whom, I believed, every other member had nothing but admiration. I cautioned myself against my own feelings, thinking I was alone in the feeling that she was a nut. After many years she left the group, allowing people to talk about her in her absence. As it turned out, everyone else, except the therapist, hated the woman in much the same way I did. Daily life is filled with surprises of this sort—discoveries that the states we feel that are ours alone are, in fact, widely shared. My feelings had kept me from seeing that I was far from alone in them, even that they were a group feeling more powerful than the woman we felt was a nut.

There is something in human nature (at least in the nature of many Americans and other European peoples) that prompts us to think of our actions, as well as our feelings, as though they were the distinctive issue of something inside us, something uniquely ours. Some (perhaps many) are. But most of the actions and feelings that help us enter into working relations with fellow members of the world are not all that private. They are, in fact, performances we execute in acceptably close conformity to widely accepted social rules. These rules are learned and held by us in such an easy way that we indulge the conceit that they are our own brilliant accomplishments. We think of them, as Goffman said, as though they were the inventions of our own utterly original psychic lives, when most of them are as familiar to others as they are to us. Social things are, as Durkheim said, quite simply social.

Social things, especially the very practical ones, must exist in their own right, apart from the individuals they affect. If this is so, then much (not all) of the time, social things have the power to persuade, even control, us—whether we realize it or not. This is the sense in which people are often "constructs" instead of free actors, which means nothing more than that a great deal of practical action is an entering into some or another social expectation that, though it was surely itself built up by folks like ourselves, was there before us as it will continue when we are gone. This may be a shocking affront to the prejudice that individuals are the original source of all that is good in the world, but you can be sure that a social world cannot exist any other way. We encounter social things, and learn how to live with them, and we do it every day. There are only a few acceptable ways to make dates, and, depending on taste, not many more to have sex. Otherwise, life with others would be an endless misery of negotiations, when what one mostly wants is to catch a bus or get some affection and companionship. The most practical social facts constitute a working knowledge that allows, not just *me* as an individual, but *we* in all our inordinately various collective comings together, to make some worlds work, even if poorly at times.

How does it happen then that, like Charlotte Perkins Gilman, so many people know what to do even while feeling quite alone? The ability to act as a competent member of a social world is, after all, an accomplishment of such regular and widespread manifestation as to justify the confidence human beings so obviously have in the superior virtue of theirs among the species of animal life. The reason humans are regularly astonished by their own kind may well be that actions we take in ordinary social life are *not* actions to which we normally give much thought. All of this practical sociological knowledge is, in fact, mostly stored as an available resource somewhere out of immediate reach of consciousness. Though it is a bit risky to say so, much of the time practical sociology is unconscious knowledge.

One of England's most admired sociologists today is Anthony Giddens (b. 1938), a professor at Cambridge University for many years and, later, the director of the London School of Economics, now an appointed member of the House of Lords and one of Britain's leading public intellectuals. Giddens has taken up the question of how these social competencies work in what might be called the social unconscious. He has been clear, and shrewd, in explaining that, when it comes to our dealings with other social creatures, the practical knowledge we possess seems to reside in two distinct states: the practical-but-not-entirely-conscious and the discursive.[9]

This distinction (and especially the use of the word "discursive") may at first appear to be a needless bother. But, as with most terms invented by professional sociologists, there is a purpose. To refer to some part of our practical knowledge as "discursive" is simply to say it is something we are able and willing to talk about.

In the eighth grade, Miss Klassner forced us to talk and write about the grammatical rules governing singular/plural accord, as in: "He hit the ball."/"They were hitting balls all night." Actually, I did not mind these assignments because, at least, I could make sense of the rules, while assigned books like *Silas Marner* were completely beyond my fidgety, teenage mind. Spoken language, we know, is a practical knowledge, the rules and contents of which are usually held more or less unconsciously. Except in schools and other institutions devoted to straightening people out, we are seldom called upon to recite the rules of the practical knowledge we possess. Sometimes we can; sometimes not. To this day I am convinced that the knowledge required to talk about Silas Marner is of another, more specialized kind— one that requires some special work. But I can tell you exactly, as you could probably tell me, why singular nouns require singular verbs. Still, the finer rules of grammar, like those necessary to read works of fiction, are among a vast number of not-quite-conscious knowledge people are able, under various conditions, to bring into discourse—to talk about.

In a similar way, Anthony Giddens distinguished between the practical sociology we possess as if by second (and not always conscious) nature and that about which we usually can talk intelligibly when required to do so. Those who suppose this to be a spurious distinction might try the simple experiment of explaining the precise rules and procedures involved in performing even the most elementary of social acts. Try, for instance, a discursive presentation to a friend of differing sexual orientation on how those of yours go about recruiting their objects of desire. Try, even, reciting the rules governing asking for bus change in a city not your own. It makes you want to recite the rules for singular/plural accord.

What people know is important, obviously. But, as I said, we usually get to knowledge first by examining what we feel and do. The formidable action Charlotte Perkins Gilman took in 1887 when she was ill was the action of someone who trusted what she *felt* to be true for her, and then, upon breaking out of the confinement, learned after a while to recite the social rules of her strong actions. Charlotte Perkins Gilman was not, in fact, the first woman to have had the idea that the man-made world was not welcoming to women. Nor was she the first to defy that world. What she did, however, was to begin to speak, then to write, thus to dramatize what was wrong with women's worlds. She was among those early feminists who put words to what millions already knew but could not say. Feminists like Gilman thus became, to use the word, discursive about their not (yet) quite conscious understandings of the world about them.

Many, perhaps most, social revolutions begin in this way—in the putting of social things into words whereby they are brought out of the dusky realm of the secrets everyone knows but, for fear of the consequences, will not talk about. When people begin to talk in public, they learn and teach and, if they are right about what they felt before they began to talk, things get done. Laws are changed, marriages are rearranged, children are brought up differently, votes are cast in a certain way, and on it goes. Social things are the buzz of such talk, and other expressions—a buzz created by truths coming out from the silences.

Practical sociology and the professional kind are different to be sure. But they come from the same mysterious place, a place of double-sided mysteries. It is amazing enough that things work so well when people get together, amazing still more that the practical beginnings of all we know in common are kept for our use in places about which we do not, and very often cannot, speak. Yet, with time and encouragement, it is possible to talk about these social things. In the course of time, most people are perfectly able to be discursive in these ways. It is also possible, for those willing to undertake the discipline of schooling of an advanced sort, to talk about such things in a reasonably professional way.

But it all begins in the private, unspeakable places from which we learn how to do what we do. There would be no professional sociology without the practical, if for no other reason than that nothing social would happen about which to talk.

THREE

~

PRACTICING THE DISCIPLINE OF SOCIAL THINGS

I once heard a radio interview with a great violinist. I believe it was Itzhak Perlman who said that musicians must begin practicing at a very young age because their instruments must become, in effect, a part of their bodies. Whoever in fact said this, it struck me as at least partly true. Over the years I have observed that musicians sometimes look like their instruments. It seems also to be true of other things.

It may not be a hard-and-fast rule that practice makes perfect, but it is fast enough. We may suppose that the practical accomplishments of daily life are performed without practice, but of course this is not so. Whether one is able to talk about it or not, most bike riders and speakers develop their skills well beyond the minimum required for daily play and talk. Practical things, including practical sociologies, involve practice, even when the repetitions are performed without calling much conscious attention to them. It might be that the practical is, in fact, the most practiced, which may explain a good bit of the second-nature effect that excuses the most practical things from discursive attention. There is no reason to believe this is any less true of practical sociologies (such as knowing how and when to defer to someone of recognizably higher status or power) than it is of practical, or habitual, behaviors of a more routine kind.

Practice, in the sense of trying it out again and again, is part of practice, in the sense of getting it right enough to do the work of daily life without thinking about it. This may be the truer meaning of the idea that musicians make their bodies into instruments. So too do people of unexceptional talents when they draw from a dark remembered past the tricks in trade of practical life. Changing a tire, fixing a date, overthrowing the local powers-that-be may be different activities in some obvious ways. But they are alike in being practical actions built with discipline into the who of what we are. As I said, practical sociologies bubble up from a reservoir of the not-yet-consciousness. They are competencies instructing the dull course of the events we produce. Then, on some occasion fraught with frightening possibility, they begin slowly to express themselves as a practical knowledge of the things all about. However timidly they thus arise into consciousness, and however surprised one may be to find herself thinking differently about social things, practical sociologies do not and cannot become new ways of talking, acting, and thinking without practice.

If we are to act with courage when courage is called for, we must work and rework how we feel and think, and this can only be done with discipline. Competence becomes knowledge able to change the way we move and live and have our daily being only when we practice the discipline of the social things at our command.

One of France's most famous, and accomplished, modern sociologists, Pierre Bourdieu (1930–2002), actually wrote on the place of habits in practical action. Like Emile Durkheim, the founding father of professional sociology in France, Bourdieu was interested in one of the most impressive of all social things, a fact that may well be the central consideration of all sociologies. As it turns out, most of the time, in virtually every social group, even those of great size and complexity, people tend to obey the rules. Though there is always talk about the lawlessness of some people—or, as the pious like to say, about the loss of values that "leads" to crime and other forms of deviance—most of the time people tend to obey the rules, even some quite stupid ones.

Take, for example, the herdlike stupidity with which nearly everyone obeys the rules of wait lines. Waiting in lines was, surprisingly, among the many peculiarities of normal behavior studied by Erving Goffman, who is often thought of as a kind of sociological kin of Bourdieu. Goffman, however, observed that not only do groups of people required to wait for some object of their common desire form orderly lines, but they do so according to surprisingly subtle rules.[10] A queue for, say, movie tickets in a big-city cinema usually forms automatically. Though its members are generally strangers, even rivals for sometimes scarce tickets, the line is held in respect (sometimes overnight, or for days in the case of especially coveted tickets). Attendees recognize certain rights of others, including the rights to leave temporarily to relieve oneself or, perhaps, the right to advance one's late-arriving partner (if she is a visibly plausible mate). But the amazing fact is that the rules work as well as they do. Some lines are superficially ridiculous, such as sex-segregated lines of march to the cafeteria among small schoolchildren in which the separation of boys from girls implies a degree of sexual interest all but completely absent. Stupid or not, wait lines form and do their job.

What distinguished Bourdieu from Goffman was that he studied the subject of well-practiced practical actions on a very much larger social scale than Goffman did. Bourdieu, for example, was interested in the question of how the habits of whole societies endure over time, even from generation to generation. This is a wonderfully interesting sociological question because if large societies did not have something like habits, then they would not, at a much later stage in their histories (say a century or two), be as obviously similar to themselves at the earlier stages as they are, or would not even be as continuously different from most other societies as they obviously are. The United States in, say, the 1890s was very much different from today. But these differences are not so remarkable as those between the United States over the last two centuries or so and some other society, say, Korea, over the same time.

In the 1890s, Korea was still in the last years of the traditional Choson Dynasty; folk culture (including Confucian practices) was flourishing, though outsiders (Russians, Japanese, and Americans) had just barely opened Korea to world trade. Today, life in Seoul, South Korea, seems to be in every superficial respect quite the same as daily life in New York—buses and subways, drink and food, cell phones are everywhere, changing the culture in small, but obvious, ways. Yet, in fact, and in spite of Korea's recent economic growth and vitality, Korean social practices are still very much different from American ones. On a date of any kind, even a business lunch, it is virtually impossible for the one invited to pay his or her share of the meal, much less to cover the tab itself. In the United States, it is customary, in the absence of an advance agreement, to argue over the right to pay, even when one would prefer not to in the case of a bad date; and the outcome of that organized show of reciprocity is open to the possibility that the invited one will pay, at least his or her share. Differences in customs of this kind are embedded in practices that run deep in the cultures. I cannot say for certain, but I suppose that this difference between Koreans and Americans has something to do with the difference between a background in Confucian culture (very orderly and prone to well-defined structures demanding obedience) and one in a secular,

Protestantized culture (obsessively egalitarian, individualistic, a bit more chaotic, and definitely competitive). Even the smallest gestures (like insisting on, or deferring with respect to, payment of the shared costs of dates) usually are reflexes of very much more complicated (one might say larger) features of the society as a whole. Not always, but usually.

How well-cultured habits are kept alive and influential throughout such complicated societies as the American or the Korean has interested professional sociologists since the days of Emile Durkheim to the present. How do the widely accepted rules of the social whole affect, and how are they affected by, the mundane practices of daily life? Bourdieu was one of those who closer to our time helped people think differently about this question. Bourdieu insisted that the relation between social rules and practical actions has mostly to do with the habits that inform the practices—or with what Bourdieu called the *habitus*.[11] Still again, one might ask why he, like other academic sociologists, was so ready to invent words of this sort. What is wrong with the word "habit" here? Bourdieu had a rather exact reason for inventing the term "habitus." "Habit" conveys too much the sense of social or personal inertia. Nail biting, drinking too much, smoking, accepting dates with people who really aren't very nice—these are generally considered bad habits representing some alien feature of our natures we are unable to shake. Habits, in this sense, are controlling practices sometimes considered beyond our will to alter.

Habitus is something else. It is a sociological term, a concept, that aims to account for the central problem of all sociologies, whether practical or professional. Why do the collective habits of groups, or even of entire societies, work so conveniently well with the habits of individuals? When asked this way, the question implies that groups or societies and individuals are things belonging to two separate and distinct categories. Bourdieu thought the problem of how they work together can never be solved when one thinks this way. Thus, "habitus" is a word that means to allow that habits are real, as surely they are, but to get us beyond the idea that they work one way in groups and somehow another among individuals.

In trying to get us to think differently about the practical ways individuals and large social groups cooperate, Bourdieu's writings challenge two very old and revered sociological doctrines.

In the dreamy not-quite-consciousness of practical life, we seldom think of ourselves as individuals somehow different in kind from the larger social things about us. We don't, that is, until we are called upon to join in with others in doing something big and different (like, say, electing someone to run things for the rest of us) or, as another example, until we find ourselves in a situation so intolerable that we figure out that we are mad as hell about the way we are excluded (like, say, when workers, as they occasionally do, decide they've had it with the bosses). Though there are other reasons besides challenges to join with others or the discovery of social anger, these are two of the more important ones. Each has been the basis for one of the two classic ways of explaining the individual's relation to what today are called social structures. Let us call the one the *individuals-first* theory and the other the *society-first* theory.

The former of these puts individuals first because its proponents believe that societies, even large ones, are composed of individuals who choose to act in concert in order to avoid the chaos that would otherwise result. Without leaders, governments, and rulers of various kinds, there would be no obvious way to prevent all the individuals from struggling with each other over the goods and necessary things they want or need. According to this theory, it is better to have bad rules or evil rulers than social disorder.

The *individuals-first* idea is the older of the two solutions, at least in modern times. It is one that dates to the beginning of the modern era in the seventeenth century, to the English philosopher Thomas Hobbes (1588–1679), whom many consider the first to ask a truly sociological question. Hobbes himself was actually not nearly so individualistic as many of the English and Scottish social thinkers who came after him. But he did put the emphasis on the power of the individual to create social things. Thus he (and those who think as he thought) creates the impression that individuals are the true and first source of the actions that lead eventually to collective social habits.

The problem with the individuals-first theory is that it entails an assumption that, especially today, seems to fail the test of personal experience. Individuals in complex societies do not very often have the experience of actually deciding to enter into the social arrangements (or "constructs," as Goffman put it) provided them. Even less often, if ever, do they decide with others how to arrange the larger social things like governmental or economic systems. The idea gives too much credit to individual choice. If the powerful who occupy the privileged places in big societies are unable to shape the social whole to their choices, what are the chances the more ordinary, and less powerful, can?

In fact, there is good reason to believe that the central moral concern of modern men and women since the beginning of the industrial era in the mid-nineteenth century has been *alienation*, the sense that one's society or even the global social whole has become something quite alien, even hostile, to individual human interests. So, though there are still proponents of versions of the individuals-first solution to the problem, their number tends to shrink when you begin to talk to the more humble and excluded people whose own practical sociologies incline them to think that individuals are anything but the first line of action in the building up of social things. Hence, the second theory.

It hardly needs saying that the *society-first* solution to the puzzling suitedness of individual habits to social ones comes at it from the other side. The society-first idea, like its rival, is quite old, going back at least to a French lawyer and philosopher Charles, the Baron of Montesquieu (1689–1755), who was born shortly after the death of Thomas Hobbes.

The society-firsters believe that the reason individual practices conform to collective ones is that some or another institution or official agency of the larger society "teaches" (again, not quite the exact word) individuals the rules and thus influences their practices, ideally to the common good. No one who read the previous chapter will be surprised that this is a solution that appeals to those who are not afraid of Marx and Marxism. Yet, just as Hobbes's individuals-first theory was only one of many of that kind, so Marx's version of the society-first theory is but one of a good many (including the theories of sociologists who absolutely cannot stomach Marx).

The society-first theory has somewhat greater surface appeal in a world in which individuals are tempted to think of themselves as alienated from some or another aspect of collective life. Very few people I know, or have heard of, are not angry about the taxes they pay, but when it comes to agreeing on which governmental service to cut, people seem to hate the thought of losing their benefits as much as they hate the taxes. Yet, curiously, in actual practice most Americans more or less religiously pay up, even when they are aware that the taxpaying practices of their cousins in other countries demonstrate that, if people refuse to pay, the government must work very hard, with limited success, to excise the tax. Why do people in some places engage in practices, even ones they hate, while others in other places do not? The answer is often put forth that they do because, to again use the word loosely, they are "taught" that paying up is good and they are thus taught by many seemingly innocent means—citizenship classes in school, moral lessons at Sunday school, oaths administered by righteous clubs like the Boy Scouts, public threats by the tax men, pleas by political leaders, and the like.

One of the words often used, though less so today, for this so-called teaching method by which societies get their individual members to think and behave in a proper way is *socialization*. The idea is, you might guess, that the individual is somehow sucked into the bigger social things, much as children who are lucky enough to have families of some kind usually end up believing more or less what their family elders taught them. My oldest son grew up through any number of social roles—at one time a punk rocker, at another an agent of the Navy special forces. Neither of these was a pursuit exactly in keeping with my parental values. But, as the years went by, Matthew cut his hair, lost his leather jacket, and quit the Navy. To our mutual amazement, he seemed to think and act much as his mother and I do, notwithstanding that she and I divorced years ago. In like manner, socialization is about the fact that Koreans think and act like Koreans; bankers, like bankers; prize fighters, like other boxers; and so on. We will come back to socialization later on, but for the moment you can see that anybody who thinks individuals become who they are because they imbibe the rules and values of some bigger social things, like a family, holds a society-first theory. The society-firsters are attached to the notion that the common will produces individual practices, while the individuals-firsters believe that individuals are the source of the common will.

Those in the society-first camp very often refer for evidence to the more salient institutions of modern societies that do, in fact, seem to be devoted to instruction of this very general but powerful kind—families, of course, but also clubs and patriotic associations, television and the movies, political parties, and, most notably, schools. Huge collective investments of time, money, and faith are entrusted to schools in the belief that individuals will get something good from the schooling, as they often do. But those same schools seem also to be institutions that demand a return in their trade with pupils. Schools offer their instruction, and eventually their certification, on the condition that those who give themselves over for instructional processing learn how to behave in ways the authorities define as proper and constructive. There is, to be sure, a lot of rebellion in high schools and on college campuses, but less than one would expect given the age of most students, and much less always when there is reason for the rebels to fear that their refusal to obey will cause the school to expel them or otherwise deny its public blessings. Though they seldom have to, schools are like other powerfully structured institutions in being able to force their individual members to comply with the rules. Most often they just teach obedience, with the result that, in spite of what you read and hear, students are not that different from older, extramural folk in their willingness to toe the official line.

Among professional sociologists, Durkheim was an early proponent of the society-first idea. It is not by accident that Durkheim and others in this camp (as well as many, like Bourdieu, who pitch their tents on its margins) are interested in schools, schooling, and education. At the least, schools are places in which, as any schoolchild knows, a great deal of monkey business goes on that has little to do with the expressed intent of imparting instruction on various subjects. Durkheim, in his day, spent much of his time teaching schoolteachers. He believed that if France's schools could teach children the foundations of modern knowledge, including knowledge of French culture and social life, then the French people would think about their lives in a generally French way. This, he thought, would make France as a whole more stable because its citizens would know just how to integrate their individual practices into the common good. In the process, they would enjoy the benefits of knowing the social rules that could inform their practices and, in principle, reduce the anxiety of social isolation—what Durkheim called the *anomie* of modern life.

One might suppose that Bourdieu, being French, would have been more impressed with Durkheim and Montesquieu than with Hobbes and the other English and Scottish thinkers who, by and large, gave the greater weight to the individual. If he had been forced to choose only between the tradition of Hobbes and that of Montesquieu, Bourdieu probably would choose the latter. Like Durkheim, Bourdieu devoted himself to the sociological study of schools and the cultures they teach, or otherwise pass on, from one generation to the next. But, as I said, Bourdieu felt that we will never solve the puzzle of the individual's relation to larger social things if we keep thinking of these as the only two alternatives. As a result, Bourdieu believed that both the individuals-first and the society-first positions are wrong, and wrong for a quite specific reason.

This, then, is where habitus comes in. Bourdieu was among a growing number of professional sociologists who believe in the maxim: Modern solutions for modern problems. He insisted, most importantly, that both of the two traditional theories force people (most especially professionals who are paid to worry about such things) to define the problem in a way that causes them to misunderstand and underappreciate what goes on in the practice of practical social life. Though he would never have said it this way, Bourdieu's idea is that, once we get beyond the older theories to what people actually do and think, it becomes obvious that their most habitual practices are *simultaneously* a result of the force of social rules *and* of their own individual flourishes. When the social rule is benign, we may well obey it without thinking. This, no doubt, is why we stand passively in wait lines. Yet let the demands of the larger social order piss us off or otherwise call attention to themselves, and we may well obey but perhaps belligerently. I pay my taxes at the last possible moment and often write the check to the Department of Revenue "Services," with quotes, just to convey that the "services" I get from government do not come from the tax collectors. Such a puny gesture of complaint may do nothing more than make me feel a little better, but it is a sign of my freedom to resist a bit—a freedom that is perfectly able to grow into some more important protest.

Habitus accounts for the fact that the practical actions by which we comply with the rules are always loaded with potential for the individual to obey or resist society's demands and to do either in sometimes highly inventive ways. The obedience keeps things humming along with only minor glitches, but over time the resistances may well change the way social things are put together. Either way, the practice of practical social things takes place, not at some mystical meeting point between "the individual" and "the social structures," but in the practical improvements or glosses by which individuals do, or refuse to do, what society expects of them. It's all in the practice of social things and not in the way one thinks about them.

Think, for example, of first dates of the potentially romantic kind. Mine (that is, the very first date I ever had) was with Darlene Loving. I was at the time just barely thirteen years old. I asked Darlene to meet me at the skating rink one Friday evening. This is how these things were done in those days in conservative, middling Midwest suburbs. It was roller skating and it provided the occasion for the excitement of acceptable touching between the sexes that we all had in mind. To my utter relief, Darlene accepted my invitation. The date itself consisted of not much more than the two of us sharing, and acting upon, the understanding of a right to more than the average number of joint tours around the crowded, dusty oval. By mutual consent, sealed by visible nervousness on both sides, the right of joint skates extended to the expectation of hand-holding beyond that required to steady the flow of forward movement, as well as the exclusive right to skate together during the last dance tune ("Good Night, Ladies"), played with the house lights dimmed, at about 9:30.

The accomplishment in my successful practicing of the first-date routine had less to do with our ultimately feeble romantic communications than with the asking and the accepting of the date itself. It had taken me days, weeks actually, to summon the nerve to ask Darlene for the date. I feared the possibility of rejection almost as much as the feelings of an impossible sexual desire that stirred within me. I was convinced I could never succeed in this to me new, but much-talked-about, sphere of human endeavor. In fact, to be honest, it was not new to me at all. I had already been the beneficiary of much, mostly reliable instruction by media as different as the gossip of friends, radio stories, movies, and a notably uninspired sex manual I once found in my parents' bedroom. Though Darlene, the immediate object of my practice, was a very real and formidable threat by reason of her powers of rejection, the practice itself was already well enough formatted onto a soft disk of amply available social knowledges at hand. No one, not even then, who grows up in a modernized society, exposed as we are to televisual and other instructions in the ways of sexual life, could possibly not already know what is expected of white, middle-class, presumptively heterosexual boys, or girls, in such a circumstance. As an individual, I did something quite my own, but I did it in passable conformity to well-structured social norms.

This is the point of a concept like habitus. The practice itself is *both*, at one *and* the same time, that which I experience as original to me and reasonably normal social behavior common to nearly everyone of a relatively similar social kind. The practice of social life is not ever so simple a matter as an individual spontaneously proposing and organizing a social coming together, nor is it simply a mechanical thing mass-produced by society's expectation that individuals execute a particular practice. As I said, practice, in the sense of trying it out again and again, is part of practice, in the sense of getting it right. But the practice itself—an actual several hours of fooling around in a noisy skating rink of a Friday evening—is a result of, first, the coming together, not just of Darlene and me, but of our respective normal senses of how these things go down and, then, our making them work that one evening just as though we were making them up as we went along.

Darlene and I were, as I say, already well taught by the narrow range of social experiences that we, in spite of our strangeness to each other, had already shared. It was, after all, roller-skating we chose. Most of the poorer working-class kids from our school lived in Price Hill, where the rink was located. They could watch us arrive at the rink, but few could afford the cost of admission, and many found our type of kid, well, weird. None of the black kids who lived but a mile down the hill in the city's West End could have gone had they wanted to. In those days in Cincinnati, Ohio, long before the better white people got civil rights religion, blacks and whites just did not mix. Nor was it the case that any of us gave the least possible public thought to the question of whether we might enjoy these delicate tastes of sexual desire equally well or better with a skating partner of our own gender. Darlene and I were strange to each other, but we both were thoroughly familiar with the well-structured forces of our white, middle-class, hush-hush heterosexual worlds. We were, that is, products of the then unquestioned dominant social things. In Cincinnati, and most of America, it was the well-off white boys who counted most. Their girls ran a far second. Few others counted, and some who didn't were told so in so many words. Some just did not exist. It would be nearly twenty years before I ever knowingly met and talked to an openly gay person. The big social things affect us, often, in silence, but affect and produce us they do. And we can never realize how important they are in our lives until our sociological imagination breaks out of the silences by looking at the practical realities. This looking about, and the practices that ensue, are what habitus attempts to explain.

Bourdieu, exercising the right of cultural sophistication the French admire so much, put it this way: A habitus is a "system of durable, transposable dispositions"—that is, in his very elaborate definition, Bourdieu means to say that social structures are real and powerful, but they do not so much get inside the heads of individuals as create a social environment that is neither purely outside the individual nor completely inside her:

> The structures constituitive of a particular type of environment (for example, material conditions of existence characteristic of a class condition) produce *habitus*, systems of durable, transposable *dispositions*, structured structures, that is, as principle of the generation and structuring of practices and representations which can be objectively "regulated" and "regular" without in any way being the product of obedience to rules, objectively adapted to their goals without presupposing a conscious aiming at ends or an express mastery of the operations necessary to attain them and, being all this collectively orchestrated without being the product of the orchestrating action of a conductor.
>
> —Pierre Bourdieu, *Outline of a Theory of Practice* (1974)[12]

Behind all the seemingly obscure words, Bourdieu is trying to get at one of the riddles of social life. We do things more or less as others do them; yet we, as individuals, often are not aware of why we are doing them. Riddles cannot always be explained in plain language.

Practices arise out of our practical disposition to obey the durable social things within around us. Yet, as we work with them, they are transposed in that we lend them our own local and individual inflections. That evening with Darlene, I tried a few skating flourishes I was not ready for, causing one unceremonious dusting of my rear end. But even that did not wreck the show Darlene and I performed in such socially predictable ways. Most others were doing what we were or wishing they could. After I picked myself up, we skated on in bliss. Before long, no one noticed this most amazing of all accomplishments of two thirteen-year-olds, already with pimples.

In the winter of 1886, just a year before Charlotte Perkins Gilman fell ill, a young German man was just finishing his qualifying studies for law school. Years later his widow described the young scholar's work habits that winter:

> He continued his strict work routine, regulated his life by the clock, divided his day into exact segments for the various subjects of instruction, and "saved" after his fashion by preparing his evening meal in his room—a pound of chopped raw beef and four fried eggs. The last hour of his day was reserved for a game of skat with a very simple friend who had failed his examination. . . . From the time he stopped dueling, he was tempted neither by the winter fun that jingled past his windows nor by spring wanderlust.
>
> —Marianne Weber, *Max Weber* (1988)[13]

This young man of but twenty-two years soon rose to prominence in the German university, then the very model for university scholarship worldwide.

Max Weber (1864–1920) became the most distinguished founder of professional sociology in Germany. While little good can be said of the food he ate, once he settled down and gave up the pleasures of bourgeois adolescence (including dueling), Weber became one of the greatest of all professional sociologists because he was so famously disciplined. His capacity for disciplined work was so extreme as to have been, even, a well-integrated aspect of his idea of how professional sociology should be practiced.

In 1918, near the end of his life, Weber said that "no sociologist should think himself too good, even in his old age, to make tens of thousands of quite trivial computations in his head and perhaps for months at a time."[14] He did not believe that the continual practice of such tedious work was the final end of good science, but he was convinced that science depended on the disciplining of the body and mind such that the brilliant idea might, just possibly, one day come to life. In this respect, Weber's famous scholarly discipline was not unlike that of the violinist I mentioned earlier.

Discipline is what we do to ourselves, including our bodies, by the continual and well-organized practice of some or another action—calculations, jump shots, skating moves, backstrokes, chords, soufflés, meditating, plumbing, getting places on time, dance steps. Clearly, these kinds of discipline are already practices about which we have given some thought and had a few words to say. No one practices that much according to schedule without some reasonably well-understood idea of the nature and purpose of the practice in one's life. At first, Weber may only have wanted to prove his father wrong (they did not get along). Soon enough, he was so disciplined that he devoted himself to the life of scholarship, with such brilliant success that even his German colleagues were impressed. The academic practice of sociology came to be a prominent feature of the institutional landscape in Weber's country largely (not exclusively) because of the impressive scholarly results of Weber's personal discipline.

One might even say that all academic disciplines come to be as a result of the personal discipline of their practitioners, not exactly an idle play on the word. An academic discipline, or profession, like sociology is indeed founded on the willingness of men and women to submit to the discipline in which they are trained, and trained mostly to discipline themselves so they might be independent practitioners in the field.

Weber was far from the only fabled self-disciplinarian among the early sociologists. For his famous book on suicide, Durkheim surely made as many endless calculations in his head as Weber did. Charlotte Perkins Gilman, for a stretch of seven years, was editor, publisher, and writer of a monthly magazine. She wrote every word of *Forerunner*, including the advertising copy. For twenty-five years, another sociologist of that era, W. E. B. Du Bois (1868–1963), did almost the same for *Crisis*, the magazine of the National Association for the Advancement of Colored People (NAACP), which he helped found. Du Bois followed nearly the same daily schedule of discipline as Weber, each hour of the day devoted to a clearly defined task. For years, Karl Marx went every day to the library at the British Museum to do the research that resulted in *Capital*, in which he retold the story of capitalism. And on it goes. Few professional sociologists do much less. The work that results from the collective efforts of a discipline may be opaque to persons not similarly trained. Students are at first quite perplexed when asked to read Weber's most famous book, *The Protestant Ethic and the Spirit of Capitalism*. But the personal discipline with which some become professional sociologists is not at all different in kind from the discipline with which jump shots, date making, skating, or soufflés are practiced.

Practices may not make perfect, but they do make the social world go round. The why and how of the ambivalent relation of individuals to the big social things that make them who they uniquely are—like the flip-side puzzle of how they persist in fooling around on their own in spite of the social pressures—come down to the practice of practical things. This is why it is not by accident that fields of academic teaching and research are often called "disciplines." Like the modest social performances of kids in roller rinks, the practices that lead to the formulation of enduring fields of knowledge arise from discipline—a discipline that is as important to practical life as it is to science. When Max Weber gave up raw meat and dueling to enter the discipline of academic work, he committed himself, as did the others of his day and since, to a life of countless calculations, as he said, but also of countless attempts to figure, to talk and write about, to work through in his head what he must have known in his life. The calculations and figurings and musings may have taken place according to schedule as he worked alone, but they were prompted by a very practical moral question neither he nor other sociologists of his day, nor any since, could ever quite answer.

Weber, in particular, wanted to know how individuals, like himself, would be able to continue to practice their individual lives in the face of the growing force of industrial capitalism. Though, as we shall see, their answers were different, Weber's question was no different from Marx's, or Durkheim's, or Gilman's, or Du Bois's. What bothered Weber about the rise of large, industrially based bureaucracies was what troubled Marx about the factory system, and what drove Gilman crazy about the man-made world, and what made Du Bois indignant about the color line in America. Though today the issues that may trouble us are in some ways the same, and in other ways different, practical social life remains much as it always has been.

In our lives, we do what we must do, and we do most of what society expects of us. In so doing, we are at the terrible risk of losing our sociological imaginations if we trust too much the instructions and orders of the powerful social institutions. The way out into the wider truths beyond our little worlds is, as I have said, personal courage. But personal courage is never simply given to us. It is gained at the cost of practicing our routines in the face of the social rules, and learning from these doings just how to think freshly about the big worlds that sneak down ever so quietly into a firm place in our guts and hearts and heads. When we look at what is there, at what we do with those expectations, we very often like what we see. Other times, we do not and we begin to look again—practically, with discipline. And then, if we stick to it, we may well imagine the world as it is, even imagine a better one. All sociologies must do thus what we must do alone—the professional ones no less than the practical.

SOCIOLOGY

FOUR

~

SOCIOLOGY AND THE LOST WORLDS OF THE NEW WORLD ORDER: 1848–1920

All children grow up as best they can, comfortably or miserably, in what sociologists are inclined to call *worlds*—a term meant to suggest not so much global geography as the force of all the social things into which a child is born. Social worlds, thus, comprise everything from the social events occurring near about a crib or playroom to the larger, hard-for-a-child-to-imagine global structures.

All sociologists, we should remind ourselves, were once children. In the 1940s, Darlene Loving, David Bennett, and I grew up with the playthings set before us by the then rising tide of white, middle-class American affluence. Some seventy years before, in the 1870s, many of the first generation of professional sociologists grew up with what their worlds structured into their lives. Max Weber, as a child in Germany, played with upper-middle-class social toys provided by his demanding but well-off father. Somewhat the same, Charlotte Perkins enjoyed the intellectual and artistic benefits of Providence, Rhode Island. Yet, because her father (Frederick Perkins) essentially abandoned them, Charlotte and her mother suffered economically—a fact of her world which may well have shaped her views of the man-made world, just as little Max Weber's adult interest in authority may have been influenced by his boyhood fears of his father's ugly temper. The worlds, small and big, into which children grow very often determine who they become and how they think about social things.

At about the same time in the 1870s when Max and Charlotte played in Berlin and Providence, a boy of African descent grew up among whites in Great Barrington, a small town in the Berkshires of western Massachusetts. Willie, as he was then known about town,[15] was even less well acquainted with his father than Charlotte had been with hers, and he was decidedly poorer even than she. Nor did Willie and his mother enjoy the bourgeois splendor of the Weber home in Berlin. Just the same, Willie grew up to become a famously disciplined scholar—just as disciplined and just as much a lover of European culture as Max. Like Charlotte and Max, Willie came eventually to practice his sociological competence in public life. Little Willie of Great Barrington grew up to be W. E. B. Du Bois—sociologist and historian, journalist and man of letters, political organizer, and, through much of the twentieth century, for many, the acknowledged spiritual and intellectual leader of black people worldwide.

Kids grow up by coming to understand the lost worlds of their childhoods. The sociological imagination is first practiced early in life as children try to imagine the meaning of their experiences with others. Their attempts to understand may at first find expression in the way they play. Those frightened children in Poland did not comprehend the structured world of secret police, but they hugged each other in a game of mutual understanding—a close enough grasp of the situation. Willie Du Bois had such an experience when he was a schoolboy in the 1870s. More than twenty years later, in *The Souls of Black Folk*, his most famous book, Du Bois remembered the story from his world of white children's play, and retold it:

It is in the early days of rollicking boyhood that the revelation first bursts upon one, all in a day, as it were. I remember well when the shadow swept across me. I was a little thing, away up in the hills of New England, where the dark Housatonic winds between Hoosac and Taghkanic to the sea. In a wee wooden schoolhouse, something put it into the boys' and girls' heads to buy gorgeous visiting cards—ten cents a package—and exchange. The exchange was merry, till one girl, a tall newcomer, refused my card—refused it peremptorily, with a glance. Then it dawned upon me with a certain suddenness that I was different from the others; or like, mayhap, in heart and life and longing, but shut out from their world by a vast veil.

—W. E. B. Du Bois, *The Souls of Black Folk* (1903)[16]

One can only guess what he might have felt at the very moment of the refusal. The first rush of feeling must have been confusion followed by embarrassment, if not quite yet indignation, at this surprising intrusion upon a world in which he had known little of what he later came to call the color line.

You can be sure that Willie the child did not at the time have in mind the ideas with which he would later describe his feelings. Like Charlotte in her sickroom, Du Bois could have been crushed by the terrible force of the dividing lines of late-nineteenth-century America. Like her, he was not. Instead, he grew into indignation and the determination to change the world. After years of schoolwork at Fisk University, then Harvard and the University of Berlin, and experience with life in the world beyond that New England village, Du Bois learned to think through the experience of his childhood. From these reflections and musings came such mature sociological ideas as the famous one with which he began *The Souls of Black Folk*: "The problem of the Twentieth Century is the problem of the color line." Few social ideas have been more true, as we who live close to the end of the twentieth century realize full well. A very great many of Du Bois's writings thereafter were devoted, one way or another, to the historical and sociological analysis of the *color line*—of the way arbitrary racial divisions are at the foundation of social organization in the United States and most European and other societies.

Sociology, the academic work, is always and necessarily the work of bringing back to life social worlds lost from an earlier time. But this scientific work is rooted in the practical labors of people like Du Bois who suffered the lost world of his childhood. The very fact that late in life he retold the childhood story of the party card suggests that Du Bois's professional sociology of the lost worlds of the people of the African Diaspora was rooted in his practical sociology of the lost world of racial innocence that little white girl stole from him. Had she not, who knows what would have happened? The sociological life is a process of many rememberings by which individuals go back deep into their earliest years, even to the days few can remember at all, in order to reconstruct, as Du Bois did, the social meaning of those lost worlds.

Lost worlds may seem a strange phrase to use in relation to the sociological imagination. One supposes that the imagination is a kind of dream of the future. But dreams cannot come from nothing. The imagination draws on past, as well as present, experience for its material. Just as it can be said that adult life is a continual retelling of the stories of childhood, so the sociological life is a reliving of the events of the past—an attempt to put into new stories the pains and pleasures that shaped us when we first stepped into the world such as it is. In Du Bois's life, the actual events of that little schoolhouse party may not have occurred exactly as he later retold them. Few of us remember the past exactly. Whatever the precise facts of that party were, they helped make Du Bois who he was to be: "Then it dawned upon me with a certain suddenness that I was different from the others; or like, mayhap, in heart and life and longing, but shut out from their world by a vast veil." The veil by which the color line in many societies shuts out blacks and others is produced throughout, and by, those societies at every level of their organization. But the veil works its effects in such little moments as the childishly vicious refusal of a party card. People thus refused, like those in a position to refuse, begin to understand their social worlds, if they do at all, when they remember the lost worlds of the past, and retell those worlds in stories.

The sociological imagination includes, with rare exception, a coming out from a dark, isolated personal place into the light of possibility. The coming out is easier, and the possibilities are greater, when it occurs in an already somewhat well-developed collective life. Children, including heterosexual white ones like Darlene and me, who come out to their adolescent world of sexual feelings present themselves to a world already well advertised. Others, like all those kids of my generation who only later found pleasure in life as gays or lesbians, usually suffer in a dark closet of social shame. For them, especially those who still do not dare to present themselves for what they are or wish to be, coming out is much harder—as it must be for children, even for adults, who face social things they do not fully understand. Great Barrington, white and rural, offered little to Willie Du Bois that would have taught him about the color line, just as Charlotte Perkins Gilman as a girl had only the vague image of her female relatives, notably Harriet Beecher Stowe, to suggest that women can be in the world on other than man-made terms. This is what makes sociologists like Du Bois and Gilman so amazing to behold. They did what they did with little or no support. Though there were race-men and feminists before them, they were available at best as shadowy forms, as whispers between the lines of adult talk. Du Bois and Gilman learned to recover the lost worlds of their early days largely on their own.

Whether one does it alone or in the company of others, the recollection of the lost worlds of the past is that without which the sociological life cannot move forward. But this, most definitely, is *not* an exercise of the individual alone. Even Du Bois and Gilman learned from the wider social worlds of their times. Du Bois's rejection at the hand of a snotty white girl must have festered inside for years. The imagination arose when he rethought and retold that story in his head, even perhaps years later in Europe, where his black skin made no evident difference, not at least to the German girl who wanted to be his wife and whom he refused out of love because he knew what they would face upon returning to the United States. But the retelling of these rejections can reach the imaginative heights necessary to a sociology of the world in all its powerful social reaches only when the true past is remembered for what it is. This is what Du Bois did. It may be too simple to say that the story of the children's mean little party led to his sociology of racial division in the United States and throughout the world. But it would not be wrong to suppose that that story and many others were the stock in which he stirred subsequent learning and experience. The sociological imagination is a soup boiling up from leftovers. It whets the appetite because it is familiar yet sustaining for the days ahead.

The days of childhood, like all those along the course of life, are people-filled. To speak of our social worlds is to speak of lives with the pals and bigots of our playgrounds, and many others as well. If one is to live the sociological life fully, then it must be lived in the wider worlds. Hence, the surprising, but true, idea that just as the individual life must reimagine the lost worlds of its childhood, so the collective life of even the modern world itself is built out of, and requires, a retelling of stories of its collective pasts— of the pasts out of which the modernized and westernizing portions of the globe created the social structures in which, for better or worse, nearly everyone must live.

The social worlds in which we live locally are often several in number and different in kind. Upon encountering the white, excluding world in Great Barrington, Massachusetts, Du Bois realized that he must ever thereafter live in two worlds at once. This experience was at the heart of his most famous line about the twoness of African-American experience:

> One ever feels his twoness,—an American, a Negro; two souls, two thoughts, two unreconciled strivings; two warring ideals in one dark body, whose dogged strength alone keeps it from being torn asunder.
>
> —Du Bois, *Souls*[17]

If a person's soul is double, then it is because he must live in two worlds at once. Du Bois's idea of *double consciousness*, or twoness, applies to the experience of many in addition to those who suffered as he did. Though she did not put it the same way, it is plain that Gilman also understood that she lived in two social worlds at once—the man-made one that defined reality for nearly everyone, and the silent one of women confined to their rooms.

It is more common for those who live in the excluded, veiled places of the world to be vividly aware of the twoness or many-ness of their social realities. But even comfortable white boys like Max Weber and Emile Durkheim had the experience. Emile, for example, came from many generations of Orthodox Jewish rabbis. His father wanted him to follow in the tradition. Yet something in his childhood experience in rural France in the 1870s exposed him to the world of secular learning and nudged him out into the wider world of Paris, and the modern urban world, where he was accorded much respect even while being subject to those who hate Jewish people. Though some have safer passage than others, few are given a free ride through the world that stands outside their childhood streets and villages. The infant is born into a small world surrounding her crib, but soon enough, over the years, she grows into awareness of other worlds—first the worlds of gossipy stories her caretakers chat about as she plays, then the worlds of small differences in early school, then eventually the wider worlds of state and nation, of the global situation. All the great sociologists of the past followed this path of discovery, leaving behind the worlds of their youth in rural France or Massachusetts, or urban Berlin or Providence.

Professional sociology, as it is practiced in the colleges and universities, differs from practical sociology chiefly for having accepted the obligation to speak about the modern world and its powerful structures. Pure, practical people have the option to pretend, at their peril, that the bigger social things won't bother them. The professionals do not. Needless to say, as we know from the stories of Du Bois and Gilman, this does not mean that the professionals ignore the stories of their childhood, any more than it means that the practical cannot understand the modern world. But what distinguishes the professionals is that, one way or another, they come to an understanding of the modern world as a whole. It's their job. That they do this work is what can make the professionals excellent field guides to living the practical sociological life. Professional sociology's dedication to describing the modern world is a constant encouragement and reminder to the rest that the sociological life is also a life in a world of big, usually national or global, social things. Such intimidating worlds as the modern one have their characteristic features about which we must learn to speak.

The work of the academic sociologists, like that of practical, is arduous enough but made even more so by the fact that the structures we study are always lost to us. Whether we study for our survival changes in the welfare system upon which some of us depend to feed the children or study the long past of the slave trade that built the modern colonial system, what we look for is no longer there. The structures that cause a mother to be cut off from social support for her children may come down just that morning as she left the government office. But the denials are always provoked by structures that came into place years before. And if the mother is African American one of those structures, some say, may indeed have been the slave trade that brought her ancestors here centuries before. Then, to make matters more arduous, sociology, the science, came to life just when the new worlds of modernity were reminding people of the old worlds they were losing.

Sociology, the academic field, began late in the nineteenth century when it was widely thought that the new industrial order was bringing forth a new world order. Ironically, much of the new sociology of that period from 1848 to 1920 or so was devoted to the search for lost worlds—those social orders that were thought to have disappeared.

Infatuation with new world orders rises and falls according to the temperature of social things. The faster social things move, the hotter they get and, it seems, the more people wish for, and think they see, a new world order. But even at the beginning of the modern era, after those earliest explorers in the sixteenth century settled into their new colonies, they lost the blush of new world adventure and had a good smoke. After that, they got down to the hard work of colony building. When the thrill of the new fades, reality dawns. The head aches and the throat chokes with phlegm fighting the toxins. These are the sort of dull, dirty days when adventurers and colonists dream of the homes they left—in much the same way that many Russians, soon after the fall of the communists, dreamt of returning to the good old days of Soviet rule when, at least, there had been bread in the markets.

Dreams of new world orders are not easily sustained when the winter of life sets in hard about the windows. Sociologies, if they are to imagine this-worldly reality, must always be skeptical of the modern world's faith in the inevitability of progress and of its seductive, but seldom delivered upon, promise of new world orders. Though the temptation is strong to join the crowds, sociological restraint requires, as I said, a willingness to lace the easy dreams with the hard work of remembering. This is why, from the beginning, and especially today, professional sociologists have studied the near and distant history of the modern world.

Immanuel Wallerstein (b. 1930)—a sociologist who today divides his time between Yale University, the Braudel Center he founded at the University of Binghamton, and the *Ecole des hautes études* (roughly, the School of Advanced Studies) in France—is prominent among those who have described the ways in which the new world order of the sixteenth century evolved into a global economic and social system. It may well be that the idea (as distinct from the reality) of a coherent, orderly world can only be explained by reference to the impressive organizing force of the economic interests of the early European powers who colonized the globe around principles of capitalist profit. Though they did a good bit of social evil, the colonizers moved quickly to build their colonial empires, out from which flowed the fuel of capitalist development.

Wallerstein, following a respected tradition of French historical scholarship, has shown that the idea of the modern world as a system is, in fact, built on the historical realities of the *modern world economy*. In brief, his idea is that, since about 1500, capitalism increasingly organized its colonized world into a system in which *core states*, like the Spanish or the Dutch in earlier times and the British and Americans in recent centuries, drew resources from *peripheral areas*, like Africa and the Caribbean, that are rich in cheap labor and natural wealth. The modern world economy is, thus, a global system in which the powerful core states exploit the resource-rich, but politically weak, periphery. Instances of exploitation in the name of modern capitalism are everywhere to be found, even within regions. In North America, for example, the United States exploits oil deposits of the Artic North (often in tandem with Canada), while similarly using Mexican workers in the *maquiladoras* as a source of unspeakably cheap labor. Wallerstein's work, which is much debated and highly influential, includes many historical illustrations of this theory.

In his three-volume study, *The Modern World-System*, Wallerstein tells the story of the infamous slave-trade triangle that became the economic foundation of the modern world economy, thus of the modern world itself.[18] Enslaved African people were brought, beginning mostly in the seventeenth century, to the Americas, where they were pressed to the labor that produced commodities like spice and coffee or raw materials like cotton. These, in turn, were traded back to Europe for refinement or spinning into sugar, coffee, or clothing. When these desirable market goods were sold across Europe, the profits were available to pay the price of taking more slaves from Africa, thus completing the triangle. There would have been no new world order had it not been for this world system that grew into a truly global enterprise, symbolized best, perhaps, by the global colonial system of the British in the nineteenth century—the empire upon which the sun never set. So, when in 1991 President George H. W. Bush spoke of a new world order after the cold war with communism, he had in mind a world order in which the capitalist world-system could return to the usual business of ordering as many corners of the globe as might have useful supplies of natural resources or cheap labor.

To imagine the so-called modern world as a *world system* is to put a damper on claims that modern social things are not all that different from lost older ones. In fact what distinguishes the modern world-system from, say, the lost imperial civilizations of Rome or Babylonia is that modern colonizers indulge themselves the belief that what *they* were (and still are) doing was much more like raising children than slave trading. In 1804 and 1805, when Lewis and Clark explored the upper Missouri River of the newly acquired Northwest plains of the United States, they were accustomed to addressing the Mandan and Nez Percé Indians as "children" when they spoke on behalf of the great white "father" in Washington, D.C., Thomas Jefferson. Lewis and Clark were actually very nice young men. Their problem was that they thought as all good early modern European and American colonizers thought. Little did even they suspect that the indigenous peoples who saved their lives and opened the riverways to them would soon be victims of American avarice. Modern world colonizers tend to be caught in a sociological contradiction. Colonizing is dirty business, by any standard—whether it is the taking of slaves and lands or, as today, the hawking of capitalist commodities to third-world villagers who need peace and clean water more than basketball shoes and deadly cigarettes. Yet these modern colonizers generally want to think of themselves as doing good even when it is usually bad they are doing to the people whose worlds they take away.

One might even say that a significant aspect of modern cultures in the West is that they tend to emphasize the alleged good of their new world orders as a way of comforting themselves over the terrible things they do that are, in effect if not in name, no different from what their ancestors did in the ancient worlds now lost. Thus they see the modern as always moving ahead toward a better world.

The idea of a new world order renewing itself through time may well be one of the most important themes in the culture of the Western civilization that has arisen in the modern world since 1500. At the very least, it is widely agreed that the sociological condition that most distinguishes modern Western societies from others (those considered premodern or traditional, and those of Asia, Africa, and the Latin American forests and highlands) is that modern ones are organized around the expectation of continuous change and growth. Just think of the role the idea of progress plays in modernist collective dreams, and the place of history as witness to humankind's capacity for improvement. Think too of the centrality of growth as the cornerstone of economic policy in the modern societies, just as development is the expectation imposed on less developed, relatively impoverished areas of the world. So pervasive and powerful is the idea of new and improved world orders that, in most of the middle-class cultural areas of the modern world, individuals measure their personal worth by their ability to get ahead. To this end, individuals engage in numerous educational practices designed for their self-improvement, in order that they might have a good career, conceived in terms of steady progress along an upward path of social and financial gain. It is not that these ideals are in themselves ludicrous or otherwise objectionable. Hardly. The point is that the collective and personal search for new world orders is a big part of what makes the modern world and its members modern. The main business of sociology in this modern world has been to render account (sometimes critically) of modernity's new world orders.

Sociology was founded, as I said, as a recognized profession in the quarter century from 1890 to the beginning of the First World War. This accomplishment may be accurately represented by reference to three individual men in Europe and a group of them in the United States: Max Weber in Germany, Emile Durkheim in France, Karl Marx in England, and the members of the Department of Sociology at the University of Chicago in the United States. Of all of these founders, only the early Chicago sociologists succeeded from the start in introducing sociology to the general public as an official science of things social.

The University of Chicago department, founded in 1892 (just one year after the university itself was founded), was the first department in a major research university to offer a Ph.D. in sociology, the first thus to train in significant numbers a generation of professionals in the field. From this one department came the oldest, and still one of the most prestigious, scientific journals in the field, the *American Journal of Sociology*, as did many of the early leaders of the most important learned society in the field, the American Sociological Association. Still today, the Chicago department is considered among the best in the country. If you trust popularity contests of this sort, the Department of Sociology at Chicago is functionally equivalent to the old New York Yankees or the Boston Celtics. No other department has been ranked first in the country, more or less justifiably, some many times over such a long time.

At Chicago in the 1890s, sociology first fully took the form of an organized discipline of professionals. One of the department's early members was a leader in the new field and coauthor of sociology's first important textbook. Robert Park (1864–1944) is said to have been led to sociology by reading the German poet Goethe's epic story, Faust, of which he remarked: "You remember that Faust was tired of books and wanted to see the world."[19] For Park, and most of his early colleagues, many of whom had also been previously engaged in some practical political, social, or religious work, the desire to "see the world" was second nature. This was just as true of many of their first students like Jane Addams (1860–1935), the famous founder of Hull House and the settlement house movement, and coworker with Charlotte Perkins Gilman in feminist causes. In the United States, at least, this very first generation of professional sociologists was drawn from among the ranks of those most attuned to the practical world of human suffering and social change. Remember that the first department of sociology to offer a Ph.D. had no pool of previously trained Ph.D.s to draw upon for its faculty. They were, like Robert Park (a newspaperman and social activist), recruited from other fields. Thus it is not surprising that the tradition still today known as "Chicago sociology" is one founded in the study of the varieties of urban life—of street gangs and immigrants in the early days, or of the urban *underclass*, the term now in use which was made famous by William Julius Wilson (b. 1935), for many years a University of Chicago professor (until 1996, when he moved to Harvard). The books the Chicago sociologists wrote over the years arose from their desire, first of all, to see the world as it is. This can be said of most sociologists, especially in the United States, but at no place was the commitment more deeply ingrained in the early days than at the Chicago department.

The world most of the first professional sociologists saw, and wrote about, when they looked in a disciplined fashion was itself a new world order. If people today think of the post-cold-war world as new, they should stop to compare today to the newness of the world in the first days of academic sociology. Already by the time of the fire caused by Mrs. O'Leary's cow in 1871, Chicago had been transformed from a raucous western frontier town to a major city, the railroad and trade center of the American plains and Midwest. Chicago had become the economic capital of one of the world's most productive regions. As the city was rebuilt after the fire that had destroyed eighteen thousand of its buildings and left ninety thousand people homeless, it became a virtual exemplar of the new industrial city then emerging worldwide. At the time of the founding of the University of Chicago's department in 1892, the surrounding city was, as a whole, prosperous, but prosperous because of the labor of wave upon wave of immigrants—ethnics with their many and strange customs and languages from Europe and, as the First World War cut off the flow of European labor, blacks from the American South.

New York, London, Paris, and other of the great Western metropoles were undergoing changes of a similar kind, but few cities anywhere in the Western world changed more rapidly in such a short time than did Chicago in the decades at the end of the nineteenth and the beginning of the twentieth centuries. Yet, in spite of differences in the kinds of changes, including differences in the ethnic and racial compositions of the immigrant populations throughout the world, the word of the day was that the order of the world was changing. In the span of a few generations, North American and European societies were transformed from dispersed rural and agrarian locales into an increasingly urban and industrial world of global proportions.

It hardly need be said that when people move from strange places into a far-off new world, they encounter foods, values, laws, and customs offensive to their own, all sold, enforced, and taught in languages they do not speak; and there will be trouble, sooner or later. In Chicago in those days, trouble arose from labor conflict between the organizing workers and the industrial interests. But conflict and violence were also a regular feature of daily life in the ethnic neighborhoods. One of American sociology's most famous urban studies, *The Polish Peasant in Europe and America*, was published in 1918-1919 by William I. Thomas (1863-1947) and Florian Znaniecki (1882-1958). (Znaniecki was himself a Polish immigrant, though of the upper, educated classes.) Among this book's rich documentary history of the daily lives of the new immigrants were stories of mistrust, confusion, even murder. Yet the point of *The Polish Peasant* was that, "in spite of the social unrest and demoralization . . . due to the decay" of their social traditions, the Poles brought to the new world "precisely the attitudes upon which cooperative enterprises can be built."[20] Consider the sociological irony here—though they were in a state of unrest, they were basically cooperative people, as are most immigrants. The sociological idea was that, upon looking out into the then new world, the sociologist saw good in the social evil all about.

A very similar conclusion was reached by Frederic Thrasher (1892-1962), whose 1927 book *The Gang: A Study of 1,313 Gangs in Chicago* explained that gang life, though the cause of crime and violence, has as its underlying social purpose the attainment of a social status. Again, out of evil, good; or, as the idea would be rephrased by Robert K. Merton

(1910–2003), one of the most important of a later generation of American sociologists (of whom we soon shall have occasion to say more), behind the appearances of things there often lies a *latent social function*. Though such an idea may seem to be either a terrible contradiction or a foolish rationalization of bad behavior, any sociologist of new and changing worlds can hardly avoid coming to some such conclusion.

Think of it this way: If you are living in a place and time of rapid social change, many social things will not be tomorrow what they appear to be today. I recall as vividly as though it were yesterday the day some thirty years ago I had to face my first, sharp rebuke by a fully conscious feminist. The subject of our confrontation was an unthought through, hence thoughtless, remark I had tossed out in casual conversation. I had believed, in the most naive way possible, that the "obvious" differences between men and women are many, absolute, and immutable. In particular, I made some reference to the then widely alleged "irrationality" of the female of the species. Since then, I have learned a great deal more about this subject (not the least important of which is a very intimate acquaintance with my own seemingly limitless wealth of irrational emotions). At the precise moment of the confrontation, it was not so much what was said to me as that she said it with such swift certainty. This caused me to think again, and slowly reconsider the world of gender differences in which, until then, I had lived rather thoughtlessly. Even today, a person of my gendered kind could hardly claim to have achieved a perfect understanding of this subject, yet there are few men anywhere who are not vividly aware that they are at warranted risk when they fail to keep their tongues in check and hands to themselves. Women, on the other hand, are right in their rage that the change is not more complete. But a change has taken place. For me it began one day; for other men, some other day. When change takes place, there is usually some moment when what had been thought to be incontestable truth became something else altogether. This may well be the most fundamental law of daily life in changing societies. From it comes the sociological idea of the latent, or hidden, meanings of social things. Latency simply refers to the fact that a good many social events may appear to be one thing on the surface, but quite another upon close inspection. Stealing, for example, is bad, unless, of course, the one who steals is penniless and homeless. Taking milk for one's starving babies may not be good, but neither is it bad in the same way as stealing for drug money.

Social things truly aren't always what they seem, and certainly not when one finds herself in a new and unforgiving social world. Whether a Polish immigrant fresh to Chicago in the 1890s, or a sleeping-car porter in the

1920s working the New Orleans line from Chicago, or an obtuse white guy of the early 1960s in a new order of gender relations—what one thought in the past, even a not so distant past, suddenly comes open to inspection. This was the near universal state of affairs in the Western world upon which the first professional sociologists looked. It was certainly as much the case in Europe as in America.

The European sociologists of the 1890s were somewhat less successful than the Chicago ones in establishing a formal institutional base in the university. Max Weber in Germany eventually gave up his university professorship. Much of his famously disciplined work was first read, not by students, but by a circle of colleagues, many of whom met for years on Sunday afternoons in the home he shared with his wife, Marianne. Weber also, of course, published his work in noted academic journals, one of which he helped establish and edit, the *Archiv fuer Sozialwissenschaft* (roughly, Journal for Social Science). So far as I know, Weber never thought of organizing a teaching department of sociology.

In France, Emile Durkheim succeeded famously in the French university system of which he was one of the brightest stars. He held the first official position with the word "sociology" in its title, but he held it only because of his prestige, which allowed him, at least, to name his own job title as he wished. He never organized a formal teaching department in the field. In fact, it was impossible even to get an undergraduate degree in sociology in France until the 1960s. But, like Weber, Durkheim worked closely with a group of influential research peers with whom he founded and edited the journal *L'Année sociologique* (roughly, Sociological Yearbook). Thus, though sociology's institutional development came much later in France, Germany, and most of Europe (including Great Britain) than in the United States, it enjoyed a good enough beginning, mostly through the leadership of Weber and Durkheim and the brilliant scholarship they themselves published and encouraged among their followers and friends.

The sociologists at the turn of the nineteenth century, Americans and Europeans alike, were equally committed to sociology as a way of interpreting and as a way of changing the world. The Americans, being somewhat more inclined toward the practical, drew this value from their engagements in social work, journalism, and religion. The Europeans, being somewhat more influenced by high culture, drew it from the literary traditions. Thus, Weber and Durkheim followed the earlier example of Karl Marx, the first of the great European social thinkers, who was long dead by the time they came of professional age. Marx, as is well known, was every bit as interested in the practical politics to which his social ideas led as in the ideas themselves. It is less well known that Marx read all of Shakespeare's plays over and over again for the sheer pleasure of it, and was himself an elegant writer. Marx wrote the sociology of the modern capitalist world with a poet's ear for human suffering. He wrote thus in order to inspire the revolution that would transform the world. As an organizer of the first international union of working people, Marx was among those who directly provoked the industrial conflicts that so interested the Chicago sociologists, who, though they knew relatively little of Marx's writings, were as concerned as he was about the world's injustices. And Weber and Durkheim, who knew Marx's ideas very well, both saw the pathos of the industrial world, at least partly, through the lenses Marx had already ground.

Weber and Durkheim, writing a full generation after Marx's death in 1883, could not help, therefore, defining their sociologies by taking into account Marx's earlier attacks on the evils of economic exploitation. But both Weber and Durkheim went beyond what they considered to be the oversimplifications and ethical insufficiencies of Marx's sociology. While their respective politics were more mainstream and cautious than Marx's (and accordingly less threatening), Weber and Durkheim were every bit as much public figures engaged in the politics of their day as Marx had been in his.

Just the same, Max Weber's most famous book, *The Protestant Ethic and the Spirit of Capitalism*,[21] is still not to be found among those at grocery store checkout counters. But it was, and still is, widely read because of the way it responded to the two most urgent practical sociological questions of the day: Why has the world order changed as it has? What will become of us in the future? *Protestant Ethic* sought primarily to answer the first of the questions, but in the end it addressed the second as well. In his book, Weber argued against Marx's famous idea that capitalism produces *class conflict*— that is, against Marx's fundamental principle that the exploitation of workers comes about because workers belong to a different class of men and women than their bosses do. The working class is that class of people whose life chances were, in Marx's day (and still in ours), largely determined by their economic vulnerability to the dominant class. By contrast, the dominant class comprises those whose life circumstances are privileged because they own (or, more often today, manage) the resources and factories without which there would be no industrial work. Class conflict is the result of the contradictory interests of the working and owner (or manager) classes. Because he believed that class conflict was inevitable under capitalism, Marx thought it was impossible for those in the working class to gain a hedge against the voracious greed of the capitalists' search for profit, economic growth, and (again) progress—at least not without a revolution.

Because Marx's ideas had been formulated and well known long before Weber ever thought of giving up dueling to become a sociologist, Weber and others who wanted to discuss capitalism had little choice but to defend their views against Marx's. One of the issues that Weber, especially, wanted to deal with was the question of the foundations of modern society. Is modern society based primarily on economic or on moral concerns? Weber was skeptical of the economism many Marxists found in Marx's writing.

Economism is the informed belief that all societies, at their foundations, are driven by economic interests; and, accordingly, that the ethics or religious values or political ideas people profess are of no true importance in defining their real-life situations. Weber, we shall see, sought a more balanced view that would include the moral along with the economic side of social things. Thus, in order to understand Weber's sociology, it helps first to know more about Marx's.

Marx's preference for an economic interpretation of social life was especially compelling in the nineteenth century, when it seemed that religion was losing its influence and that modern industrial society was the wave of the future. Put simply, Marx thought that modern capitalism was the most fundamental structure of the modern world because the capitalist class was so effective at depriving working people of any right to profits from the commodities they produced with their hands. Capitalists seldom get their hands dirty with anything more than the money they take from the toil of poorly paid workers.

While Mississippi slaves without whom cotton would not have been produced in the American South enjoyed none of the profits of their labor, the early generation of workers in the factory system were not appreciably less excluded from the vast profits made in the burgeoning cloth and steel milling operations. Indeed, for a period of time in the nineteenth century, the early factory workers in the north of England and the northeast of the United States wove, under capitalism, the cotton that had been picked by slaves under feudalism. Cotton picking then depended on the fresh supply of healthy bodies. The slave's body was, in effect, the principal tool of early cotton production. The slave earned no profit because she was, literally, the chief tool of the production system owned by the planters.

In much the same way, Marx might have argued, nineteenth-century weavers mill workers in New Hampshire or turn-of-the-century meatpackers in Chicago were tools of these new industries. Legally, they were not the property of the factory owners. But, just as the planters paid no wage to their slaves, the factory capitalists were free to pay as low a wage as possible to their workers. If you come from Poland or Alabama to find a job in meatpacking, and that is the one skill you possess, what "freedom" do you have to sell your working body's energy, when the only work is at relatively few meatpacking establishments, each owned (then) by capitalists more willing to cooperate to fix wages than to satisfy the human needs of workers? What, then, is the worth of ideals and laws freeing workers from slavery, if workers are virtual slaves to the capitalist system?

Marx's ideas were powerful sociology in the 1860s, when his most famous book, *Capital*, was published. His ideas drew notice because he wrote with good evidence and clear thinking about the essential greed of the early factory system in which, in contrast to today, there were no meaningful legal limits on the industrialists' right to press children and mothers into service, to extend the working day to the limit of human endurance, to introduce machinery without regard to the safety and health of those forced to operate it, or even to suppress the organization of trade unions. The world of work today is far from perfect, but in Marx's day it was an unmitigated nightmare—real bondage underneath artificial ideals of progress.

This is where Weber and the founding of official sociology come back in. Weber, as I said, felt that Marx did not see the new world with enough subtlety. Weber, in *Protestant Ethic and the Spirit of Capitalism*, largely accepted Marx's claim that capitalism aggravated and enforced deep divisions between the economic and social classes in industrial society. It would have been difficult for anyone at the end of the nineteenth century to overlook the new *social division of labor*—that is, the way in which people fell into different social classes according to the advantages or disadvantages of their place in the factory system. Workers and bosses did different work; as a result, they were socially different people. Even people like Weber, who lived in the relative ease of a bourgeois life in Heidelberg, Germany, could see that the factory system had changed the world and that something was wrong with the new industrial order. Whatever the profits and progress, people were suffering. It was so bad that some workers were ready, at the extreme of their endurance, to enter into open conflict to improve their circumstances.

But, in spite of this fact of life in that new world, Weber believed that capitalism was not merely a product of economic greed but every bit as much a product of something even deeper in human nature. In brief,

Weber's idea was that the modern world could not have come simply from economic things, because greed is a feature of most economic systems. Therefore, greed and class conflict are not, Weber thought, the most definitive features of modern society. Rather, one of the more astonishing facts of the modern world was, and still is, that millions of people had ended up thinking and behaving differently from those who had come before. In other words, it was evident already by the last years of the nineteenth century that along with the new social division of labor had come a new social consciousness, a different way of thinking about, and behaving in, the world. In particular, people had come to believe, often in spite of the hardship of their own lives, that the new world held out to them the hope of progress. As I said, Marx thought this was false consciousness. Weber, in particular, thought the new consciousness, even if false in some ways, was real in its own right, and worthy of scientific inspection.

One of the distinctions Weber drew in order to account for the importance of consciousness, or ethical attitude, was between the traditional and modern ways of thinking. In the traditional world prior to modern times, and especially before the industrial system, people were not so much worried about the future as about how to organize daily life in order to protect the traditions to which they were accustomed. *Traditionalism* obviously has to do with keeping traditions, keeping faith with the past. In other words, people living in a traditionalist culture are not likely to be willing migrants to some foreign place like Chicago—unless their economic plight forces them to move in order to survive, or unless (like the Polish peasants in Chicago) they can be assured of living among people who are traditionalists like themselves. One of Weber's most memorable lines was that the traditional world was the world of the "eternal yesterday." And this was the world that was very rapidly passing away as he and the others wrote. Even the immigrants to Chicago found that, though they settled with others of their traditional kind, it was very hard to keep the old ways—if for no other reason than that factory work demanded a different orientation to work.

Working in the fields is strenuous, but there are times when one cannot work—at night, in the rainy seasons, winters. Rural life is ordered to some degree by the rhythm of natural events that (except, of course, for slaves) allows time to enjoy the religious, family, and culinary traditions in which one has been brought up. But, in a factory job, one starts at a time dictated by schedule and works until released. The worker must adjust her movements to machinery, and must think always about what is coming next, under conditions that dull the mind and numb the fingers. Meanwhile, on their side of the shop floor, the owners invest their money in factories, new production machinery, and wage costs because they know that this system is the most efficient means of production and, thus, the most profitable. But, of course, the entrepreneur would never take the risk, would never be able to take the risk of such an investment if he did not already have a modern outlook on things. Investment risk demands a definite attitude—an ability rationally to calculate the cost of things and the profits expected, a willingness to work long hours, sacrificing the pleasures of life in order to supervise the operation (in those days owners were also the managers), and most importantly an ability, that is, to "see" the future profit to be gained from the risk and sacrifice. For many of the early capitalists, the risk paid off, but it could not have if they had not been able to envision a payoff in the imagined future and then, importantly, to calculate and coordinate all the details required to make the thing work. Whatever you think of capitalists, then or now, this is a mighty accomplishment.

Weber was not all that more favorable toward capitalism than was Marx. But he was better able to appreciate the possibility that the capitalist could be motivated by more than greed. In fact, though he believed that the workers were themselves influenced by the spirit of capitalism, it was the capitalist entrepreneur whom Weber pictured as the new modern man, so to speak. This new man's rational, entrepreneurial ethics were the new attitudes that had come gradually to displace traditionalism. In the older, agricultural past, people could afford to observe the feast days, eat the foods, and dance the dances by which traditions are passed through the generations. But in the modern world of industrial activity, thinking had to be directed to the future—the future of the jobs the workers had migrated to find, the future of the profits the capitalist bosses had saved in order to gain.

Weber concluded, therefore, that traditionalism had declined and a new modern attitude he called *rationality* had arisen gradually over the several centuries after the Protestant Reformation until the time Weber wrote at the end of the nineteenth century. Rationality, Weber thought, is an attitude of future-oriented calculations. More than an attitude, rationality was so pervasive that it could be called an ethic—a widely shared social value that motivates practical behavior. In order to survive in a future-oriented world, modern individuals must be on the lookout for ways to use their energies and wealth in order either to have some place to live and something to eat after the migration, in the case of the workers, or to have some surplus to reinvest in newer and better equipment, the case of the bosses. According to Weber, the new economic world could only come into being if it included a new ethic inspiring new ways of thinking and acting in the world. This is the now-famous work ethic that spread gradually among people in parts of

Europe and North America where capitalism arose most vigorously and is still today highly valued and necessary to economic survival.

Weber believed that this new attitude, or ethic, was originally the basic idea of the Protestant religion—and, thus, was an attitude that associated a person's spiritual fate less with participation in the rituals of the church than with doing work in the world. While I omit the details of the argument, you might well appreciate that there is something to be said for Weber's reasoning in that even today we speak of the "work ethic," by which is meant the "Protestant work ethic" that was, in fact, more generously diffused in the very Protestant regions (England, Holland, parts of Switzerland, New England) where, by no coincidence, capitalism also arose first and most emphatically.

Weber's book on capitalism made sense to many, though perhaps more sense to those who had a reason to defend the role of the capitalist in the new system. It was, in any case, considered by many an effective reply to Marx's idea that capitalism is nothing but an evil economic practice determining all else in social life. (Marx's view, of course, was preferred by those who took the side of the workers.) Weber believed, and many would agree today, that modern society is at least as much a result of the attitudes, values, and cultures of modern people as of their economic greed.

Hence, again, the basic sociological principle: Things just plain are not what they seem, at least not always. Capitalism, an apparently economic thing, is also an ethical thing. In this respect, Weber may properly be considered the sociological source of our understanding today of how the habits of big social things like capitalist societies are rooted somehow in the habits of rational individuals. Bourdieu's concept of habitus is, in fact, a more advanced version of Weber's theory of the ethical spirit behind capitalism. The modern world came to be because the habitus of modern people changed, and with it changed the daily practices, not only of millions of people who migrated to Chicago, and other thriving urban centers, in order to labor in dreary manufacturing firms, but also of those who calculated the cost, and took the risk, of forming the firms in the first place. Modern thinking requires modern habits, and vice versa. Both together must exist for a modern world to come into being, however long it may take.

Weber was not, however, happy with what he saw in capitalism, not even with the ethical values it required. At the very end of *Protestant Ethic*, he turned directly to the question of what he felt about the practical human effects of modern life. He expressed himself in a poetic style that some think was borrowed from Goethe. Referring to the negative side of modern efficiencies with all their calculated indifference to the human spirit, Weber wrote of this new world as an *iron cage*:

> No one knows who will live in this cage in the future, or whether at the end of this tremendous development entirely new prophets will arise, or there will be a great rebirth of old ideas and ideals, or, if neither, mechanized petrification, embellished with a sort of convulsive self-importance. For this last stage of this cultural development, it might well be truly said: "Specialists without spirit, sensualists without heart; this nullity imagines that it has attained a level of civilization never before achieved."
>
> —Max Weber, *Protestant Ethic and the Spirit of Capitalism* (1905)[22]

Though writing in the high literary form of the German cultural elite, Weber was speaking with passion of the debilitating effects of his day's new world order. Where Marx saw the degradations of early capitalism behind the scenes of the industrial workshop, Weber saw another human threat in the more subtle aggressions of modernity's rationalizing culture upon the human spirit. If everyone was constantly calculating the most efficient means to get to some future goal, then what, he asked, remained of the quiet reserves of human spirit, of those places and times in which people discover meaning simply by opening their hearts to others, to their gods, even to the values of their pasts? This good question troubled Marx every bit as much as Weber. Their sociologies were different, as were their diagnoses of the evils of their world, but each was equally concerned, in his way, with the consequences of the new world for the practical lives of ordinary people.

Emile Durkheim could hardly have been expected to disagree. It was he, more than the other two, who had struggled in his youth to give up and leave behind six generations of Jewish village life to find his way in the big cities of modern France. Durkheim, though more austere and remote than Marx, even than Weber, was otherwise of much the same mind as they. Just as Weber disagreed with Marx over the question of the role of ethical value in the rise of capitalism, so too did Durkheim. Durkheim's view was that the new industrial order inevitably introduced the very divisions that were already apparent in France, as they were in Chicago at the turn of the century. What Marx had seen as class division and struggle under capitalism, Durkheim viewed from the point of view of social effects of a new division of labor. Though his interpretation of the crisis in the new world was different from Marx's, Durkheim was no less bothered by the way the industrial world divided people from each other. Industrial life, and the urban environment that supports it, aggravates differences and breaks apart the deep need Durkheim believed people have to live in a morally cohesive community. No doubt Durkheim's faith in the local community's ability to guide and support the individual was born in the experience of his native village, which was, in most ways, more traditional than modern.

There were, Durkheim feared, no social bonds strong enough to unite the separated parts of the socially divided labor force. Workers work with the machines; industrialists, with the books and their calculations of profitability. Though their economic destinies are bound to each other, the two classes come in no real social contact with each other. One social consequence is that they share few of the same experiences and fewer still of the same values and hopes. There is nothing, that is, at the heart of social life to support, guide, and encourage individuals to heal their social divisions and resolve their individual senses of confusion and isolation. For Durkheim, the most fundamental threat of the new world order was neither the alienating exploitation Marx saw nor the dispiriting iron cage Weber saw, but the loss of social cohesion. This, as I said, he called anomie, by which he also meant, roughly, the absence of moral rules able to instruct the individual in the ways of the world. Without a cohesive society able, at least minimally, to guide individuals with all their differences, society will incline toward greater confusion. As a result, individuals in that world are left in an anomic state.

Durkheim felt the struggles of modern life just as strongly as his German contemporary, Weber. Durkheim's sociology, as well as his work as a teacher of teachers, was motivated by a deep conviction that good professional sociology could produce a new knowledge that would move slowly and steadily through society, providing thereby a renewed sense of the values of social life, of the wider society. As religion did in a former time, Durkheim felt, knowledge, including sociological knowledge, must serve in modern times to integrate the individual into the collective life.

Professional sociology came into its own as an academic science just at a time when an earlier world was straining under the pressures of its terrible newness, of the changes that, as Marx put it, made "all things solid melt into air." Marx went on to say that whatever progress there may have been in modern times, the gains were always at the cost of a sobering destructiveness that Zygmunt Bauman later described in the title of one of his books: *Wasted Lives: Modernity and Its Outcasts* (2004).

Constant revolutionizing of production, uninterrupted disturbance of all social conditions, everlasting uncertainty and agitation distinguish the [modern] bourgeois epoch from all earlier ones. All fixed, fast-frozen relations, with their train of ancient and venerable prejudices and opinions, are swept away, all new-formed ones become antiquated before they can ossify. All that is solid melts into air, all that is holy is profaned, and man is at last compelled to face with sober sense, his real conditions of life, and his relations with his kind.

—Marx and Engels, *Manifesto of the Communist Party* (1848)[23]

Many are the benefits of the modern world. Even Marx granted this. But modernism came at such a high cost to human life. This was the fundamental moral contradiction for which all of the major lines of early sociology sought an answer. When the old worlds are lost, what are we to become in the new ones?

SOCIOLOGY BECOMES THE SCIENCE OF WORLDLY STRUCTURES: 1920–1960

The First World War (1914–1918) was not really the first world war. Nations, empires, city-states, families, and tribes the world over had been fighting each other for centuries. Nor was this war the first in which a foreign state sent troops across the seas to enter on the side of one or another European power. In the eighteenth century, for example, the Dutch and the French sent support to the Americans during their revolution against the British, who were rivals for control of shipping and the New World. In these ways among others, there had been world wars aplenty. Why was this one called the first of the world wars?

It is likely that this one war in the early twentieth century was thought of as the first world war because, by then, it was difficult to think of the more important events of human society as having any less than global implications. Then began a process we take for granted today. It was not yet, of course, a time when people spoke of globalization. Today the world, in spite of its troubles and differences, is brought together by the genius of information technologies, which seem to have united many in a global culture that arises, in turn, from the rapacious power of multinational corporations and states seeking world markets. One of the more puzzling, yet apparent, realities of today's world is the degree to which the cultural values and ideals that, more than a century ago, seemed to Marx to be so sneakily subordinate to economic interests are, today, produced in open and intimate correspondence to the interests of those very economic structures. Capitalists today may be just as greedy, but in Marx's day they mass-produced, say, woven cloth for profit and profit alone; today they often produce, say, software products for profit and social communication. The process of globalization, which is well advanced early in the new millennium, was just beginning to make itself known at the dawn of the previous century, in the days of the so-called First World War. The wars the world has since fought, and the big one it still fears might come, are thought of as worldly because, from the days of the early twentieth century, people have been increasingly required to think of the world as a whole comprising parts whose destinies are linked.

Max Weber's despair over the negative effects of capitalism, for example, was based on his fear that the ethic that drove the capitalist was like the sorcerer's apprentice. Once the magic words were said by Calvinist preachers in the sixteenth century, the earnest, hard-working ethic just kept hauling bucket upon bucket of enterprises until, it seemed, one day we all might be drowned in a sea of calculations. One of Weber's most often cited convictions was that the world had been "disenchanted." He meant that, as people gave themselves over to the rational calculations that lay at the heart of the modern ethic, they inevitably began to see the entire world in rational terms. This we recognize very well today in the avarice by which corporate interests are more than willing to clear-cut primitive forests in the American Northwest, or strip-mine the fertile farmland of southern Illinois, or pollute the waters and air of the industrial centers of Europe and Asia in order to maximize their profits.

From Weber's point of view, the actions of capitalists are not just greedy (though greedy they often are). More profoundly, Weber believed they are the inexorable result of the calculating spirit of the entrepreneurial ethic. If the world is meant to service the economic goals of mankind, then the entire world is at mankind's disposal. Nothing is spared. Few corners of the globe retain the natural enchantments that might cause people to think of forests and streams as, say, sacred places of the gods. Disenchantment, in this sense, is the unforgiving fellow traveler of globalization. Though Weber did not write of globalization, he was completely and utterly consumed with the problems he thought accompanied its earliest beginnings—that is, with the beginnings of modernization. Whether it is modernization or globalization, the temptation is strong to think of any such process as one that cannot be stopped, as one that will affect all men and women everywhere, eventually.

Modernization, by whatever name, is obviously not a process likely to end at the territorial borders of any given society. Though capitalist manufacturing did not spread to many parts of Africa, the Middle East, and Asia until much later (mostly after the second of the twentieth century's world wars), it was obvious that, once it began, modernization would eventually conquer the globe. This was plain to see even in the late nineteenth century because European or North American enterprises depended one way or another on world trade. Just as the first capitalists, in the sixteenth century, bought and sold slaves from Africa or cotton from the American South, the industrialists of the late nineteenth century took the profits that had accrued over the years from a rich system of world trade, to invest in steel and oil production, in the building of railways and skyscrapers. The modern factory system and the cities in which it thrived were built with capital drawn from all parts of the world, and built on the backs of workers enticed to come from all over the globe. Even in relatively more traditional corporate enterprises, like the meatpacking firms in Chicago in the late nineteenth and early twentieth centuries, one could hardly miss the fact that the industrialization that was the most salient form of modernization was a world process. All the founders of sociology understood this, one way or another. Weber called it rationalization, where Marx had seen it as the inexorable law of capitalist exploitation. Durkheim, the least global of the early thinkers, saw it nonetheless in the widespread anomic effect of the modern division of labor. Even the Chicago sociologists, seemingly narrowly focused on the social problems of their city, spoke of the universal laws of urban ecology that explained the wild differences in the life and chances of people in differing parts of a large city like Chicago.

So it would not be far wrong to say that professional sociology began at the end of the nineteenth century both as a science of the new world order and as a science of the world itself. It would be a long time until professional sociology, in the last quarter of the twentieth century, would develop its own explicit theories of the world, and look systematically beyond the borders of the distinctive social forms of the West's nation-states. But the necessity of thinking in global terms was there from the beginning. It was present in the undeniable fact of the times that, whatever one's theory of it, the world was caught up in a powerful process whereby even the most sacred of local customs and habits were disenchanted, transformed eventually into habitual practices so global that, while sitting cross-legged on a floor mat eating *kimch'i* in a provincial city in South Korea, an American and a Korean soci-ologist would be perfectly comfortable speaking of the world as though it were one. Those who have not had an experience like this need only think of the products they consume each day—jug wine from Chile, videos of Madonna romancing a bullfighter in Spain, rap music down-loaded from an internet pirate in China, Japanese cars made in Ohio, and cocaine illegally transported by go-fast boans from Columbia. Though there is little reason to believe that the first founders of sociology had sufficient sociological imagination to picture the world that today we take for granted, they did realize that sociology, if it was to be science of some respectable kind, had to be a science of global structures, of the world as a whole.

The period from the beginning of the First World War in 1914 through the end of the Second World War in 1945 up to the beginning of the 1960s was one in which the new modern world of the late nineteenth century was sorely tested by economic and political events that were felt to call into ques-tion the most basic values of human civilization. The economic crisis that became the Great Depression of the 1930s was not the first such economic crisis. Nor was Hitler, with the evils he wrought across Europe, the first such tyrant. Nor was the Second World War all that much more fully a global war than the First, or than, in relative terms, earlier clashes of great civi-lizations. What made the years between the First and Second World Wars so terrible was the concatenation of world events and the collective havoc they visited upon the spirit of the times.

One need only sample the opinions of leading social thinkers of the day to see just how desperate things were thought to be. Early in the period, in 1922, Georg Lukács (1885–1971), a Marxist social philosopher from Hungary, wrote that it was a time when "history must abolish itself."[24] Such a dire, fatalistic idea was, in Lukács's opinion, the necessary condition for considering the fate of human beings in an aggressively alienating world, one in which Marx's alienated laborer and Weber's lost soul in the iron cage were increasingly seen as the universal condition of all men and women. It was not just the effects of industrialization and modernization that led everyone into dire straits. Rather, it was the hard-to-avoid evidence that, everywhere one turned in the early decades of the twentieth century, the original hope of the modern world was being defeated, or reserved for the very well-to-do.

In the early years of the Great Depression of the 1930s, Reinhold Niebuhr (1892–1971), a theologian who was to become a leading political thinker in the United States, introduced the pessimistic idea that the modern democratic state, originally considered the guarantor of individual freedoms, was an essentially and unavoidably immoral and selfish institution. State politics, Niebuhr said, were hopelessly unable to operate with regard for the morality of their actions. Those, especially those of German descent like Niebuhr, who watched events in Germany in the early 1930s as Hitler rose to power needed no convincing. Even the leading liberal economist of the period, John Maynard Keynes (1883–1946), writing before Niebuhr and the Depression, saw enough evidence in the economic implications of the First World War to insist that the coming economic anarchy could never be avoided by a traditional, but naive, reliance on the free market and the enlightened freedom of individual entrepreneurs. Keynes's economic theories, which influenced American and European policymakers as they struggled with economic failure in the Depression (and with a surprising affluence, after), essentially taught that governments, as guardians of the common good, must replace free individuals as the prime movers of the economic world.

Not even the most sacred areas of social life, such as science and art, were exempt from this pall of gloom. Max Horkheimer (1895–1973), a German sociologist and social theorist, was chief among those who believed that even science itself, modern society's source of progress and hope, was corrupted by the political and economic evils of the day. Horkheimer had gotten his start as a sociologist in the years when Hitler's fascism overwhelmed the politics and culture of Germany. He understood very well that the numbers of intellectuals and scientists who supported Hitler's cause meant that scientific knowledge was no antidote to political evil.

Perhaps the most despairing voice among those who shared Horkheimer's concerns was that of the German writer Walter Benjamin (1892–1940). Benjamin, who is today widely read for the brilliance of his cultural and literary criticism, committed suicide while fleeing Hitler. Benjamin saw in fascism and the terrors of the war Hitler provoked in Europe the terrible logical outcome of the rationalizing effects Weber had written about. In 1936, Benjamin quoted a fascist writer's bizarre attitude on the relation between fascism and war: "War is beautiful because it establishes man's dominion over the subjugated machinery by means of gas masks, . . . flame throwers, and tanks."[25] In this terrifying idea, Benjamin saw evidence for a worry many were beginning to feel. Hitler was not just an aberration, but a logical outcome of the rationalizing tendencies of modernization. Weber's idea of the iron cage of modern society might be thought to have reached its final expression in the Nazi war machine that sought to purify society of all it hated. Those who glorify the machine will love war and seek it. All this and more was a far cry from the still hopeful, if concerned, speculations of the earliest sociologists.

One of the most important schools of sociology to have emerged out of these conditions was the now-famous Frankfurt school, sometimes called the German school of critical theory. Lukács, Horkheimer, and Benjamin were among those affiliated with this tradition in its early days. In the 1930s, Horkheimer, along with Theodor Adorno (1903–1969), founded the Frankfurt Institute of Social Research. After Hitler came to power, many affiliated with the institute fled to the United States. This tradition thrives today, long after the subsequent generation of critical theorists returned to Germany. It influences sociology the world over.

The German school of critical theory began, however, as an attempt to reconsider social thought and sociology during the events of the interwar period. Its goal was to invent a new form of social thinking that took seriously the threats to human life posed by the extreme effects of economic failure, fascism, and war. Most of those in this tradition borrowed heavily from Marx and Weber, among others. But what was new in their thinking was that they took the critical concerns of those from whom they borrowed even more seriously than had Marx and Weber themselves. They were less inclined than Marx to trust a coming revolution to correct the evils of capitalism, and more suspicious than even Weber of the iron cage of the rationalization process capitalism promotes. What most distinguished the Frankfurt thinkers in this era was that they completed the sociological arguments of the earlier time. They thought of the world as caught up in a process that, while its effects varied from place to place, was thoroughly, irreversibly global. As a result, they turned their attentions to the task of designing a critical theory whereby all human beings might be able to see themselves against the conditions the world as a whole imposed, and to understand their circumstances in ways that could possibly emancipate them from the exploitation and disenchantment of the world. Hence, the name "critical theorists."

To think of sociology as critical work is, of course, to abandon much of the naïveté of the early time. In their different ways, Marx, Weber, and Durkheim—and most sociologists of the earlier period—had believed it might be sufficient to provide men and women with knowledge capable of informing their intellectual and political judgments. If people knew how bad capitalism was, Marx had thought, they would know how to react and know what to do once the revolution came. But, in the 1930s, though many were attracted to communism's high ideals, most people knew enough of what was taking place in the Soviet Union to realize that this was not a trustworthy doctrine. Or, Weber had thought, if only there would come along some great charismatic prophet, he might lead the world out of the iron cage. But such a prophet came in Hitler, who was, in fact, sealing up even the few openings in that cage. The ultimate cage was the gas chamber. Or, if only sociology would teach people modern values, society would overcome the divisions of class conflict, Durkheim had thought. But, by the 1930s, it was plain that no such values were available and that the economic crisis of the Depression promised anything but a lessening of economic disorder. The Frankfurt sociologists, in effect, gave up the dreams of simple solutions, and began to think of sociological knowledge (all social knowledge, for that matter) as knowledge that must be understood, not as the enlightenment of well-informed individuals, but as the hard-won effort of people struggling with inhuman social conditions.

Critical knowledge, including sociology, was therefore considered knowledge gained, not in the autonomous and isolated freedom of intellectual contemplation, but always in some evident relation to the political realities of the world with which it was concerned. One of the more straightforward proponents of this idea was Karl Mannheim (1893–1947), a sociologist loosely affiliated with the Frankfurt thinkers. Mannheim invented the *sociology of knowledge* out of his conviction that all ideas arise from the social conditions of those who think them. He said, at one point: "Strictly speaking it is incorrect to say that the single individual thinks."[26] What he meant was that all thought about the world (including, of course, sociology) is largely determined by the social position of the thinker. Marx had long before thought the same thing, but Mannheim and many of the Frankfurt sociologists took the idea to its extreme. As in politics and economics, so too in sociology and science: Neither action nor thought is the pure invention of the free individual. In those days, few people were ready to think of the individual as free at all. Most understood that the overwhelming social forces of the modern world, especially in their worst manifestations in war and fascism, were so powerful as to leave the individual in a precarious position. This idea was exactly the same one that led to the next advance in professional sociology.

When in 1945 the Second World War ended, most of the world was in ruins. Japan had been devastated by the atom bombs at Nagasaki and Hiroshima, and repeated firebombing of most of its cities and industrial centers. Western and central Europe, likewise, had been torn asunder by bombing and land war. Parts of Africa, India, and China were similarly scorched by the war. Only the United States was untouched. Where the industries of all other modern societies had been broken by the war effort, those in America had thrived. This war established the United States as the one supreme world power. Though the United States soon began to dismantle its mighty military machine (until the cold war got it revved up again), its economic system remained vital and unrivaled, able to produce most of the world's steel, electricity, and consumer products. There really had never been a world power so brilliant by contrast to the conditions in which the rest of the world lived.

American supremacy would not last long. In but a few years after 1945, it would become clear that the Soviet Union, America's ally in the Second World War, was intent upon challenging the United States' position as world leader. Thus began the cold war. The rivalry between the American system and communism would define world affairs until the 1990s, when the fall of the Soviet system would stimulate the dreams of still another new world order.

During the late 1940s and 1950s, the world became a strangely contradictory place. On the one hand, the booming economy of the American system encouraged many people the world over, but especially in the United States, to think that mankind had finally discovered the means to true, unending progress. As the United States contributed materially in the late 1950s to the reconstruction of Europe and of its former enemies Japan and Germany, there were those who believed, even, that the skepticism of the previous years had been in error. Perhaps Reinhold Niebuhr had been wrong. Was not the United States a state power able to engage in acts of uncommon moral decency? Though this view overlooked the fact that the United States had important economic and strategic interests in redeveloping Western Europe and Japan as potential markets for American goods and political buffers against communist states in Russia and China, it was not entirely strange to think of this as a new era, one led by the moral force and economic might of America. Americans had always thought well of themselves. Now at last there was manifest evidence to confirm their destiny as the last best hope of mankind, as Abraham Lincoln had once said (and American presidents ever since have never stopped repeating).

At the same time, however, the chastening effects of the interwar period could not be forgotten. For one thing, the cold war was itself a continuation of the political realities of the Second World War. Whatever one might want to say against Soviet imperialism, it was not entirely foolish of the Soviets to seek a buffer of their own in the East Bloc countries. The Nazi military machine had, after all, come terrifyingly close to conquering the Soviet Union. From the West, it looked as though the Americans and their Allies had defeated fascism only to be left with communism. This was true, in a sense. But, from a more sociological point of view, it would have been just as accurate to say that the combined effect of the historical crises of the early twentieth century—economic failure, Holocaust, wars—had changed things forever. No longer would the comfortable elites in the United States, or Europe, be entirely free to think of the world as a playground for the liberal pursuits of free men. Though, of course, they tried, as elites always do. But each successive shock to their faith—like the attacks on American power on 9/11—was less by the contrast to the first.

The Enlightenment ideal of the emancipated individual rationally seeking a better world had been dealt a crippling, if not fatal, blow. The ideal would remain a vital part of the modern West's imaginary—that is, of the collective dream life by which politicians and other secular preachers encourage the masses to trust deeply held, but hard-to-prove, beliefs about the truth of society. But, in the real world of practical politics, hardly anyone thought in these terms. The cold war was conceived as a battle of one system against another, not just as a contest between differing types of "men." The renewal of economic growth after the Second World War was led as much by governmental interventions in the marketplace as by the ingenuity of individual entrepreneurs.

The political virtues of the "free" democratic societies were likewise accepted now to reside as much in their capacity to assure a decent standard of living through social welfare programs as in their capacity to protect the individual rights of citizens. It was a time of the activist state, in the United States as in Europe. Though such a theory of the government would eventually come under the severe attack it faces today, in the days just after the Second World War the upper hand in real politics was held by those who believed that the institutions of the larger society, governments and corporations above all, were chiefly responsible for the world's progress. There was good reason to think, at the least, that, in order to keep the world from falling back into the terrors of war, depression, and holocaust, the care and management of social things could not be left to the good intentions of free individuals.

This new idea in the practical life of Western societies was fundamental to the growth of professional sociology. In the years following the Second World War, professional sociology enjoyed its greatest institutional success, especially in the United States, where sociology was among the social sciences that would most support the government-led, and corporation-sponsored, social development of American society. Flush with success in war and economic life, many Americans believed their society was on the verge of being, at last, the truly Good Society of which moderns had dreamed for years. Sociology, which in those days considered itself the queen of the social sciences, was indeed looked upon as a major contributor to social progress. If any society were to eliminate poverty, educate all its citizens, assure the basic decency of living conditions, and work harmoniously toward continuous economic growth, it would surely have to understand itself scientifically. This was professional sociology's considered role. For a while, the field seemed ready to do just that, thanks largely to the efforts of two major schools, led by the two most influential sociologists of the postwar era.

By the time the affluent 1950s had come, things were much changed in the United States from the days when the University of Chicago's Department of Sociology was the dominant center of professional sociology. The waves of immigrants had stopped with the First World War; industrialization had reached the very peak of its development and was already turning from manufacturing in heavy industries like steel to the industrial assembly of consumer products like televisions, automobiles, and washers; and, for a moment at least, social unrest was not in the news as it would soon be after the beginning of the civil rights movement in 1955. If people in the United States and the rest of the West had concerns, it was with the communists who were supposed to be creeping into the fabric of American life, while they were conquering Cuba, China, North Korea, Hungary, and parts of Africa. But even communism did not abate the widespread satisfaction most middle- and working-class white people in America enjoyed. As a result of all these changes, the new schools of sociology were very different in their emphasis from the early University of Chicago department.

The new schools emerged as powerful forces in the discipline at Columbia University and Harvard University. They were (and still are) associated in popular imagination with the names of their most prominent leaders: Talcott Parsons (1902–1979) at Harvard and Robert K. Merton (1910–2003) at Columbia University. Though there were important differences in their respective definitions of sociology, both Merton and Parsons believed that sociology must become a rigorous science with its own, well-defined vocabulary of concepts, and with clearly articulated principles of investigation.

Parsons, for one, devoted himself to the task of working out the universal laws he thought governed all functioning social systems. This led him to what most commentators consider a highly abstract series of books and articles that, though they left many students puzzled, were highly influential among graduate students and scholars in the field. On the basis of his *general theory of social action*, as he called it, Parsons led a reorganization of Harvard's social science departments into one super-department of "social relations," which brought together anthropologists, psychologists, and sociologists. The integrating theme of this project was the notion that it was possible to describe the general and universal laws governing what Parsons called "the social system."[27] His "the" begins to suggest the ambition of the work. He and his followers were not speaking of this or that society or social system, but of all social systems. The global references of the scheme were intentional. Parsons had obviously learned at least this lesson of the interwar period. Sociology, he thought, must be a general science of the social in which the actions of individuals must be judged in relation to the conditions and expectations established by the larger social whole. Though some time later, in the 1960s, Parsons would be bitterly attacked by more radical social thinkers for what they considered the liberal naïveté of his ambitions, he was one of those in sociology who made genuine, and successful, efforts to apply the stern lessons of the early twentieth century. For him, the individual and all social action had to be viewed in disciplined relation to the global features of social systems. The individual was not a freestanding moral agent. This was a principle with which Merton agreed.

Like Parsons, Robert Merton was a serious student of the European traditions of social thought. This is why they both based their ideas on the problems that had been worked on by Europeans of the earlier generations, including those who had struggled with the terrible crisis of the interwar years. Merton, for example, benefited from the intellectual work of two important sociologists who had once maintained relations (though admittedly heretical relations) with the Frankfurt school in its early days in Germany. One was Karl Mannheim, to whose ideas Merton devoted an entire section of his most famous book, *Social Theory and Social Structure* (1949).[28] What Merton found appealing in Mannheim was the idea that knowledge and ideas are rooted in society. While at Harvard, Merton had been trained as much in the history of science as in sociology. He was thereby well prepared to advance the sociological importance of Mannheim's ideas. One of Merton's many lasting contributions to sociology was the founding and developing of the sociology of science, one of academic sociology's most important and intellectually mature specialties. It should not be surprising that professional sociologists, given their obligation to think back to the social origins in practical life of their own ideas, would be interested in the sociology of sciences, including their own. It sometimes annoys academics in other fields that sociologists spend as much time as they do thinking about, reflecting upon, and otherwise studying their own field. But this, as

I have suggested already, goes with the territory. One can hardly imagine a professional sociology that is not *reflexive* in this way, that is, one that does not constantly look back upon itself in order to understand how its own social circumstances affect its knowledge. So it is not by coincidence that one of the founders of sociology after the Second World War would have also been a founder of the specialty that took sociology and other sciences themselves as a subject of sociological investigation.

But the sociology of science was not Merton's most important contribution to the field of sociology. He is just as well respected for the work he has done to develop sociology as a science based on empirical research. This is his most famous difference with Talcott Parsons, who, though sharing Merton's goal, wrote in such a way that many thought it difficult to draw the connections between his general theories and concrete research work. The impression that Parsons was ignorant of the facts that lay behind his theories is more a malicious rumor than a reality. Parsons's best students at Harvard were every bit as much the researchers as were the students of the Columbia University department. In fact, for a long while these two departments produced the most important empirical work in sociological subfields like science studies, industrial sociology, modernization and economic life, social movements, mass communications, education, and social psychology. Just the same, it was Merton who was more overtly concerned with showing the way by which postwar sociology could be empirical social research.

At Columbia Merton joined forces with another former associate of the Frankfurt school, Paul Lazarsfeld (1901–1976), a Viennese mathematician. Like many of those associated with the Frankfurt school, Lazarsfeld had settled in New York City. By 1940, after a number of years engaged in research on radio and its social effects, Lazarsfeld had established the Bureau of Applied Social Research at Columbia. Shortly thereafter, Merton entered into collaboration with Lazarsfeld, and soon the bureau and Columbia's Department of Sociology were hand in glove—advanced research in a superior teaching department. These two men brought differing skills to a common enterprise. Lazarsfeld's knowledge of the mathematical foundations of empirical reasoning, combined with Merton's appreciation of the historical and theoretical principles of sociology, was one of those once-in-a-generation happy coincidences of genius. There had been good theory in sociology before, and plenty of quantitatively rigorous empirical research, but never before had the two been combined so fortuitously, just when the United States most demanded good sociological knowledge.

These were the golden years of sociology in the United States. Students came from all over the world, and from all parts of the United States, to study at Columbia or Harvard. A very great many of the most accomplished sociologists of the next generations were either trained in or influenced by the Harvard or Columbia school. This does not mean that the still-important Chicago school had disappeared, not by any means. But during this time it was somewhat more an alternative to the then more dominant schools led by Parsons and Merton, even though some of Chicago's most brilliant students—like Erving Goffman, who would teach for a while at the University of California at Berkeley in the 1960s, after finishing his doctoral studies at Chicago—were considered every bit as important as Merton and Parsons. One of the ironies of that day is that the original Chicago tradition migrated to other institutions, like Berkeley, while in due course the Chicago department took up the traditions of the Columbia school. Until his death in 1995, James Coleman (1926–1995), a former student of Merton and Lazarsfeld, was a leading member of the Chicago department. Generally speaking, today Chicago is noted for its scientific sociology every bit as much as are the Harvard and Columbia departments.

The details of how ideas and sociologists migrated from place to place may not, in themselves, be of keen interest to all. But they do suggest just how important the changes were that took place in academic sociology in the 1940s and 1950s. Thereafter, though professional sociology welcomed quite a varied lot of unruly and divergent ways of thinking, the field nonetheless had at its center the example of the Columbia department's ideal of sound *middle-range* sociological thinking, in which theory was to be expressed in working concepts that could lead directly to empirical research. Still, the commitment to middle-range, as opposed to grand, theory did not prevent the Columbia school from paying attention to the reflexive sociology of its own knowledge. Today, many sociologists, especially those who came into the field after the 1960s, do not approve of the scientific concerns of the sociologies of Merton, Lazarsfeld, and Parsons. But they forget, or never realized to begin with, that, for better or worse, sociology's reputation in the public eye, and especially its reputation as a serious science of modern society, owes largely to the work of men (and, until the last generation, a few women) like these, and their students.

It is also easily forgotten that deep in the culture of these postwar sociologists was a recognition of the travails through which the world had passed between the two world wars. I have suggested how Parsons insisted that the individual actor is always "conditioned," as he put it, by larger system, or structural, factors. This is one example of the theoretical maturity of that era. The same can be said of Merton. His most famous essay, "Social Structure and Anomie," was written in 1938 when Merton was still a young man.[29] The Second World War had not quite broken out, though anyone could see what was happening in Germany. In the United States, the suffering caused by the Great Depression was still very much evident. So it was not by accident that in 1938 Merton took up an idea of Durkheim's. Anomie, Durkheim had proposed, was the condition of uncertainty that arises among modern people when their society becomes too disrupted by change to be able to provide a steady line of moral guidance. One of Durkheim's examples of such a condition was, precisely, economic depressions (though of course Durkheim was long dead by the time of the Great Depression of the 1930s). When the economic system collapses, Durkheim argued with good evidence, people are left without their customary expectations in life. Without a steady income, one can hardly predict the future. This leaves the individual in anomie, without the practical norms or rules that in more stable times guide daily life.

Writing more than a half century after Durkheim, Merton took up this same idea with reference, evidently, to the economic conditions of the 1930s. But Merton put a quite different spin on the notion. He argued, for one example, that when the economy fails to provide individuals with jobs, they do indeed fall into anomie. In America, he said, one is supposed to work hard in a job to be a good American. If "America" provides no jobs, then what is the "good American" to do? But here Merton diverged from Durkheim. According to Merton (but not to Durkheim), one of the things the individual can do is to "innovate," that is, find some other way to gain the income necessary at least to provide for his or her family and perhaps even for a semblance of the decent life. One example of "innovation" would be the poor who steal, not out of avarice, but to provide milk for their babies. Legally, the theft is still a crime. But, sociologically, it is one of the means by which the individual might adapt to anomie, the state of not being able to be a good enough provider, hence a good enough American. Innovations of this sort are not ideal, obviously, but they serve their purposes—and once again they suggest the sociological importance of always looking below the surface of social things, to their sometimes unintended consequences and latent effects, just as the Chicago sociologists had done with respect to the social benefits of gang and immigrant life, and Weber had done with respect to the dehumanizing side of modernization.

Merton turned, in this work and others, to the sociological tradition, while seeking to advance the empirical knowledge of the field. His version of the adaptation to anomie is a clear indication of just how far sociological reasoning had come. With Merton, the crime of the innovator is, sociologically speaking, caused as much by the structural conditions of the society that fails to provide the job as by the individual himself. This is a big step from Durkheim, with whom the anomic person was just plain lost, bewildered to the point of committing suicide. With Merton, years later, the anomic person acts, but not as a free man. He acts in response to the conditions in which he must live, and chooses the alternatives, however undesirable, available to him. Once again, the individual is much more rigorously portrayed as an actor caught up in, and required to obey, the structured conditions of the larger society.

Since the generation of Merton, Lazarsfeld, and Parsons, academic sociology has been, by and large, much more consistently structural, that is, much more inclined to begin the study of social things with their larger, society-wide manifestations, like the economy, than with the actions of individuals like adaptive crime. The contributions of the postwar Harvard and Columbia schools thus encouraged professional sociology to become, for a good while, more disciplined after the fashions of the natural and physical sciences. The study of structured events, like the impact of the economy on social life or of global warming on plant life, is always more susceptible to the mathematical rules of scientific procedures than is the study of, say, an individual's motives.

Today, professional sociologists disagree on many things, sometimes angrily. But rare is the sociologist who does not think that, whatever else it does, sociology is the study of the enduring, not always just, structured relations among men and women in a structured world. This growing recognition of the importance of structural analysis to the study of society was the great advance in the field in the years between 1920 and 1960. Where sociology successfully stakes a claim to be a science, it does so in the name of this idea. Even when sociologists refuse to consider themselves scientists of any kind (and many do), most will take into account the question of *social structures*. The study of social structures—of the unrelentingly large and powerful social forces that so often determine the ways and means of individuals—is what makes sociology an academic field, just as the study of markets does for economics, and the study of minds for psychology. Social structures are not more concrete things than are markets or minds. Some even consider them vastly more vague than the subject matters of other social sciences. But they are what sociologists have to study. Social structures are to sociology what birds are to ornithology. They are the social things we most often talk about when we speak sociologically.

SIX

~

SOCIOLOGY DISCOVERS ITS COMPLICATED VOCATION: AFTER 1960

In the heartland of the American plains, small towns are dispersed far and wide over uninhabited expanses. It is possible to drive for hours without coming upon much more than a one-room schoolhouse or ranch house here and there off across fields of grain or grass, perhaps a simple store selling gasoline and fat-clogged snacks. Every so often, a town of some size and importance presents itself.

One such town is Pine Ridge, South Dakota. Few would plan a trip to Pine Ridge unless they were on government business or, perhaps, trying to find Wounded Knee, the site of what American whites so innocently call the last of the Indian "wars." Though the town is superficially of little interest to the outsider, to the people of that area it is a center of cultural and commercial importance. Pine Ridge is the business and administrative center for the Oglala Lakota Sioux, a native people of proud traditions whose tribal lands cover nearly two million acres—from the Badlands, many miles north, to the Nebraska border, just two miles south of town.

I visited Pine Ridge in the fall of 1996 at the invitation of Thandi Emdon (b. 1974), then a young sociologist who had just that spring graduated from the college back east where we had met as teacher and student, and become friends. Thandi, a Jewish woman who had grown up in South Africa, was volunteering as a teacher at Our Lady of Lourdes School in

Porcupine, South Dakota, a tiny hill-town north of Pine Ridge. She and the dozen or so other young volunteers lived and taught in simple, but well-equipped, quarters and classrooms. They worked hard at their teaching and at learning how to respect the cultural differences and needs of the Lakota children they teach. For Thandi, sensitivity to those of different cultures comes naturally because of her childhood experience in South Africa under its now-collapsed whites-only apartheid government. Her mother was one of the whites who under the old regime struggled courageously, and at considerable personal sacrifice, against the vicious racism that had been the foundation of European colonial rule in Africa. Thandi and her mother understand the nature and effects of colonial rule as well as any who are not the intended victims of it. She could see the meaning of what lies behind the superficially ordinary and deteriorated outward features of a town like Pine Ridge.

The town's new high-school buildings are modern and designed to incorporate emblems of the Lakota culture, but one must leave the main street to find them. A new and modern hospital, the most striking building in town, sits on the hill just to the northeast. It is the Indian Health Service, a native-peoples-only hospital. In a rare turn of the racial table, whites must drive forty miles off the reservation for hospital care. At the town's main intersection, there is a Lakota-owned convenience store, Big Bats. Whites are welcome enough, but they soon see that the store is a social gathering place for local Lakota people, including those from the several public housing projects outside town, or the teenagers making social noise over video games. The large supermarket just down the street is like supermarkets everywhere except that it is rare to find fresh fruits and vegetables on the shelves and, it seemed to me, the prices on the cellophane-wrapped, but browning, iceberg lettuces were high for what was offered. Otherwise, but for the buildings of the United States Bureau of Indian Affairs and some other public buildings, many of the houses were in need of repair; some were boarded up.

The Lakota nation officially bans the sale and consumption of alcoholic beverages on the tribal lands. This is a move necessitated by an extraordinary rate of alcoholism, which in turn is usually attributed to the desperate economic conditions throughout the Indian tribal lands. There is no real productive work to be had for the twenty thousand Oglala Lakota people. The damage done by being excluded from the economic benefits of the wider society is truly beyond belief. Life expectancy is twenty years less than national norms. On the average, Lakota men die at fifty-five years. Suicide rates and infant deaths are twice the national average. Heart disease and diabetes are epidemic, mostly because of high fat-content and overall poor quality of food available through government food subsidy programs. Nearly 70 percent of Lakota children live below the poverty line.[30] Alcoholism is a killer of so many of the Lakota because, in the absence of social hope, many Lakota people turn to drink. Yet, with all this misery, there is a dirty little town just off the reservation, over the Nebraska border, where the only evident commercial activity is the selling of liquor by whites to addicted Lakota people who drive or walk the two-mile road from Pine Ridge to Whiteclay, Nebraska. It is said that there are more traffic fatalities on that stretch of road than on any other in the country—people struck down by the accidents of their deprivation.

Ventures off the reservation (to use the official government term) can be demoralizing journeys into the wider American world of indifference to the racism in which the theft of Native American lands is veiled. In Martin, South Dakota, to the east, the white-dominated Bennett High School "Warriors" celebrate their homecoming by playing Indian games. Before the football game, local white kids prance about in borrowed Indian dress, elect an "Indian Princess," poke fun at a made-up "Indian Chief," and foolishly dance about in a Hollywood version of "Indian dance." The Lakotas and other Native American people across the nation consider practices like these degrading to the indigenous cultures. But when political activists and students from the Oglala Lakota communities, supported by the national American Indian Movement, protested, school officials in Martin adamantly refused to stop the festivities. One older white from Martin is quoted as saying to a Lakota youth: "You're in Bennett County Warrior Country. This is the white man's sacred ground."[31] Oh, how the colonizer thrives on degradation and how the colonized are subjected to mockery.

Pine Ridge is what a colonized village looks like, if the outsider will only stop and look. Behind all that is of local value lies the strain of years of disregard, abuse, and intrusion by the colonizing power, in this case the United States government. The power of the intruder may, at first contact, be the raw power of military or corporate takeover. In the nineteenth century, Native American people were forced onto reservations by the federal government in order to make way for white settlers and railroad corporations. But, after the first rush of brutality, colonization slows to the low drone of the rational administration Weber wrote about.

The towns and rural villages of Native American people are economically depressed enclaves dispersed across arid reservations. The colonizing powers are interested chiefly in the natural resources of an area and not at all in the people themselves unless they are useful as cheap labor. In Pine Ridge, there are no international business corporations, unless one counts the small Pizza Hut next to the supermarket. From the point of view of capitalist profit making, there is little of marketable value in the treeless, rolling hills, and empty spaces. Most of the large-scale, corporate farming and ranching in the Dakotas are off the reservations, where few Lakota people are employed. In the Oglala Lakota tribal lands, the largest single employers are government agencies dispensing health and welfare benefits. There is no other work yielding real incomes. Unemployment is 85 percent!

Outside Pine Ridge, the most enduring monument to American colonial rule is the mass burial ground at Wounded Knee, where in 1890 the United States Army—fearing reprisals after the murder of Sitting Bull, one of the last great chiefs—slaughtered three hundred defenseless Lakotas, ill and shelterless in the late December cold. This was the action some American whites still refer to as the last of the Indian wars. It was anything but war. But, as I said, colonizing does not always require such brutality. It more often works in the daily affairs of administrating subjugated people out of their lands, lives, and dreams.

When Immanuel Wallerstein spoke of the world as an economic system in which a core state exploits peripheral regions, he was referring to effects like those one finds in Pine Ridge. North Americans tend not to think of themselves as colonizers, much less bullies. But what the American, Mexican, and Canadian governments have done to the indigenous people of the Great Plains, tropical rainforests, and the far north is not different from what their European cousins have done in Asia, Latin America, and Africa. These were, and in some ways still are, the effects of a worldwide structure that has done good for many, to be sure, but usually at great cost to millions more.

The structures of colonial rule are one among numerous different kinds of structures about which sociologists talk in order to be truly sociological. Charlotte Perkins Gilman spoke indignantly of the confining structures of the man-made world, just as W. E. B. Du Bois spoke of the no less abusive structures imposed along the color line. Marx studied the structure of the factory system, as Weber studied the dehumanizing effects of capitalism's rational systems on people's lives. To use one's sociological imagination, whether to practical or professional end, is to look at the events in one's life, to see them for what they truly are, then to figure out how the structures of the wider world make social things the way they are. No one is a sociologist until she does this as best she can.

Yet, strange as it may seem, even professional sociologists fail to use their imaginative powers to the fullest. It took the better part of a century after Du Bois's *Souls of Black Folk* (1903) and Gilman's *Women and Economics* (1898) before professional sociologists caught up with more practical sociologies and began to think seriously, without embarrassment, about the color line and the gender-caste system as major structures of the modern world. Still today, some who are otherwise well-trained balk and mumble before the evidence that the epidemic of violence against gay people, far from being local pranks, is a structural feature of the world's order. It is not easy to look social structures straight in the eye, because one is likely to see social things that stir the deeper feelings of social discomfort. Usually, however, sociologists overcome their resistance and begin to look and talk, especially when their worlds are shaken.

One of the more unspeakable structures of the modern world is the one upon which it was founded: the structure of the world colonial system. It was not until well into the 1960s and the decade following that sociologists like Immanuel Wallerstein and others began to examine the world economic system, thus to see just how fundamental the colonial system that began in the sixteenth century has been to the present world system. One of the reasons sociologists began to look at the world as a whole was that, as young men and women in the 1960s, they were forced by the political turmoil of the times to think in even more global terms than their sociological elders had. When the streets are ablaze with protest, as they were in the 1960s, sociologists will listen—just as, in the 1930s, an earlier generation of sociologists listened to the cries of those deported to the Nazi camps and came to the conclusion that the individual alone was insufficient to the task of holding the world together.

Popular culture mass-produces the flimsy impression that the 1960s were a kind of unruly national rock concert in which naked hippies drugged their minds looking for the next appearance of the Grateful Dead, while their more intense brothers and sisters protested the injustices of the world. The 1960s are not, however, well explained by the most memorable icons: Richard Nixon's awkward V sign in defeat; young John Fitzgerald Kennedy, without a topcoat on a cold January day; police dogs in Birmingham, Alabama; Martin Luther King's dream speech; long hair, pot, beards, and sex in Haight-Ashbury, Woodstock, or Altamont; a little Vietnamese girl, now grown and forgiving, running naked from the napalm; a young student at Kent State University screaming in agony over her friend's dead body; bricks thrown across barricades in Paris; students slain in the Tlatelolco plaza in Mexico. These searing images come down through the years as reminders that something important, if occasionally wild, happened for a stretch of time.

The events of the 1960s were important not because a new generation of young people was suddenly overcome by a good toke of moral and cultural inspiration. In the larger history of social things, outbursts of desire for change arise from an abiding, subterranean disarray in the world's structures. If, at such times, there is lightning, it strikes because a prior, slow-moving glacier has begun to melt, opening fissures that expose a weakness throughout the mass, to which the celestial fire and thunder are drawn.

One prophet of the world weakness exposed in the years just before the 1960s was Frantz Fanon (1925–1961), a colonial subject of French Martinique. Like many other brilliant students from France's colonies, Fanon studied in Paris. Afterwards, he became a psychiatrist practicing in Algeria, which in the 1950s was still a French colony. His experience as a physician and a colonial subject led Fanon to write books that were among the most widely read by civil-rights, student, and antiwar activists in the 1960s. In *Black Skin, White Masks* (published in 1952), Fanon described one of the effects of colonial rule on its subjects:

> The crippled veteran of the Pacific war says to my brother, "Resign yourself to your color the way I got used to my stump; we're both victims." Nevertheless with all my strength I refuse to accept that amputation. I feel in myself a soul as immense as the world, truly a soul as deep as the deepest of rivers, my chest has the power to expand without limit. I am a master and I am advised to adopt the humility of the cripple. Yesterday, awakening to the world, I saw the sky turn upon itself utterly and wholly. I wanted to rise, but the disemboweled silence fell back upon me, its wings paralyzed. Without responsibility, straddling Nothingness and Infinity, I began to weep.
>
> —Fanon, *Black Skin, White Masks* (1952)[32]

In words like these, Fanon and others spoke for the other-than-white colonized people who, in the 1950s, began slowly but surely to refuse to accept their amputations—refused any longer to play the cripple dependent on meager mercies of the colonial system. They arose, with much pain and wrenching, to change the world. These were the revolutionaries who, in Africa, the Caribbean, and Asia, threw off the colonial rulers and thus brought about *decolonization*, the worldwide challenging and partial breaking apart of the European and American colonial structures. Decolonization involves, that is, the world-system as a whole. In 1961, just before his death, Fanon said in *The Wretched of the Earth*: "In decolonization, there is . . . the need of a complete calling in question of the colonial situation."[33]

Decolonization was the global event that, more than any other, led to the events people today think of as the sixties. Behind the civil-rights and black-power movements, before the counterculture, before feminism and gay politics, before the American Indian Movement, there was a long, heavy shifting in the order of world politics. The first lightning struck in parts of Africa, India, and China where the social landmass had been worn bare by the long marches of colonial people out from under colonial rule. The clash of protest in the American and European cities and campuses in the 1960s was largely, if not entirely, the delayed thunder of the decolonizing of world structures. Though the world is still largely ruled economically and militarily by Europe and America and their business allies, the way in which the ruling is done is far less neat and complete than it had been under the colonial system. People in the used and abused parts of the world are today far less likely to obey the precise expectations of European and Japanese bankers or to tremble before the threats of American generals. Very little in the world is untouched by the breaking apart of the colonial system. Though partial and incomplete, decolonization means that the world powers must pause before the resistances of those nations and ethnic groups that no longer accede to their will as if it were the natural law of things. Simply put, the world today is a much more rebellious place. Contention crops up where superficially calm discussion had previously prevailed.

Professional sociologists in the 1960s may not have seen these changes coming, but they soon caught on, mostly because their students were demanding attention to the changing world. It was black students who began the second wave of the civil-rights movement by their lunch counter sit-ins in Greensboro, North Carolina, in the early months of 1960. Later, white students from the North joined the movement in the American South, as others began protests on university campuses around the world, and still others, still later, protested against the Vietnam War, and against sexism and homophobia. The role students played in these political events could not but have had an effect on the intellectual and academic work of their teachers, some of whom took up protest themselves. Though students were not by any means the only, or even the most important, participants in the events of the 1960s, they were among those who brought worldly changes home to the thinking of sociologists and other academics.

Sociology soon fell under the sway of change. Its once unlimited prospect as the science of the structures of the good society soon faded. In the 1950s and early 1960s, the field was at the height of its influence and prestige. In the early years of the Kennedy administration and well into the administration of President Lyndon Johnson after Kennedy's death, until Johnson himself gave up in 1968, sociologists were among those called upon regularly to advise the White House, Congress, and the courts. It is not an exaggeration to say that Johnson's Great Society was a sociologically informed dream of the liberal prospects for America. But, at the same time, a younger generation of students was reading sociology, and many of them were putting it into practice. They had different ideas from their elders.

One such young sociologist was Richard Flacks (b. 1938), who, in the early 1960s, was a graduate student in social psychology at the University of Michigan, and is now an emeritus professor of sociology at the University of California at Santa Barbara. Flacks had been a red-diaper baby; that is, his parents had spent their lives and careers devoted to left-ist political causes. Both of Flacks's parents lost their jobs as public school teachers in New York City in the 1950s to the vicious right-wing, anti-communist henchmen who tried to destroy people who sought to change their world. But Flacks learned from his parents not to yield on moral and political principles. Thus it was perfectly natural that, while a student at the University of Michigan in the early 1960s, he would have read the writings of C. Wright Mills and put his sociological imagination to political work. Richard Flacks was among the early leaders of the Students for a Democratic Society (SDS) and was a coauthor of SDS's famous 1962 vision for America's future, "The Port Huron Statement." That document was influential among students then attempting to bring into reality their own version of a domestic decolonizing movement. There is no doubt that the student movement was inspired by the civil rights movement, which in turn had been inspired by the decolonizing movements around the world. As Martin Luther King had learned from Gandhi's success in India, young white students learned from the first, courageous wave of black civil-rights activists in the American South. "The Port Huron Statement" begins with the ringing words: "We are people of this generation, bred in at least modest comfort, housed now in universities, looking uncomfort-ably at the world we inherit." Though mild by comparison to Fanon's wrenching pain and forceful insistence on world change, "The Port Huron Statement" goes on to present a point-for-point case for just how politics and economic life in America ought to include, and be built out of, the personal politics of individuals without relinquishing the attention that must be paid the larger structures. It was, in effect, a statement based on C. Wright Mills's definition of the sociological imagination as the capacity to "understand the larger historical scene in terms of its meaning for the inner life."

Elsewhere, in Europe, sociologists were awakening to the demands of students, workers, and former colonial subjects. In France, Pierre Bourdieu developed his famous theory of the *habitus* on the basis of prior field studies he had made in Kabylia in Algeria, which from 1954 to 1962 had been engaged against France in a decolonizing war. You can begin to imagine why Bourdieu felt it necessary to invent a more subtle idea of how the individual solves practical problems in daily life. A European woman in the Latin Quarter can follow the established French courtship practices in deciding whether to respond to a public flirtation. An Algerian woman, torn by the rules of her local traditions and those imposed by colonizing France, must develop a vastly more complex *habitus* in dealing with advances by, say, a French gendarme.

Meanwhile, back in France early in the 1960s, Bourdieu had been studying the effects of a traditionally elite educational system on students from working class backgrounds. These studies led to a book, *The Inheritors: French Students and Their Relations to Culture* (1964), which helped spark the rebellion of French students in the Paris revolution of 1968. Here Bourdieu introduced another of his important concepts, *cultural reproduction.*

Reproduction theory, of which there are several versions, basically attempts to answer the central riddles of modern societies. If education is meant to make individuals free, why is it that educational systems in modern societies do NOT produce a narrowing the social equalities in a given society? Bourdieu's version of reproduction theory argued that the schools actually serve to teach children from, say, working class backgrounds that they are *incompetent.* Hence another example of sociological incompetence—a system designed to make things better, actually makes things worse for some. Cultural reproduction reproduces social and economic inequalities when the schools give an unfair, if not always visible, advantage to students from cultured families. A child who grows up with working parents who had little education and no time for reading books will start school with a cultural disadvantage compared to a child of the elite and cultured class. The bourgeois child comes to school familiar with books, arts, language, and all else necessary to succeed. Working class kids come with the disposition to fail as their parents did. Schools teach them, in effect, how to fail.

As one might expect, such a vision of sociology did not please everyone. Many older sociologists were disgusted by the student movements around the world, all of them radically left wing, angered elders who had a stake in preserving the advantages liberal society had provided them. It was not easy for professional sociologists to face the internal criticism of so many of its young, but most did. By 1970, many younger sociologists, students, and new faculty had come to think of sociology as a sociological imagination that would remake the world, while the older generation had thought of it as a profession that would help manage the world.

In France and Europe, Bourdieu was just one of a new generation of intellectual leaders who challenged the status quo. In the United States the younger generation made Alvin Gouldner's *Coming Crisis of Western Sociology* a bestseller. Gouldner's book was one much like Mills's earlier book *Sociological Imagination*. Both called sociologists to return to the field's roots in political and moral concern for the social problems of the world. Gouldner (1920–1980), for example, attacked any sociology that pretended its knowledge could be universally and objectively true. In so doing, his book, like Mills's, expressed the younger generation's bitter denunciation of the older generation's sometimes uncritical faith in scientific sociology.[34]

Across the years of the 1960s, from Mills's *Sociological Imagination*, published in 1959 and Bourdieu's *The Inheritors* (1962), to Gouldner's *Coming Crisis*, published in 1970, and Bourdieu's *Outline of a Theory of Practice* (1974), academic sociology changed, once again. Though sociology never gave up its midcentury commitment to the study of structures, it soon lost its belief in itself as the science of modern society. Many, after the 1960s, refused to consider sociology a science of any kind, and many of those who still believed in its science applied their scientific skills to the study of topics that were of urgency because of the 1960s. Sociological feminism is one example, among many others, of these changes.

Prior to the early 1970s, there had been very little feminism in sociology except for the work of pioneers like Charlotte Perkins Gilman and Jane Addams early in the century, and, later, Jesse Bernard (1903–1996), among a very few others. But, early in the 1970s, after feminism had quickly established itself as a major force in American intellectual and political life, a new generation of feminist sociologists began to do work that would change the field.

Dorothy Smith (b. 1926), a Canadian who studied at the University of California at Berkeley in the 1960s and who now lives in British Columbia, was one of the first and most important post-1960s feminist pioneers. Smith's enduring contribution was to methodically criticize until-then male-dominated professional sociology for its systematic ignorance of the unique position of women in social life. Her argument, simply put, was that sociology's claim to objectivity would always be false so long as practical experiences—in particular those of women—are left out of the equation.[35]

Not all feminist sociology was as devastatingly critical of male-dominated scientific sociology as Smith's, but much of it set about to rethink the basic categories of social thought in terms that traditional sociology had ignored. In a 1978 book, *The Reproduction of Mothering*, Nancy Chodorow (b. 1944), a professor of sociology at Berkeley and a practicing psychoanalyst, reexamined the basic sociological and psychoanalytic categories for describing sex roles. Her idea was to explain that a woman's competence as a mother is not so much an automatic result of a mechanical "role" as a consequence of the ways in which middle-class families are organized.[36]

In the years that followed, feminism came to be a major intellectual force in scholarly sociology. More and more research was conducted in creative new ways that would not have occurred to the earlier male-dominated generations of academic sociology. For example, in a 1991 book, *Brave New Families*, Judith Stacey (b. 1943) challenged commonsense beliefs about the middle-class families Chodorow had in mind.[37] Stacey teaches sociology at the New York University after many years at the University of Southern California where she held a special chair for the study of gender relations that was funded by, and named after, the movie star Barbra Streisand. One of Stacey's more daring innovations was to rework the methodological principles of sociological fieldwork. Stacey's method, not unlike Dorothy Smith's, was that, when the sociologist looks with a different, more engaged eye at how families are actually constituted, she sees a system vastly more complex and irregular than the idealized traditional family of two biological parents and a certain, usually modest number of kids. People live together and raise kids in all manner of oddly divorced and recombinant households. Families, like sex roles, are not what they are often thought to be.

In a similar but even more stunningly original way, Susan Krieger has helped us see that the nature of community life can also be very different from what the textbooks and sitcoms teach us. Krieger lives in northern California, where she teaches at Stanford University but devotes her work life largely to perfecting the art of sociological writing. One of her most important books, *The Mirror Dance* (1983), is based on systematic observations made while living in a lesbian community in a small town in the Midwest. With evident appreciation for the life-choices of the women she lived among, Susan Krieger has written about their community in a way that brings the changing forms of their personal and social relations alive on the page. Reading her book, one actually feels something of the dance of relationships—some intimate, some not. It is very hard to experience life in that community through Krieger's book and not begin to rethink what is meant by community life anywhere it occurs, which is exactly what Krieger intended. She concluded *The Mirror Dance* with the elegantly simple idea that women struggling with the particular issues of life in a lesbian community have much to teach all of us who may long to belong without having to give up too much of our individuality:

> The women of this community express contradictory desires for one-ness and for separate identity. They struggle together and alone. They speak of experiences particular to lesbians. At the same time, they inform us about problems we all face. Like the women of this study in relation to their group, we are all to some extent outsiders in the com-munities to which we belong. Yet we need our communities to take us in when we seem to fit in, when we merge and conform. There is per-haps no more worthy endeavor in the social life than the struggle to build communities that might be truly accepting of their members.
>
> —Susan Krieger, *Mirror Dance* (1983)[38]

Feminist scholarship in sociology has studied many different topics—sex roles, family structure, and community life are but some of the subjects feminists have reanalyzed, causing professional sociology itself to recon-sider its ways. Needless to say, feminist scholarship is not always received with appreciation by those whose habits it questions. Just the same, it is one of the most important discoveries to have resulted from the contra-dictions of the 1960s.

Other areas of sociology in the post-1960s period have been more explicitly focused on the new social movements, like those for civil rights and women's liberation. One of the most important of these is called *resource mobilization theory*, which seeks to account for the social and political resources social movements use to organize people for protest and social change. It should not be surprising that a topic like this would be of inter-est to sociologists writing after the decade that gave birth to so many of the social movements active in social and political life today. Civil rights and black power, feminism and gay rights, environmental and peace movements were among the most agitating features of the public sphere in the decades following the 1960s.

One of the questions of interest to sociologists is, simply: Why, then? Why did all this social unrest gush forth at once in the sixties? It is obvious that concern for racial justice, or gay rights, or the environment did not suddenly appear from nowhere so late in the twentieth century. Throughout the modern era, there have been social movements organized to fight for justice in many areas, especially since the middle of the nineteenth century, when Marx was among those early agitators for social change. Many of these movements enjoyed modest successes in the earlier years. In the United States, the abolition movement finally led to the emancipation of the slaves in the 1860s; and women won the vote in the 1920s. Just the same, over the years of the modern age, there have been very few, if any, periods quite like the 1960s when so many social movements fueled the fires of change.

What happened in the 1960s that might explain this sudden explosion of social movements able to sustain themselves even against opposition? Resource mobilization theory was, thus, the result of attempts to answer this question. One of the most influential proponents of resource mobilization sociology is Charles Tilly (b. 1930), a historian and sociologist who now teaches at Columbia University. Though some disagree on various details of the theory, what Tilly clarified was the importance of the relationship between movement resources and the structures of the societies in which the movements take their actions.

In one of his earlier books, *From Mobilization to Revolution* (1978), Tilly explained with elegant simplicity that the resources a social movement requires are many, of which two of the more important are money and ideas.[39] Social movements obviously must have the financial ability to pay for meeting rooms, to get their grievances covered in the media, to call people to sit-ins or marches, to train them in what to do if they are arrested, to pay the bail bondsmen, and much more. Demonstrations, marches, and mass meetings may seem free, but they are very expensive. At the same time, resources necessary for movement success also include less tangible commodities like the ideas and languages by which leaders analyze the situation they want changed, and then rally the masses. Without people like Du Bois and Charlotte Gilman writing and publishing over the years, there would have been no tradition of knowledge that people seeking redress of injustices could draw upon. Movements must have a good stock of ideas, as well as cash, if they are to move social things to their cause.

But resources alone seldom lead to a successful movement or to social change. Since the 1860s, after the Civil War, African-American people, for example, have lived in well-ordered communities, with strong churches and community groups, and they have had very clear ideas about what was wrong with the racist structures of American society. But there was never a time before the civil rights and its successor movements (like the Black Panthers and the resurgence of the Nation of Islam) in the 1960s, when American blacks were so successful in joining forces and so effective in forcing the changes that had to be made. Again, why then? Tilly's theory would say that the resources for a movement will lead to changes only when the society's opportunity structure allows people to act. The concept opportunity structure refers to variations in the degree to which a society's political and economic structures either limit opportunities for protest by, say, the threat of suppression and punishment or, on the other hand, tolerate protests when those in power are less able or willing to suppress.

The opportunity structure of a society can be open or closed to social movements and the changes they demand. It is closed to change when the ruling powers of the society, most especially the governmental authorities and parties and their agencies (like the police and military), are in firm control of the reins of power. One of the reasons the Jews in Germany could not and did not resist deportation and eventual extermination is that, while they might have had the resources to do so, the Nazis were in such complete control of Germany that they were able to crush any opposition. In a similar fashion, in the United States in the 1950s the right-wing anticommunists held so much of the country in fear of being accused of disloyalty to America that, for a while, they had a free hand in their attempts to destroy the lives of people like Richard Flacks's parents.

But, in the 1960s, things were different. Then the opportunity structure for social action was more open because the political and government leaders found themselves in a surprisingly weakened position. Many leaders were, for example, surprised by the conditions of racial oppression in the South. Many northerners, including President Kennedy, had lived sheltered lives and had no idea of the extent of the racial injustice in the South. When the nonviolent actions of the early civil rights movement drew southern racists into bombing churches or siccing attack dogs against innocent children, even the most powerful in Washington, D.C., could see what they had never seen before. At first, they did not know what to do. Eventually they acted, though cautiously, to support the civil-rights activists. When the federal government stepped in on the side of the protesters to enforce school integration in Mississippi or to protect freedom riders in Alabama, the opportunity structure was opened throughout the South. Because its opponents were less able to stop it, the early civil rights movement could put its resources to work, and social things began to move.

Then the movements came one upon another. Later in the decade, many social movements contributed to the sudden change in public opinion in 1968 against the Vietnam War. By then, however, the opportunity structure in American society was already wide open after years of civil rights and student demonstrations. Then, too, the American war in far-off Indochina had met with a rising chorus of international protest. Among the voices of opposition were recently decolonized peoples in Asia and Africa. In a like manner, the new social movements in the United States and Europe were deeply influenced by Mohandas Gandhi (1869–1948), the moral leader of the first successful decolonization movement in India in the 1940s, and by decolonization (or, as it is said today, postcolonial) leaders who had followed in the tradition of Frantz Fanon and others in Africa. By 1968, the opportunity structure was so opened to protest that the president of France fled the country for a while and the president of the United States, Lyndon Johnson, gave up by declining to run for reelection.

The opportunity structure in the United States and many European nations was open to protest movements because, in part, there were internal troubles that weakened the ability of the powers to block the protests. But, even more importantly, in the 1960s the opportunity structure of the world had been opened by the decolonizing movements in Africa, Asia, and the Caribbean. This is why it is possible to say that the most important social fact of the 1960s was decolonization. It was not the only social process, but it was a very important one in loosening the freezing grip that the Western core states had on the world-system. Then, for a while, the powers were shaken, and changes happened. While some of the control has since been reasserted, the world is still not what it once was before decolonization began. In the 1960s, millions of people who had only the vaguest, if any, understanding of the struggles for decolonization in South Africa and Kenya, or in Vietnam and India, still rose up to seek a better life.

In 1971, for example, members of the American Indian Movement took over the burial ground at Wounded Knee. It is said that for years after the massacre in 1890, Lakota people could hear the voices of the dead crying from the grave. The takeover held the ground for seventy-one days. Federal agents once again surrounded native people. This time two Native Americans died. One is buried today alongside the mass grave. After the confrontation, local Lakota, joining other Native American activists, embarked on what they described as the Red Road, a journey of cultural affirmation of what the whites had tried to kill. Some years later, in the early 1990s, the voices of the dead at Wounded Knee were silent. These are truly sacred grounds, sanctified by people who at the time may not have been thinking of Gandhi or Fanon, but who in 1971 had the resource of sociological imagination to seize the day from their still-belligerent, but now less overtly brutal, colonizers, thus to free the souls of Lakota people, living and dead.

Lakota sociological imagination was encouraged by changes in the world structures—changes they may have felt only by the odd occurrence that one day for some reason federal agents surrounded them but did not fire, just as earlier in the South one day white sheriffs had not sicced the dogs. It may have been that some agent of the Bureau of Indian Affairs insisted on restraint, perhaps because he had remembered the days a decade before when presidents in the far-off capital sent their troops to protect black children on their way to school. Once structures open up, people remember. Sometimes structures change their ways. The powerful may be more cautious; their opponents, more bold.

Professional sociology too was changed in ways that could well be explained by resource mobilization theory. Being part of the world, academic sociologists could see what was taking place. Some who were committed to older ways of thinking may have privately hated the feminists who began to speak up in class, or felt unappreciated by the students of color who all of a sudden refused white politesse and demanded a deeper, more real respect. It is not that most academic sociologists were ever among the more recalcitrant members of the society. Rather, academic fields of study, being well-institutionalized and very human things, can get trapped in their ways. But, just as the generation of Parsons, Merton, and Adorno responded to the crisis of the earlier years of the century, so sociologists like Wallerstein, Tilly, Stacey, and Smith saw the meaning of the 1960s in real-world terms and responded, thus to change again the way sociology is done.

Few in the 1940s and 1950s would have predicted that professional sociology, at the end of the twentieth century, would become so much like what it had been at the end of the nineteenth century—a field of moral and political concern for the world's troubles. Today, sociology is, to be sure, very much more accomplished than it was at the beginning. Its methods and knowledge are more sophisticated by far than they were in the days of Marx and Weber, Gilman and Du Bois, and scientific sociology is rigorously pursued. But, as it has moved out of the troubled, if partially liberating, times of the 1960s, professional sociology has rediscovered the moral passions that inspired it at the beginning. In this respect, academic sociology has recaptured its true vocation as a science, where it can be, and even more, as a practical activity whereby individuals and societies attempt to understand the changes taking place in the worlds near and far to their homes.

This is why the professional sociologists deserve the attentions of practical people, who are the original sources of the moral concerns, the ideas, and the dreams with which the professional work is done. The professionals, so-called, are after all people who each evening, as the shadows lengthen, turn down the artificial glow of their computer screens and descend into the true light of the streets, there to meet the social realities we all must face.

SOCIAL THINGS

CHAPTER
SEVEN

~

THE MYSTERIOUS POWER
OF SOCIAL STRUCTURES

Early in the 1980s, the peace of Clarendon Heights was regularly disturbed by a gang of high-school boys. The Hallway Hangers were mostly white and, without exception, tough guys who made their presence known by an unrelenting readiness to challenge the rules, damn the system, and start a fight when the lesser forms of rebellion proved insufficient to the occasion. Their parents, who were of working-class or poorer circumstances, had settled for the time being in Clarendon Heights, a public housing project for the poor of an American city. But most of their homes were broken either by death or by the separation that so frequently follows upon poverty and the loss of social hope. The Hangers were all in, or on the verge of, social and criminal trouble.

Not surprisingly, the leader of the Hallway Hangers was the toughest in the group, a boy of medium size but with a fierce rage for street fighting. Frankie was, just the same, a natural leader as much for his cool style under pressure as for the temper that gave way in the heat of battle. Frankie was also a good practical sociologist of the social prospects he and the other Hangers faced:

> Well, some of them are going to do okay, but, I dunno, some of them are just gonna fuck up. They'll just be doing odd jobs for the rest of their lives, y'know. Still be drinking, y'know; they'll drink themselves to death, what's some of em'll do. That's what I hope I don't do. Yeah, some of them are gonna drink themselves to death, but some of them,

y'know, they're gonna smarten up. Get married, have some kids, have a decent job. Enough to live off anyways, to support a wife and kids. But some of them, they're gonna fuck up; they'll be just a junkie, a tramp. They'll be sitting out on the lawn for the rest of their life with their fucking bottle. Going to work every morning, getting laid off. Fucking, y'know, they're just gonna fuck up. That's what I hope I don't do. I'm trying not to anyways.[1]

—Jay MacLeod, *Ain't No Making It* (1987)[40]

Years later, Frankie's predictions came to pass. Most of the Hangers failed to complete high school; most failed at work. Several were caught up in lives of crime and drug trafficking for which they did time in prison. Frankie was one of the few who smartened up, at least enough to find steady, if poorly paid, work, and to support the child he had by a woman he never married.

If you look closely at Frankie's hard-nosed, earthy description of the social chances of his gang, you can see that even in his teen years, he had largely understood that their hopes for a good life were meager, already defeated. Frankie imagined that many of his companions would be trapped in drug and alcohol abuse, odd jobs, and a life of hanging around, doing little that even they, in their bitterness toward the wider world, could respect. Though Frankie knew nothing whatsoever of the statistics pertinent to young people born in the modest or impoverished conditions in which his gang lived, he was right on the money in analyzing what may be the most discouraging fact of social life in modern, democratic societies.

Today, if you are born poor, you will grow up to be poor. There are exceptions, of course, but the exceptions are rare when measured against the ideals of social progress in which those societies believe. In the mid-1980s, shortly after Frankie and the Hangers entered adult life, the wealthiest 40 percent of all Americans gained 67 percent of the country's total income, while the poorest 40 percent received only 15 percent. The United States is one of the modern societies most honorably committed to the ideals of equal opportunity and social progress. Yet the gap between the income and wealth of the richest Americans has remained in roughly this range for most of the last two centuries. By the 1990s, the gap had grown into a canyon. In 2005, the wealthiest 5 percent of the population enjoyed 22 percent of nation's income and the top 20 percent raked in 50 percent of the total income, while the poorest 20 percent eked out but 3 percent of all that was earned that year. Or, worse yet, the richest 5 percent of the population earned 18 percent of all income, more than four times that earned by the poorest 20 percent. Worldwide, by 2000, the 20 percent of all humans living in the richest countries earned 86 percent of the world's income, while the billions in the very poorest nations struggled along on 1 percent of the global income. In 2002, the world's richest 1 percent earned more than the poorest 57 percent. Well into the 2000s, the United States, once the most equalitarian of societies, was well had firmly established itself as the modern nation with the highest level of economic inequality in the world. Some who are poor better their situation, but most do not. The problem is getting worse, not better.[41]

Though the facts of social inequality raise many questions, four are the most important for a sociologist: (1) What goes on in the larger structures of society to produce the reality with which Frankie and millions of others must live? (2) How do people, whether poor or not, live with the effects of those structures that so obviously shape their thinking about whether or not, as Frankie put it, they are going to fuck up? (3) How do individuals measure their own social chances in comparison with whatever opportunities their world provides? (4) And what methods do they use? Simply put, these are questions of social *structures*, of the individual *subjects* who must live with them, of the social *differences* these structures create, and of *methods* for figuring out the sociological life. Hardly a person alive does not face these questions one way or another, even if only in the crude but astute way Frankie did. All sociologies, practical and professional, must address them.

It would be nice if the answers were as straightforward as the questions, but they are not. One (but only one) of the reasons the answers are so hard to come by is that there is a good deal of mystery surrounding the stark facts Frankie knew so well. This chapter and the two following it will consider each of these mysteries in turn, beginning with the most difficult of all—the mysterious power of social structures.

What, after all, is a structure? We use the word often, but, as with many common terms in our daily speech, we seldom examine it.

We may speak, for example, of doghouses, apartments, caves, nests, rocks, or even subway grates as structures within, under, or upon which a creature sleeps or, even, "lives." We recognize that most living things are themselves well-enough structured. Flowers have stems, trees have roots, beetles have shells, other bugs have wings; on it goes. An animal's body, for example, is structured around or within skeletons of some kind, just as most plants can be said to be structured with respect to a system of trunks and roots. Rising a bit higher in the food chain, it is not uncommon to speak of the structure of one's marriage, the structure of one's work organization or school, or the structure of professional sports, network television, or the American family. We seem to recognize that things are structured in certain ways, as if by nature.

Even when the word "structure" is not the one used, people recognize that, for the most part, it is a word that applies to the ordering of some set of things. Once, astronomers even spoke with confidence of the structure of the universe, just as physicists used to speak definitively of the structure of subatomic particles. Even though, now, science in its wisdom has progressed to such a point that we know that neither universes nor subatomic matter are particularly stable or orderly structures, still, it is not wrong to speak of them, and other things, as though they were "structured." "Structure" is a word of many applications, from the largest to the smallest of things. Yet, again, it is very hard to say exactly what one of them is.

A structure can, on occasion, be a most temporary, even artificial, sort of thing. One day, when I was about ten or so, the bulldozers came to the woods behind my house. I loved those hills and creeks, shaded by tall trees inviting play. For many summers, this had been the garden of my dreams. I slept out overnight beside the creek, pretending I was a true man of the woods. Daniel Boone, someone like that. Other times I leapt from limb to limb as Tarzan. On a path that had been beaten down over the years, I even practiced my losing effort in the fifty-yard dash at the grade-school track meet. When the bulldozers came to carve the land for still another postwar subdivision I was angry—at first.

In the first days of clear-cutting, the workers left a huge stack of fallen trees. With the limbs unsevered, and slowly dying leaves still attached, this accidental, unintended, temporary structure was for a few weeks a place of summer play. My pals and I climbed high on the fallen wood, slithered down into hidden crevices, cut away hiding places amid the branches. In those crevices and caves that would soon be hauled away, I had many an adventure, including even the first memorable, if futile, sexual act of my dimly approaching adolescence. For so long as it endured, this pile of construction rubbish had become a temporary, but wonderful, structure in and around which I organized a moment in my young life.

I have since heard of other children doing much the same. Even children who are poor—or those, poor or not, who are deprived of parental attentions—make their rooms, or their beds, or a corner of a closet into some little structure that, for a time, shelters their emotional lives, allowing them as best they can to organize their understanding of the world about. Dollhouses, train sets, Barbies, and toy soldiers are the occasional furnishings of the worlds imagined and played with in these corners. Structures like these (which, in the end, may not be all that different from social structures of all kinds) are able to support life, and give it order, even when they endure only for a short while.

Perhaps, to begin, we can agree that structures, including social ones, have at least two defining characteristics: (1) They make *order* out of some set of things—cells, stars, bodies, sleeping places, playrooms, imaginations, sex, and the like. (2) They do this work because they *endure* for a time, even if a very short time. In other words, structures organize some set of things because they lend them at least a minor degree of permanence. The set of things may eventually decay, come apart, or fade away, as did that stack of fallen trees and the fanciful experiments of my late childhood. But while they remain, they remain because some hard-to-define structure holds them together.

Of all the things sociologists concern themselves with, structures are, as I said, the most distinctive subject of their professional attentions. The same might be said of scientists of all kinds. Astronomers concern themselves with the structure of stellar things, just as psychologists are preoccupied with the structure of mental things, and microbiologists with the structure of organic matter.

This fascination with structures is especially remarkable among the social sciences. Economists study *markets* (a name for the structures within which economic transactions take place, fixing prices and values of other kinds). Political scientists study the structure of *political systems* (a name for the systematic, if not always fair, methods by which social groups decide who gets what among scarce resources). Cultural anthropologists, and many students of literature and the arts, study the varieties of *culture* (a name for the structures whereby societies organize myths, legends, stories, and other representations of what they value, hate, or wish to repress).

Sociology, it has been said, studies all of the above; it studies, that is, the structure of *social worlds* or, it is sometimes said, of *societies*. Unfortunately, though we often think we know what structures are, this confidence does not bear up under attempts to say with compelling precision just what realities terms like "social world" or "society" are meant to name. Social structures, somehow, are even less definite than others. A social world obviously includes everything that constitutes the collective life of groups of people, up to and including societies—their economics, their politics, their shared mental lives, their cultures, and more. Even when the social world is very small, like Frankie's hallway in Clarendon Heights, reference is made to some coherent order of social life that encompasses the economic, political, and cultural life of its members. This was an idea that Talcott Parsons made famous in the 1950s and for which his opponents, thinking he was a bit too ambitious, never forgave him. But Parsons was surely right in believing that sociology is in some sense the social science that aims to provide a general account of all that takes place in all the social worlds. Sociology, thus, is supremely interested in structures.

However uncertain social worlds may be, we know that social structures are real because differences among societies are easily spotted. Any particular enduring organization of an ongoing *social world* of people like the Lakota, the Russians, or the British is, simply, a *society*. The ongoing social worlds of members of a recognizable society can, therefore, be said to be structured such that their economic, political, and cultural practices, including any number of peculiar customs and manners, are as a whole distinct. Of this, illustrations are everywhere. Though the practices and structural forces of American society assault the Lakota society, still the social world of Lakota society is different and unlike any other. When we recognize differences of this kind, we understand that the very existence of a variety of social worlds is evidence of the powerful work of structures.

Still, structures appear to people in the course of daily life as through a mysterious fog. As I've said, it is very hard to say with precision exactly what a social structure is. Yet we must, if only because the practical sociologies by which people live and move are constantly drawn toward attempts to explain how and why structures so inexorably determine what individuals can and cannot do, even who they are. Behind the swagger, Frankie was bemoaning the structured destiny of his pals to be fuck-ups with few real options in life. Others, who might have been luckily born among the wealthiest 20 percent, have many more options than the Hallway Hangers, or for that matter the Lakota people. The privileged enjoy many more options than they need. But they, too, are who they are, and they do what they do, because of the mysterious work of social structures.

Power is the means by which social structures do this not-exactly-fair work of sorting people according to the few or many life-chances they get. Power may simply, if incompletely, be defined as the social energy of structures. Power is the determining force that causes some people to get less and some more of whatever is considered desirable in a social world.

It is power that accounts for the most important difference between social and other kinds of structures. In the structure of the universe, some stars die, while others burn on for eons. Yet no one but a poet would consider the uneven fates of stellar bodies far into darkest space a matter of unfairness. Still, strictly speaking, the death of some stars and the eternal spinning of others are the effects of cosmic energy empowering the shape of the universe into a definite structure. Though one can say that the extinction of some species of animal life is a tragedy, even this sad fate is normally felt to be a far lesser injustice than the suffering of colonized people or, even, of the urban poor like Frankie. It is only in relation to social things, to life in social worlds, that the question of power becomes a matter of binding moral intrigue. And, until we know what exactly the ants and dolphins truly think and feel, it is safe to assume that it is only in human society that the lack of power with all its sad consequences is felt so bitterly, with such terrible loss of possibility.

Perhaps the reason this is so is that power comes into serious consideration only when scarcity affects the moral as well as physical, well-being of living creatures. All living beings, we know very well, are subject to the effects of scarcity, but these effects are different when the loss of life, or of life's chances, is found to be a consequence of one group's theft of that to which another has a preexisting claim, perhaps a prior right of possession or ownership. Some people think that animals and plants have their distinctive rights to life. But, inasmuch as cows and trees are unable, at the present moment, to argue their case, their rights can be viewed as of a different kind. Yet, when human avarice enters in, suddenly the problem is beyond reasonable doubt.

The great herds of buffalo that possessed the American plains before the white people came died as much because their home grazing lands were divided artificially by the railroad as by the voracious stupidity of hunters for sport. When their natural access to food was diminished, the buffalo began to die. This was one scarcity-effect. But also, as the buffalo herds disappeared, the people native to the plains, including the Lakota, suffered a scarcity of meat upon which their way of life depended. Scarcity injured the buffalo as it did the Plains Indians. But its effect on the human societies can more reasonably be viewed as a sociologically interesting effect of social power. The white settlers and corporate bosses who took the plains for their use made life marginal for both the buffalo and the Indian. Only the moral confusion that did, indeed, prevail in the period of pioneer settlement could treat the danger to animals and people with equal indifference. What the Lakota lost was a direct and unequivocal result of the social power of the American society forming itself by a greedy grasp of the vast continental lands. That the whites viewed the theft of land and life as a right of their god's providence only masks the harsh reality. The current social structure of American society, based on its absolute control of a resource-rich continental landmass, was built and energized by social power taking a vast, but ultimately scarce, land from a weaker people.

When power works in these ways, it is relatively easy to see its effects in the structures that arise from the struggle for scarce but desirable goods like food, land, water, and much else. The sociological imagination would not be as demanding as it is if power always worked so openly. Sometimes it does; sometimes not. It is one thing, for example, to see the powerful effects of slavery on slaves and of colonization on the colonized, but quite another to see the effects of social power in the lives of people like Frankie. Compare, for example, Frankie's complaint at the beginning of this chapter to the reflections of Black Elk (1863–1950), an Oglala Lakota holy man, on the massacre at Wounded Knee:

> I did not know then how much was ended. When I look back now from this high hill of my old age, I can still see the butchered women and children lying heaped and scattered all along the crooked gulch as plain as when I saw them with eyes still young. And I can see that something else died there in the bloody mud, and was buried in the blizzard. A people's dream died there. It was a beautiful dream.
>
> —*Black Elk Speaks* (1947)[42]

Black Elk saw clearly that what had happened to his people by the force of American power was devastating to the structures of his Lakota world. He was a holy man, a visionary. But this alone does not account for the greater clarity of Black Elk's understanding. Frankie's complaint is much more uncertain in that he places the responsibility (and blame) on himself and his fellow Hallway Hangers. Their plight was, he felt, a result of their own fuckings up.

It is true that poor people, including the Lakota, are perfectly capable of screwing up their own lives. But it is just as true that the energizing power of modern social structures does not very often do its work openly as it did at Wounded Knee and, thus, may be a powerful, but hidden, cause of trouble for many. This is the difference. The Lakota knew beyond any reasonable doubt that the land was theirs to use and respect and that the slaughter at Wounded Knee was a result of terrifyingly direct power. But Frankie did not so clearly see the wider powers of American social structures, even though it was these structures, every bit as much as the boys themselves, that caused their social failure.

Why could not Frankie see as clearly as Black Elk? This question leads to a still finer aspect of the mysterious workings of structuring power.

In most modern societies, most (but not all) of the time, people encounter powerful structures, not directly, but indirectly by the effects those structures cause, such as the ways teachers treated the Hallway Hangers as the losers they came to believe they were. Power may even sometimes work in the events that structures cause *not* to happen, as in Frankie's slim prospects for a good life. Either way, as bad as the consequences were for the Hallway Hangers, these effects of power are a far cry from the slaughter at Wounded Knee or the overt cruelty of slavery. The discouragement of the Hallway Hangers is one of the sneaky effects of powerful structures, an effect that challenges the sociological imagination.

One generic form of the sneaky epiphanies of power appears in the structures of prestige, that is, in the remarkable and systematic consistency with which nearly everyone in a society seems to agree that some persons ought to be respected highly, others less so, and some not at all. The way a society structures the distribution of prestige assigns to some people—certain championship prizefighters, for example—an incomprehensibly high status from which they usually become wealthy. At the same time, the prestige structure prevents others—most kindergarten teachers, for example—from achieving either status or wealth even though the worth of their work is certifiably more valuable than the entertainment value of public beatings rendered for pay and pleasure by boxers. We never see the actual structure of a status or prestige system, but schoolteachers (and their pupils) and boxers (and their excitable fans) experience it in all kinds of ways.

We know social structures more often by their consequences than by seeing them as such. In this sense, social structures are less like trees than stars. Trees we see. We can, as a consequence, well imagine their structures, which is why they are so often the subjects of photography, painting, art, poetry, and music. Distant stellar worlds, on the other hand, we never see. The thrill we get from those distant stars is always light-years away, long gone by the time we see it. Whatever may be the structure of the universe, its "reality" to astronomers, or lovers on a summer night, is at best a well-informed conjecture about something no one will *ever* see. Yet, were the sun to turn cold, or Jupiter to veer crazily out of its orbit, or were Darth Vader truly to invade our system, we would experience the consequences no more than we already do without realizing it. Most social structures are like this.

Most of us, for example, have distant relatives living in social worlds far from our own. They constitute the structure of our family (or kin) relations, and they make a difference. Some years ago my uncle Edwin, a quite famous professional sociologist, died after a long and productive life. At the funeral in California, I met a cousin I had not seen for more than half a century—when he was two and I was five. As he and his sisters and I and my brother shared our stories of their father, my father's brother, I felt a surprising (to use the correct term) *kinship* with them. Though differently, we were all shaped by many of the same family forces. In such ways, it is possible to catch an occasional glimpse of the social structures we otherwise experience by their effects, without ever seeing them all at once. After the funeral stories were told, we Lemerts had learned a great deal more about the particular, not-to-be-exaggerated prestige our fathers and uncles, their mothers and fathers, and each of us had come to possess, for better or worse. We understood, that is, a little more about how and why we each came to be who we are because of our kinship in this one structure among the many that influence us. Prestige bestows on individuals a sense of their status, whether high or low, in the structure of social things. This too is power, as anyone assigned an inferior status like Frankie's knows most painfully.

Alongside its sly workings in the structure of prestige, power also works through the structure of *authority*—the rules and regulations that assign to some people a limited right to tell others what they can and cannot do. Erving Goffman—the same Goffman who said "universal human nature is not a very human thing"—was one of sociology's most astute observers of the hidden effects of social structures like authority. In an intriguing footnote in one of his books, Goffman told a story of an event in the 1960s when the authority structures were very much in turmoil.

The event took place at Columbia University in the late spring of 1968 in the office of the university's president, Grayson Kirk. Rebel students, protesting the injustices of American society as they saw them in their own university, had taken over President Kirk's office and, quite literally, trashed it. This was not an uncommon form of student protest in those days, often inspiring outrage on the part of the authorities, including Mr. Kirk. Goffman begins his footnote by quoting a long paragraph from a book about the Columbia office trashing, then provides his own observation:

> "One and a half hours after the President's suite had been cleared of student demonstrators, Grayson Kirk stood in the center of his private office looking at the blankets, cigarette butts and orange peels that covered his rug. Turning to A. M. Rosenthal of The New York Times and several other reporters who had come into the office with him he

murmured, 'My God, how could human beings do a thing like this?' It was the only time, Truman [Kirk's dean] recalled later, that he had ever seen the President break down. Kirk's windows were crisscrossed with tape and on one hung a large sign reading 'Join Us.' His lampshades were torn, his carpet was spotted, his furniture was displaced and scratched. But the most evident and disturbing aspect of the scene was not the minor damage inflicted by the students. The everything-in-its-place decor to which Kirk had grown accustomed was now in disarray—disarray that was the result of the transformation of an office into the living quarters of 150 students during the past six days."

The great sociological question, of course, is not how could it be that human beings would do a thing like this, but rather how is it that human beings do this sort of thing so rarely. How come persons in authority have been so overwhelmingly successful in conning those beneath them into keeping the hell out of their offices?

—Erving Goffman, *Relations in Public* (1971)[43]

This is indeed the great sociological question. Just more than fifty years before President Kirk's office was trashed, Max Weber, a more sober commentator than Goffman, had asked the same question: "Why do men obey?"[44] Why, indeed, do people obey authorities and their rules? It may be that no question comes closer than this one to opening up the hidden workings of power. We may be drawn to people of high prestige for the magic they sometimes seem to possess. But respect for authority is more complicated by far, thus more intriguing.

The remarkable fact that people tend to keep the hell out of the offices of the authorities, and otherwise respect the rules and regulations, even those nowhere written down, is perhaps the most impressive general evidence for the power of social structures in ordinary life. While there are many kinds of social structures, those that stand behind obedience to authority—norms, customs, rules, etiquettes, and the like—are among the more telling ones. When they work in our favor, we seldom notice. When they work against us, we notice the pain of punishment or exclusion. And, in the case of President Kirk and other authorities astonished by the actions of rebels, when authoritative structures *fail* to work any longer, such an occurrence is the subject of widespread interest. Throughout the spring of 1968 when students trashed Kirk's office, there were hundreds of demonstrations on college campuses worldwide. Everyone noticed, as well they should when the authoritative structures of such a valued institution as higher education are no longer respected.

Hence another curious feature of social structures: They tend to be invisible to those who enjoy their benefits until such time as they fail to deliver. But, even then, when workers and students, journalists, sociologists, and other rebels exercise their sociological imaginations to account for their failures in life, the collapsed social structure can only be reconstructed, *after the fact*. And, like the structure of prestige, it is never a totally present entity upon which hands can be laid.

What, after all, is the social thing that keeps people the hell out of offices? One might say it is the power those in the offices enjoy to require those who must wait their turn outside to obey, respect, or tolerate what those inside say and do. This is why "office" is, in fact, the word sociologists use to describe the modern way of structuring authority. "Office" is nothing more than the English language translation of the French word *bureau*, from which we take the concept *bureaucracy*. Literally, a bureaucracy is a structured system in which the basic rule is that those with the bureau, or office, are considered the legitimate rulers of some or another organized sphere (such as universities) so long as they follow the rules of the office.

As in many other things, Max Weber was one of the first to think through the importance of bureaucracies and kindred structures to the rise of modern society. In fact, Weber was the first sociologist to write at length on the subject. He pointed out that the rational structuring of authority was the single most distinctive feature of modern social life, just as the rational principles that led to capitalism were behind modernity's most salient economic form. In brief, it was Weber who, early in the nineteenth century, saw that modern society was founded on a contradiction that arose from the fact that bureaucratic organization was one of the, perhaps even *the*, most modern of all social things.

On the one hand, bureaucracy, strictly speaking, is the form of authority that provides the greatest possible assurance to the masses that the natural tendency of rulers to become despots will be held in check. If, in modern societies, authority is created by the rules of an office, and not by the power of the person in charge, then in principle the person in authority can be held accountable to the rules. If he violates them, he can be thrown out of office. As it turned out, though the students who trashed President Kirk's office may have behaved badly, Kirk himself was eventually found wanting in his respect for members of the Columbia University community. Though none of his failures were grave enough to cause formal charges to be filed against him, an investigation revealed that he and his administrators administered arrogantly. They all soon left office, after which prestigious Columbia suffered a long period of decline from which it took several decades to recover. President Kirk had broken the unwritten rules that delicately held in place the structures of Columbia's authority. When he was called to account, he lost his power, and the institution had to reknit its system of authority in order to regain the prestige his mismanagement of authority had lost.[45]

Mr. Kirk was, however, far from being the only victim of challenges to authority that took place in the 1960s. Judges, mayors, police chiefs, sheriffs, labor leaders, student leaders, a few civil rights leaders, and others who were then, and since, found guilty of breaking the rules of their offices were often forced out. The most famous case from that era was President Richard Nixon, who was forced out because he had abused the power of his office in the Watergate affair. Nixon was so awkwardly serious about getting reelected in the 1974 elections that he looked the other way when his political agents broke into the opposition party's office in the Watergate building. He wanted them to capture the enemy's campaign secrets. But it was his crooks who got caught, and so did he. Nixon had a lot of power, but there were rules. The United States Congress used those rules to find the facts and to threaten, as years later they threatened Bill Clinton to impeach Nixon. Whatever you may think of the attempt to remove Clinton from office, years before many agreed that Nixon deserved what he was about to get. He quit because he knew he would be removed. The idea, as Weber first presented it, is that the structured rules of an office are a higher authority than any person who holds the office, which is to say that the structure of the authority is a social thing separate from, and in principle, superior to, the person who holds a temporary right to its power. *constructed. No.*

But Weber also saw that there was another side to these rationally structured rules of authority. Rules are very difficult to change when they become cumbersome or useless. On top of that, they seem to multiply at an alarming rate. Years ago, I was part of a group of friends who decided to pool their resources to rent a wonderful summer home at the sea. This was a time in our lives when we all had young children, so it was no small task to find a place big enough. To make matters surprisingly worse, once we found the place we had to figure out how to run the operation through the six weeks we had rented the house. Six families and twenty or so kids consume truckloads of food and produce mountains of trash, dirty laundry, sand from the beach, and general household filth. All of the former had to be purchased, and all the latter disposed of. The costs of the buying, like the work entailed in the cleaning up, had to be organized. Without an agreed-upon leader, all the adults, being reasonable and liberal people, decided we would handle everything by collective discussion and consensus. Soon there were work charts on the walls assigning tasks, then meetings to negotiate purchasing decisions, then more meetings to settle differences arising because always some of us hated how others did whatever they were assigned to do; then, ultimately, rules and more rules. Soon we were meeting to discuss the rules almost every evening after the younger kids went to bed. The older kids thought we were crazy. Eventually, we thought we were crazy. Yet we persevered. But the summer was a mess. Such an experience is why, if it is at all possible, one is better off spending vacations in hotels. Hotels and such establishments may be bureaucracies in the way they are internally organized, but, as far as the guest is concerned, they are dictatorships in which, within limits, the guest is a despot of sorts.

Weber saw that the problem with bureaucracies is that the reasonableness of the rules of authority usually fades as rules proliferate, creating objections of all kinds. Weber was, so far as I know, the first to write about the *bureaucratic machine*, which most people hate and some fear. Rationally structured organizations tend to become machinelike, that is, automatic, autonomous, and autocratic—thus defeating the great virtue of their reasonableness. In this, Weber saw the contradiction of modern societies as what later sociologists have called the *crisis of legitimacy*. Modern, democratic societies attempt to rule reasonably, from the people up. This is what "democracy" means strictly: rule by the people. But, as we all know, the bureaucrats eventually take over, making it nearly impossible for the people ruled to have a legitimate say in what goes on.

This is why people pay particular attention to failures in the social structures of authority. This is why Weber asked, "Why do men obey?" and why Goffman said the most interesting sociological question is, "Why do we keep the hell out of their offices?" In both versions, this is an interesting question in modern societies because, according to the ideals of modern societies, "men" ought not need to obey. They are, allegedly, the rulers. But we all know that "the people," whether men or women or kids, do not rule very often, or at least not very directly. Again, it turns out that those who benefit from the way the rulers rule tend not to mind the ruling, except when their garbage is not picked up on time. On the other hand, those who are regularly abused by the way rulers rule—the poor, gays and lesbians, women, and the otherwise discriminated (including students in autocratically run universities)—notice quite readily what the structures of authority are. They usually have sophisticated theories about what goes on. They are, indeed, some of our society's best practical sociologists because, like Frankie, they have less reason to be conned into staying the hell out of the structures.

I hate this sec. writing method: pick an entry points; ask questions; give an easy summary. It is dumb, overlooks the point always, etc.

THE MYSTERIOUS POWER OF SOCIAL STRUCTURES   **125**

There is hardly any doubt that the social structures whose failures we notice most acutely are the structures of authority. They may do their powerful work in silence much of the time, but, when they go too far, or fail too disruptively, people snap out of the state of mindless obedience and begin to see just how authority and other structures work. When authority exceeds its limits or otherwise fails, someone always gets hurt. When welfare caseworkers, probation officers, hanging judges, police, school principals and deans, SWAT team agents, admissions officers, motor vehicle registrars, ticket takers, and other agents of authority screw up, those subject to them suffer by doing more time in slammers or wait lines, or much worse.

Though social structures come in many different varieties, our common experiences with structures of authority should suggest why sociologists of all kinds must learn how to think and talk about them. In the simplest of terms, it is possible to summarize what has been said so far about the formal attributes of structures, including social structures. Social structures are social things that (1) give order to some lesser set of social things, for which purpose they must be (2) durable and enduring, at least for a time, which they are in spite of the fact that (3) they are invisible in the normal course of social life, except when they fail or otherwise *why?* call attention to themselves, on which occasion those victimized by their failure can teach the rest of us a lot about (4) just how big and powerful social structures are. *This word list means nothing!*

Or, briefer still, social structures are (1) *organizing*, (2) *enduring*, and (3) generally *invisible*, but (4) *salient*, social things we know by their effects. The larger structures of authority (governments and their courts and jailers, for example) possess all of these attributes—a fact well known to anyone who has recently been required to stand in line at a registry of motor vehicles or, even worse, a traffic court. *hah.*

⁂

But, still, what is to be said of Frankie and the Hallway Hangers? They were, to be sure, persons of slight prestige and lowly status. But one might say they brought it on themselves. Other kids hated them; even their teachers treated them with contempt. This is not surprising, given their crude and hostile behavior. But why were they so hostile? Not everyone who is poor rebels; many are resigned, others are depressed, still others carry on with great nobility. For the Hallway Hangers, rebellion and aggression, particularly against authority, were their own, not-all-that-unusual reactions to their meager social world. Clearly, Goffman's question meant nothing to them. They were quite prepared to trash any office they could get into.

To account for the Hallway Hangers' way of responding to, and being shaped by, social structures, still a third form of social power must be called forth: the power of the class structure. Class structures organize the social opportunities allocated to various groups according to a group's greater and lesser access to scarce goods, particularly income and other sources of wealth. Class structures, thereby, are the systemic effects of the economy on social worlds. The sociological study of class structures is different, there-fore, from economics because the sociological attention is paid, not simply to markets and money, but to how access to them is determined by a group's social position. Class, like prestige and authority, is a primary instrument of power—the one that best accounts for the Hallway Hangers.

The story of the Hallway Hangers and their rival gang, the Brothers, was told by Jay MacLeod (b. 1961), who worked with them, became their friend, and eventually wrote their story while still a college student. The result of MacLeod's study was the book *Ain't No Makin' It*, which has become a best-seller and a modern sociological classic. For those who doubt what I say about the power of practical sociology, it might come as a surprise that Jay MacLeod took only one course in sociology in college and did not go on to become a professional sociologist. Instead, after col-lege he studied theology as a Rhodes Scholar at Oxford University and became an Anglican priest. He has dedicated his life to work among the rural and urban poor in the United States and England. It was only as an undergraduate scholar that he mastered the professional sociological lit-erature he used to account for the hopelessness of young people like Frankie. Everyone who knows Jay MacLeod knows that his mastery of the professional ideas grew first out of his mastery of the gifts of practical soci-ological competence.

MacLeod would never have been in the housing project he called Clarendon Heights had he not been the kind of person who, as a student, would volunteer to work with young people of poor economic circum-stances. So, when he returned to his university to think about the study, it was natural that the power of economic structures, of the class system, pro-vided the puzzle MacLeod tried to solve in *Ain't No Makin' It*. He drew on ideas that had been developed by professional sociologists about, again, what is known as *reproduction theory*. As the term suggests, the theory holds that the structures of modern societies tend to reproduce themselves from one generation to the next, on and on.

Of course, it is obvious that institutions are meant to reproduce them-selves to some extent. It would hardly make sense for a society to change, say, its political system every generation or so. Even when most people hate the politicians, they seldom look for ways to change the basic rules. Overlooking bad rules is probably the better course, at least until the corruption gets out of hand. Political systems may remain the same over time because, whatever their weaknesses, they work reasonably well—at least they do in many of the democratic societies. The structure of the economic system, however, is another matter.

Economic structures in capitalist societies, in point of fact, usually work very well only for, say, the top 40 percent or, increasingly, the top 20 percent or, soon, the top 5 percent. Those who benefit from the way economic, or class, structures are organized seldom complain. Complaint, when it is heard, usually comes from people in Frankie's situation. Yet, as I suggested when I compared him to Black Elk, there is something quite distinctive about Frankie's sociology of his situation. Underneath all the bravado and hostility, he blames the people who fail for their failure! Though at other times the Hallway Hangers are willing to blame the system, sometimes in racist and other confused ways, they always come back to themselves as a principal source of their own problems.

Here, at last, is the why and how of the mysterious workings of power. There may be surprise, but little mystery, in the sneak attacks of the colonizers, slaveholders, and secret police who crush the lives of some children. There is relatively less mystery in the workings of prestige because it is not all that difficult to imagine why the people looked up to have more power than others. The riddle of powerful structures is tougher to crack when it comes to authority, but it may be toughest of all in relation to the class system. It is, after all, mostly in relation to the structure of class and economic differences that one most feels the tragic effects of social reproduction. The poor actively contribute to the reproduction of the economic and social unfairness of a society when they believe, as do the Hallway Hangers, that they are part of the problem. This, of course, is the problem C. Wright Mills tried to solve by calling people to imagine that their personal troubles are very likely structural problems of the society as a whole.

The problem with Mills's original idea is that false consciousness is so pervasive that it is seldom enough simply to encourage those with troubles to see and think differently. People who suffer from unequal opportunities are committed very early in their lives to the proposition that it is they who are no good, and no good because they cannot accomplish what they are taught to dream of. Even when the poor or socially marginal also believe that the system is unjust, they feel defeat so deeply within themselves that it is hard for them to get out of their troubles into the light of sociological imagination.

In other words, the big structures of economic power that establish and maintain the class system *also* get inside the heads of the individuals subjected to that system. The Hallway Hangers, being of poor families, were in fact dealt a losing hand by the class structures. They were born to the bottom. But being thus born does not absolutely determine one's fate. Some do overcome, though not many. Class structures are not, therefore, machinelike any more than bureaucracies are as deterministic as Weber thought they were. When even one person escapes from the lowest of classes, this means that something other than naked economic power is going on. As I said, power is sneaky, and especially in the way it reproduces the injustice with which the poor must live while they beg for small change from the well-off.

Those who beg often believe they are meant to be beggars, just as those who brush them off on the way to cocktails usually believe in their superiority. In modern societies, power works from within the wounded or cold hearts of individuals. It seldom works openly from the top down, for, if it did, the evening news would be much more filled with Wounded Knees than it is. The really bad news of the poor and excluded is that they confirm their plight in their own beliefs and actions, and thus become trapped.

The Hallway Hangers were indeed fuck-ups—drugged, destructive, and dangerous even to themselves. But do not suppose that Frankie had not been called a fuck-up by others, one way or another, long before he came to believe it about himself and his friends. They were indeed fuck-ups first and foremost because they had so few opportunities to do any better than they did. Those who have never spent long hours, much less nights, in an urban public housing project, as Jay MacLeod did, will never know how hard it can be to find a quiet place to read and study, or how powerful the pressure is to conform to what another sociologist, Elijah Anderson (b. 1943), calls the code of the street. Anderson systematically explores the concept of code-switching in his book *Code of the Streets: Decency, Violence, and the Moral Life of the Inner City* (1994) in which he reports on years of research the pressures on young black men in the impoverished cities to demonstrate their self-respect by facing up to the challenges of street life—by a readiness, that is, to respond aggressively to any gesture of disrespect.[46] Many believe that much of the violence in urban neighborhoods is partly explained by the confused need of young men to prove themselves worthy of aggression, if nothing else, against the many debilitating economic and social odds they face. To survive on the street they must be adept at switching codes—displaying manliness when it challenged, even when at home or school they may act according to the code of decency that abhors street violence. But it is not just young black men who face these impossible odds. The Hallway Hangers, mostly white, and inclined toward racism, believed and behaved according to their own code of the streets. They looked for trouble, especially with authorities, and found it at every turn. Soon enough, they had moved beyond being simply troublemakers. They were trouble.

One of Jay MacLeod's interpretations of their situation is that their aggression was, like that of the black men studied by Elijah Anderson, an attempt to confirm their masculinity in a society that expects men, more than women, to earn good money and provide for others. The problem is that the economies of such societies produce class structures that, literally, deny many young men the decent jobs necessary to meet the society's expectations. There are not enough well-paid jobs for everyone, and in the United States there haven't been since the Second World War. That is a fact. But what is its effect?

Remember that Frankie's hope for himself was that he would "get married, have some kids, have a decent job." He understood the normal path to human success in America. But read on. He immediately qualified his hopes: "Enough to live off anyways, to support a wife and kids. But some of them [he meant to include himself, of course], they're gonna fuck up." The norm is to earn not just enough to "live off" but enough to support others well. Even in expressing a kind of backhanded faith in the system, Frankie knew he and his were going to fail, as indeed they did. *Ain't No Makin' It* was their realistic situation. What, then, is a young man to do when he is faced with virtually certain failure? Some struggle on, hoping against hope, as did the Brothers, a rival gang in Clarendon Heights. But some rebel in a just as vain grasp for a modicum of respect. The code underlying the code of the streets (and the schools) was, in effect, "If I can't succeed, then at least I'll make my mark and screw up the system for screwing me."

Such a fate as this is common in modern, postindustrial societies like those in the United States and Western Europe, and increasingly in parts of Latin America and Asia. Jobs disappear in societies where the economies are now based on high-technology applications and where manufacturing is done more often by computer-driven machines than by men and women. Some economists predict that, within the lifetimes of children born since 1975, there will be so few jobs that perhaps only 20 percent of all men and women will be able to find work.[47] (And this is for the advanced societies on the globe. Think of the underdeveloped societies!) Already, it is well known, unemployment rates in the deteriorated cities can be as high as 55 percent.[48] Worse yet, across the world there are cities like Lagos in Nigeria that, like the *maquiladoras* along the Mexico-United States border, where there is either no real employment at all or work so poorly paid as to offer no real hope. Not as high as on the Lakota reservation, but a terrible number just the same. Should this prediction come to pass, as well it might, then the top 20 percent will be not just the most wealthy but the only persons with any real access to income as we know it today (unless, that is, something changes).

Such a futuristic nightmare was beyond Frankie's street sociology. But he could imagine enough to understand the odds against his ever finding work, much less a career of the kind other kids his age not only dream of but believe they will find. This, ultimately, is how the power of the class structure gets inside the heads of some children. It may work its way differently in different cases. Being white, the Hallway Hangers did not face exactly the same code of the streets as did Elijah Anderson's black youth. But, whatever the differences, the powerful work of class structures is the sneaky work of convincing those who fail that they deserve to fail as much as those who succeed believe they deserve to succeed. It does not always happen this neatly. Dirty work like this is never seamless. There is always somebody with enough sociological imagination to see the structures, and the effects they cause, for what they are. Still, modern societies, in spite of the hopes and ideals of those who live in them, reproduce themselves and all their social and economic injustices, from generation to generation.

Yes, some children born poor escape, and some born wealthy care about economic justice. But, in the grinding frustrations of lives without decent prospects of making it, the good fortune of the few escapees means little to those left behind. And the mystery is that the Frankies of this world, if they are lucky even to survive to a middle age of <u>furious</u> <u>disappointment</u>, may well down their beers to drown their self-disgust. They may never fully realize that it was the power of the structures, not they, that dealt them such impossibly rotten hands.

However power works—through raw force, prestige, authority, or the reproduction of class inequalities—it works to structure the social worlds in which people live. Some do well and some are fortunate; others don't or aren't. But the fortunes we have, or lack, are never entirely ours to keep, or regret. These organizing, enduring, invisible, but salient, social structures are necessary to hold social worlds together, but they can be deadly, and sometimes are.

EIGHT

~

THE LIVELY SUBJECTS
OF DEAD STRUCTURES

"The burial will be properly taken care of. Please return to your cars." The company of mourners obeyed slowly, leaving the casket standing in an open field. Only a statue of St. Jude, partly hiding the eager gravediggers, broke the hot, early-summer sky. The heat pressed on us as we slowly left Ted's remains.

This was the scene at the burial of my father-in-law, whose death changed life in important ways, even as it brought back a long-lost past. The day after the funeral, I walked to a park where I had played as a child. The heat was, if anything, heavier than the day before. I sat staring through the haze, looking far into the valley below. A single-engine plane floated toward a distant landing. Its forward motion was so slight I half thought it would drop were it not for the thickness of the air. To this very park, I had been brought as a small child, nearly half a century before, when the world was different but Cincinnati's summer sky just as laden. Some things remain the same.

I had been too young then to notice the human rituals that took place about me the day after Ted's funeral, as they have for years, before and since. Off in the distant shade, a young couple petted, classic public strokes of fresh affections. They touched each other as though guided by some rule of decency instinctive to couples at a certain, early moment in their loving. The same heavy sky that could hold an airplane also dampened the throttle of their passions. On certain days time does stand still.

A shirtless teenage boy pranced—chest fine, his pants fallen on the ass in the fashion of the day. He yelled to his pals. He was going to the gravel pits for a swim. It could have been me and my pals at the same age. Summers in this Ohio River town, boys without lovers go to these deep pits seeking some other refreshing danger. They left together, showing off their barely legal beer in brown bags. Even their rowdy departure failed to break the spell. A ruddy-faced man of indeterminate middle age sat transfixed, hands folded atop the picnic table. He too looked far off into the valley. The plane had moved close to its touchdown. Ted, too, was settled into the ground, properly buried as had been promised.

For the living, death is more like summer than winter. The worst heat slows things to a stop. But the more important social things remain. Loss narrows the sociological eye into a stare down and back toward valleys of the past. During the same long-ago summers when I had been brought there for innocent play, Pat, my mother-in-law, had worked in that airfield from which my father, whom she never knew, had departed for America's war with Japan. There, one day, strangers who would later be joined as kin without ever meeting may have passed each other. The airfield is mostly closed now. The air was too thick, landings too dangerous—except, it seems, for small planes on certain days. Along the Ohio River, lowlands are given to spring flooding, which comes as to a schedule indifferent to the needs of boys and girls to fly, pet, stare, swim, go off to war, or otherwise skirt the laws of their nature. Spring floods thicken summer days, just as a death slows the memory of those who remain. Death may itself be a winter, but for those left alive, it is a never-ending summer of memories.

Social worlds and their structures may be deadly, but they are also dead from the point of view of we who live and move and have our social beings in them. Do not allow the fear of death modern culture promotes to fool you into thinking that dead beings and things have no relation to the living. My uncle died some years ago; my father-in-law two years before that; twenty years before that, my mother; my father a few years before her; and his father twenty years before that in 1948. We all live in the succession of deaths. But these dead of kin and social relations continue ever to be among us. As I promised at the beginning, this is a book of mystery stories, and here is another. The large social structures that mete out privilege to some, despair to others, and modest means to those between are active forces in the lives of even the most lowly of all who are subject to their powers. Structures are, as I have said, organizing, enduring, invisible, and salient.

But what does it mean to say they are invisible, if it does not mean that in some very practical sense they are dead, or at least not alive in the same sense that we, their subjects, are?

Pause, if you can, before those Lakota dead who cried and moaned from their grave for a full century after Wounded Knee. In a world such as ours, a century later, there is little support for the conviction that the laments of the dead are real. The sophisticated might belittle Black Elk's vision of the slaughtered innocents as primitive superstition. But, from a mundane perspective, do not Frankie's lament and Black Elk's have much in common? Was not the sad anger of this poor white boy from the big city also a psalm of despair for lives he knew were already buried? And what is to be said of men of relative privilege, like my father, who was so filled with rage at the pain his father had inflicted on him that he could not keep himself from fits of temper against those who loved him? Once, at a birthday party for his mother, good old dad threw a bowl of mashed potatoes strong against the ceiling, then stomped out like the little boy he had become in that moment of terrifying regression. There was more, and worse—all symptoms of the dead father within him, just as he lives today within me. I hated my father's anger for the longest while, until I came to understand, after many years, that his pain and mine are joined across the grave. Even we who are privileged are also distant cousins at many removes of the Frankies and Black Elks of the world. Every feeling human being lives under the force of events that transpired in the past.

One might think of these effects of remembered things as figments of the psychological. To *some* extent, they are. But, deeper still, within all men and women who survive to adult life, the power of the structured social past works its way. Any society that could look the other way as its militia murders innocent children in the South Dakota territory, or while the grandchildren of those soldiers ignore, or cause, the neglect of Frankie is an enduring social thing in which *all* the deeds and misdeeds of its social past are carried forth. Structures would never endure from generation to generation were it not for the coming down of collective memories of blood shed or hymns sung in the past.

One might say that social structures are dead social things, well remembered. My memory of my father's tantrums is certainly the articulate work of my psychology. But my ability to understand other grown children when they tell similar, usually far worse, stories of the abuses of their childhoods is something more than a coincidence of individual minds. It is the beginning of a sociological imagination, a work done out of the sociological competence hidden beneath the pain or pleasure of current circumstance. Anger and abuse tear at the seams of family life for reasons that go deep into the soul of the still larger collective life. Reaching more broadly, when people dispersed across a large society meet by chance and hear each other's stories, they put the bits and pieces of memory together. They recognize themselves in the other, thus forming the first filaments of the web of social life. Then, the imagination can blossom into a full and poignant sociology of the structures of the world. We who did not grow up black or female in America can rest assured that more than a few black people read W. E. B. Du Bois's stories of the color line, as women read Charlotte Gilman's *Yellow Wallpaper*, in growing awareness that they are one with those who came before. What another black boy or young white woman experienced in the long ago (just about the time of Wounded Knee) was indeed a vision (not different from Black Elk's) of just how the injuries of the now-dead past are alive today in the invisible structures that make the world what it is.

Structures thus press upon living social individuals who are, when one stops to think about it, the same individuals without whom those large, abstractly structured social things would be utterly lifeless. Much of the time structures are a dead and deadly weight on individuals.

One of the best-known sociological examples of this strange phenomenon is reported in *The Urban Villagers*, the study of an Italian, working-class neighborhood of Boston.[49] Herbert Gans (b. 1927), a sociologist who has devoted his career to writing on sociological issues of political concern to the general public, spent a year of his youth living in the neighborhood he studied. What Gans found out about the people of Boston's West End is that they were, in his view, *unable* to think about the wider structures of their social world. They, thus, lacked all but the most limited capacity for sociological imagination, with the result that, for them, the wider social world was quite dead as far as their daily lives were concerned.

Being on the average but one or two generations removed from rural, southern Italy, the people of the urban village were still very much traditionalists. They were almost wholly preoccupied with preserving the customs and values in which they and their ancestors had been reared. In particular, they were dependent on their *peer group society*, the concept by which Gans described their emotional reliance on a circle of friends of the same age, gender, and stage of life. The urban villagers were so dependent on the approval of these groups that they were unable to see beyond them. Anyone who remembers the gangs or cliques of their early teenage years might appreciate what peer group societies are like. For a while in the eighth grade or so,

I didn't care about anything except what David Bennett and all the other popular kids thought about me. I would have done anything to get invited to their parties. I suffered horribly when I was not. My adolescent pain was, however, but a passing reflection of the enduring social world in which Gans's urban villagers spent the whole of their lives. The problem for them was that, just as a teenager often thinks of little but what the others think of him, so Gans's villagers could not imagine much of anything outside the small circle of their peer groups, and certainly not what city hall had in store for them. Middle-class teenagers usually get over the cliquish years and seldom suffer very serious effects of this stage of sociological mindlessness. But Gans's urban villagers were in a different position entirely.

It happened that the city of Boston was just then embarking upon a program of urban redevelopment, a politician's obfuscating name for taking the lands and homes of the less well-off in order to build apartments and trendy shops for the wealthy. The urban village was scheduled for destruction. Yet the West Enders, in spite of frequent official notices of their coming doom, paid no attention because they simply could not visualize such a thing. Had they, they might have organized politically to prevent the bulldozers from taking their neighborhood. Others in other parts of the city had in fact done this. The urban villagers could not because they were a people irretrievably dependent on a well-structured way of life rooted in a past that stretched back to Italy. They could not imagine the structures before their very eyes—structures that were about to kill their village society. Here is an example of how the dead structures of the social past can so blind people in the present that their way of life is destroyed.

Social structures are salient enough to organize the small deeds of social worlds because they endure, for better or worse. Their duration, like that of mountains bearing the fossils and relics of life long gone, can only be the carrying forth of effects of the deep past. In the urban village, the effects of the past of their ancestors' lives in Italy created a small and local structure that clashed, to deadly effect, with the enduring weight of a modern city's desire ever to take more land for better business. The class structure that, if you are young, may be at this very moment sorting you for a good chance at life, even as it assigns others lesser chances, did not spring up all at once. Structures are working on you as you read or nap, but their working is the slow-moving, leading edge of a social mountain, long enduring, not soon to tumble. The sociological imagination must always look up to the far peaks that define the dark valleys or pleasant streams where people live.

Mysteries abound. But it is not all that eerie to suppose that structures, like voices from the grave, press upon us out of the deep past of lost, but still powerful, worlds. Their weight may be deadly for many, or inspiring for those more privileged, but they are dead in the sense that structures do not, ever, have the same vital force as the actions individuals are generally able to take. Where the mystery persists is in how it happens that dead and invisible structures send forth so much power. Such a notion confounds the more common experience that the actions of social life rise up, instead, from individuals clustered in their many and different, but local, groups.

Mysteries may abound, but they are not altogether beyond reason. Professional sociologists, as I said earlier, are obliged to give an account of structures. Though the professionals, by their training, are usually able to give more complete and detailed explanations of structures than, say, Frankie could, they encounter many of the same dilemmas any practical sociologist does. This is especially so when a sociologist is attempting to explain the larger structural changes in society, such as the rise of modern societies out of the traditional past, which so troubled Max Weber, or the question of social revolutions that has haunted sociologists since the tumultuous times of the sixties.

One of the more important innovations in social thought to have come from the studies promoted by the sixties was *structuralism*—the view that structures are so important a cause of fundamental social process that hardly anything else counts, least of all the actions of individuals. Charles Tilly's resource mobilization theory, which I discussed earlier, is a moderate structuralism. Tilly attempts, among other things, to explain why it happens that individuals and groups can be ready to act to change an unjust system, but are unable to act until an opening in the opportunity structure allows them effectively to mobilize their resources in pursuit of revolutionary goals.

To this day, not everyone agrees with the structuralist position, but hardly anyone demurs from voicing an opinion of it. Critics of the more extreme structuralists say their view of the autonomous power of structures leaves little room for agency, that is, for the contributions of visible, breathing, concretely human subjects to the larger social actions that sometimes change society. Agents are, simply, the people who carry the message and power of actions leading to change. Those who object to structuralism consider agents the subjects, or original sources, of the actions that move things along.

Structuralism has provoked one of the most persistent and fruitful controversies among professional sociologists in the post-1960s era, and thus renewed in somewhat different terms the classic debate between the society-first and the individuals-first traditions. One of the more curious features of the debate is that both sides tend to forget about false consciousness. The structuralists tend to assume that individuals are honest dopes, passively aware of the power of structures, while those who defend the role of agents tend to see individuals as fully alert seekers and doers of the truth. Both sides should have a chat with Frankie. Just the same, though the debate occasionally ascends to heights of abstraction that take the breath away, it boils down to the important practical question of just how palpably alive individual subjects take action *against*, *with*, or *because* of structures.

One of the most influential (and not at all abstract) structuralist contributions to the debate is a 1979 book, *States and Social Revolutions*, by Theda Skocpol (b. 1947), now a professor of sociology and government at Harvard. Skocpol frankly admits that her interest in social revolutions was encouraged by her experience as a politically concerned student in the 1960s. Early in her career, Skocpol's bold affirmation of the political side of the sociological life was well in evidence in her book, but also in her principled actions against Harvard, which, at first, had denied her a permanent job. She took the action of bringing a sex discrimination charge. After a drawn-out review, the Harvard authorities relented. She won her tenured professorship because, by the time of Harvard's review of the case, it was already apparent that *States and Social Revolutions* was destined to be a modern classic. Today her work is regarded as responsible for a scientific revolution in political sociology.

What Skocpol did in *States and Social Revolutions* was to seek an even stronger structuralism than can be found in theories like Tilly's. Her idea was that revolutionary social change occurs, when it does, not primarily because of the agency of individuals (not even large numbers of them joined in collective actions), but because something world-shaking happens to the social structures. Skocpol conceded, of course, that well-mobilized mass protests are part of the revolutionary situation. But the revolution itself takes place only when, as she put it, "there is a rapid, basic transformation of society's state and class structures,"[50] and such structures change only when something happens to the structures themselves. In other words, Skocpol gives little revolutionary credit to the agency of individuals; she even reduces the emphasis Tilly put on the mobilization of resources for change.

One of the more intriguing case studies in *States and Social Revolutions* is the French Revolution of 1789. Many people are drawn to the idea that the French Revolution had mostly to do with the celebrated storming of the Bastille—that the old regime in France fell before the courageous revolutionaries who brought the evil system down on the 14th of July, 1789. In the popular imagination, glamorous revolutionary heroes are pictured as the agents of this moment of human liberation. More sober versions of this view are held by some social scientists. Skocpol disagrees.

Skocpol's idea is that the storming of the Bastille, and all the other actions taken by the masses and their leaders, would not have taken place had there not been prior important changes in the political and economic structures in France. France's heavy investments in the American Revolution of 1776 were chief among a number of costly international ventures that, when combined with internal problems (like major crop failures and famines in 1788), required the king to raise taxes. Nobody likes taxes, to be sure, but Skocpol's idea is not that the new taxes led directly to the revolution. Instead, she argued, the raising of taxes before 1789, and the trouble it caused for the king, were the early symptoms of the bigger and longer-lasting structural weakness of the throne and the traditional nobility. In other words, though the individuals, including the king and his court, were the decision makers, the real life-force that led to the revolution of 1789 was the structural weakness of the ruling classes in the face of the rising new classes of merchants, democrats, and the poor. Because the dominant classes were weakened, the new classes were able to encourage the revolt of the masses. The shift in power arrangements was a rearrangement of the structural parts of the society, not an inspired movement of fervent revolutionaries.

Skocpol's theory is not that individuals are irrelevant to revolutions but that, in effect, they act, not as free-moving agents, but as embedded members of a series of newly formed classes and political organizations in and outside of the government. In the French Revolution, it was not the angry individuals the king was unable to suppress, but the economic and political groups that had organized themselves into newly formed classes, which, in turn, broke open the structural fissures that weakened the traditional powers, thus giving the new powers their day. The implication is that individuals may be agents of change, but only as members of a structured social position. Though this proposition might come as a shock to the nobles and revolutionaries who lost their heads to the stunningly real actions of individual executioners, it is a compelling scientific argument.

A structuralist theory, even a strong one like Skocpol's, will always win a scientific debate when the alternative is an equally strong agency theory. Today, most professional sociologists would consider it vastly more foolhardy to attempt to explain the French Revolution or, closer to home, the failure of the Hallway Hangers as a simple consequence of the actions of individual actors. Fortunately, there are choices between the extremes. Though strong structuralisms like Skocpol's come perilously close to ignoring, if not eliminating, the actor-agents of social change, few professional sociologists anywhere would deny that both structures and agents must be included. The question is, How?

There are creative attempts to resolve the debate by changing the terms of the argument. Pierre Bourdieu's idea of the habitus was an attempt, as I said earlier, to get around the society-versus-individual problem by starting over with the more practical question of how deadly structures and lively actors come together in practical actions. Though Bourdieu's concept might not appease the hearty explanatory appetites of many structuralists, his example of how to begin with the practical matters of the sociological life deserves the attention it has received. Habitus, after all, is an attempt to suggest how individuals practice the discipline of living as free subjects of powerful structures. This may well be the most practical moral question there is.

One of the confusions arising from the structuralism controversy is that professional sociologists' proper responsibility to explain social things is so very different from the duty of practical sociologists simply to live and to tell the stories that account for their actions. The professionals will always be tempted to make structures more lively than they are to bad actors like Frankie or good ones like Black Elk. That is their job. The urgent question for the practical sociological life is not, How do I explain the French Revolution, or the turmoil of the 1960s, or the role of class structures in social reproduction? Those who are the breathing subjects of practical sociological life will more often feel the threat of deadly structures when the streets are ablaze or the guillotine falls, or the job is lost, or never found. Practical sociologies can learn a great deal from the causal explanations of scientific sociologies, as the story of Jay MacLeod well illustrates. But, ultimately, in practical life, the question is not one of causes so much as, What must I know, feel, and believe, in order to act in ways that will make life better for me and mine, and more just for all?

A practical sociology may be supported by the wisdom of structuralist explanations, but it will always view an analytic debate like the structuralist one with a skepticism bred of urgency. Practically speaking, structures are more often dead in the sense of being always in the background of the concerns of earning enough daily bread to feed hungry children. Those who must feed babies, or otherwise care for the needs of their human brothers and sisters, have no choice but to be agents bearing bread and milk, stealing if need be from some unsuspecting corner of their worlds.

Professional and practical sociologies are locked in the embrace of a dance that never ends. There is no last dance when it comes to life with social structures. When Darlene and I took our turns around the roller rink, we heard the music, but, you can be sure, I was so preoccupied with what the other kids might think that I gave little heed to what the music was or where it came from. She, however, seemed noticeably more alert to the wider scene. Thus it is with social structures. The professional sociologist keeps an eye on the larger scene to explain, as precisely as possible, just where and how the music of the big world comes down to us. The practical sociologist keeps an eye on the action, ahead and around, as others fall by the way or dance blithely past. But the sociological life is consummated, for richer or poorer, in a forward movement that transcends any and all debates.

To be alive sociologically, and socially, is to practice the normal rules of social participation—sometimes with a flourish of independence, never exactly as the rules are passed down, but close enough so as not to disrupt the party. The rules, however, are given in the structured mass of stuff the surrounding world makes available for individuals to learn and use. But, as usual, there is a question that does not admit an easy answer. No more than they could agree in the structuralist controversy can the professional sociologists see eye to eye on how that stuff gets from the structured social world into the living individuals.

A common, if traditional, answer is socialization—the process, as I said earlier, whereby individuals come under the influence of bigger social things. The term means mostly what common sense would suggest. An individual is socialized when she knows what society expects of her and acts more or less according to expectations. A person who remains silent and attentive while a rabbi or some other teacher is holding forth—or the guest who waits for the hostess before digging in—is thought to be well socialized. She knows her manners and, presumably, much else that allows her to move about without drawing too much unfavorable comment from others. Socialization is the process whereby a social individual learns the rules governing normal social behavior in a given situation.

Often the idea of socialization is used technically in conjunction with another easy-to-figure-out concept: *role*. If in ordinary language a role is a well-plotted script of actions and speeches an actor follows in performing, say, *Hamlet*, then in sociological usage *social role* builds on the idea that individuals are well socialized when they understand the script or scripts society provides for their actions in a particular social scene. A child who listens with superficially rapt attention to his father's oft-repeated stories about the good old days is satisfactorily socialized because he allows himself to be constrained by the weight of the role of the good child. Playing such a role may be irritating for the moment of its performance. But it is worth playing if only to sustain the peace of family relations, from which may flow social benefits like allowances, rights to car use, or overnights—not to mention the deeper, if little remarked upon, benefits of family love.

When my son Matthew was a young man of twenty-six, I told him a story of my young adulthood, when I had lost hundreds of dollars in a bad car trade. Later, having come back to my senses, I realized that I had told him that one before. Just the same, Matthew took it in as though it had been a brilliant first-telling, and went on about his business. Sooner or later, I'll hear about this foolish slip of paternal memory. It took him nearly five years to confess why he and his brother never finished their breakfasts when they were kids while I was learning the ropes of single parenting. The reason was that I, being then an improperly socialized "mother," had buttered the morning toast on a board from which I had not washed the previous evening's garlic. I myself had thought the toast was odd, but never really considered the cause that they had so filially kept to themselves. Following the rules of the role does not mean that you give up your sense of humor. But failing to follow them, even haphazardly, might mean the loss of some local structure, like the luxury of being served in the morning.

The problem with the sociological concepts of socialization and role is that they do not yield enough information as to how it works that the instruction to listen raptly to a father's old tales, and all the other instructions society offers up, actually gets inside the living individual. Talcott Parsons once provided an influential theory of socialization. He taught that one of the most important aspects of society is its culture, by which Parsons meant something like a depository of values, norms, rules, even manners, from which individuals may withdraw what they need according to the situation; or, even better, culture might be, to play loosely with Parsons's idea, the data of a hard disk on which are stored instructing signals for use in various roles. It is possible, of course, to withdraw, or download, according to the needs of the situation, but one must be cautious not to write the script so that others will not recognize the role being played. Parsons's theory of culture and roles is, you can see, more respectful of the actions of agents than are the stronger structuralisms. It is at least an honest attempt to figure out how structured things work inside individuals.

One of Parsons's best-known, but now notorious, applications of his theory of socialization made reference to the roles of the sexes in domestic and societal life.[51] In most cultures, he said, work is valued, but so are love and caretaking. The families Frankie dreamed of, but could not have, require both work and love to survive. Someone has to make the money. Someone else has to take care of the moneymaker and his kids. (You can see where this is headed.) Therefore, Parsons's theory continued, there must be roles in which some people are given instructions to work hard at a paying job, and some other people are assigned the roles of working hard to provide love and care (which meant, of course, doing the dishes, picking up dirty underwear, and generally cleaning up). You can see now, if you had not guessed, that, though he usually claimed to be writing about all societies, the man was writing about white, middle-class America in the 1950s. Parsons, having been of good middle-class background, had only to look around at those he knew in order to conclude that, by and large, the worker role was normally assigned to men, and the provider-of-care role was assigned to women. In those days, middle-class white mothers generally did not work at a paying job as they do today.

Today, sociologists are still willing to use the concepts of role and socialization, but most will use them sparingly. Some object to the fact that, in his attempt to show how structures get inside the heads, or hearts, of individual actors, Parsons was still too much a structuralist. Others, and particularly feminists, hated (as you might well suppose) the way he ascribed the worker role to the boys and the nurturing role to the girls. Since Parsons developed these ideas in the years after the Second World War when, in much of white America at least, the expectation was that men do real work for pay and women do the laundry, he might be forgiven for trusting arrangements that then were superficially normal. In the 1950s, women had not yet found a way to make men, not even the best professional sociologists, understand just how they felt about these so-called role expectations. Yet they knew that the official sex-role scheme was a bit of a scam, even if they had not yet read Charlotte Gilman. Women knew what work was, and many of them had quite definite feelings about its being unpaid. Many women had worked for pay during the Second World War, building the tanks and planes for the men who fought the war. For them, and their daughters, the idea that a woman's role was fixed narrowly upon housework and childcare was inexpressible nonsense. Even my mother, who never worked outside the home after she married, knew that a woman's sex-role was, in fact, a plethora of roles and duties, which hardly excluded the work she did to hold things together while my father was off to war for three long years. She knew it even more certainly because her widowed mother, a nurse, moved in and helped pay the bills. My mother and her mother, and Mrs. Lyons, who also lived with us for a while, well understood that the public line on women's roles was way wrong.

Socialization is not a bad idea. Far from it. But it does have its limits when it comes to explaining how it happens that some people, including most women in most societies and some men in many, usually are instructed to play a great many roles in life—some seemingly all at once. Socialization into roles is never so neat as Parsons's theory would have it. Yet socialization has its place so long as its most commonly occurring limits are kept in mind: An individual's roles are many and fluid, always open to the flourishes required by the situation or inspired by temperament.

Work for income and caretaking—a great deal of most social worlds comes down to just how structures assure that these two basic tasks are done, and by whom in what roles. Parsons was not wrong to believe that there are tasks that must be done in most societies. Where he erred was in encouraging the notion that they must be done a certain way according to official, but arbitrary, assignments. It would be hard to find very many people who are not preoccupied a good part of the day with practical problems arising from the necessity of caring for their kids or lovers or, if they are alone, for themselves. The time for deeds of practical love must be carved out of a schedule dominated by work or the search for it, or, in Frankie's case, by anger and regret over not having ever found a decent job.

Just as with structures, when the question is posed as a practical one, then suddenly the worlds of caretaking and work rise up in their all-too-often unstable, ill-defined, bone-tiring reality. One of the strengths of professional sociology since the 1960s has been, as I said, a renewed willingness to begin the search for answers with the practical realities of the sociological life. Nowhere is this more the case than in the sociology of family life, where the demands of caretaking and work confront each other so unrelentingly, and in the sociology of poverty, where the most terrible consequences of the absence of well-paid work are visited upon hungry children and their mothers and fathers, who feel the failure to provide as a deficiency of their own moral worth.

That the worlds of work and caretaking, of jobs and family life, are not segregated into separately socialized values and roles is evident in recent studies of the family. Judith Stacey, one of the leaders of American feminist sociology whom I introduced earlier, has shown just how complicated the lives of women with kids and occasional lovers or husbands can be. *Brave New Families* is Stacey's ethnography of families in the Silicon Valley of central California. This area just south of San Francisco is one of the world centers of the electronics industry. As a result, it is not only the leading edge of new forms of industrial (or postindustrial) work. But the electronics industry is also the most innovative sector in experimenting with new ways of structuring work to adjust to the competing pressures on corporations to attract skilled workers, and on workers to meet the demands of family life when both spouses are working or one is missing for any number of reasons. Stacey supposed that here is where one might best find out how work has altered the traditional ideals of family life.

What she found in the Silicon Valley surprised even her. Women still lived in households with children and other adults, sometimes with romantic partners, but the men were not always the fathers of the children. This, of course, will not surprise those who grew up with the effects of divorce and recombinant families. What most surprised Stacey was the way the two women she studied most closely, Pam and Dot, were so resilient to the difficulties they faced and so creative in inventing new ways to keep their lives in order. They had suffered the loss of work, the failure of marriages, the death of a spouse, and much else, while being well able to fashion new and unusual work and family arrangements. When Pam, Dot, and their friends separated from husbands, they sometimes reunited, and other times they entered other relations in which the children enjoyed a new father. They had no choice but to work, so they entered the world of work with zest, if not always success. When they lost their jobs, they invented new careers. And, when they became intentional feminists, they held on to their feminist values while also finding comfort in institutions that would seem to be obnoxious to a feminist. Pam, for example, was a feminist but also for a while a member of a fundamentalist church that instructed women to be obedient to their husbands. And their families were anything but normal by traditional standards. On special occasions, Pam's or Dot's gathered clan could include members of the divorced husband's family along with members of a new family coming together with apparent ease.

When Stacey first published the family stories of Pam and Dot in 1991, many recognized the trends these brave new families represented. Today, well into the 2000s, few would any longer be shocked by them. Call them what you will—modern or postmodern—families are not all that often in the form of a mom and a dad, still married after many years, with a couple of kids. Parents divorce, or never marry. They may be heterosexual or gay. They may never have, or desire to have, a steady household partner. Families are what families are. Whatever the allegedly *normal* structure of "the family" is thought to be, *actual* families into which kids are born or adopted are local, always reinventing themselves. *The* family, like all structures, has its effects but, if it ever once was, it is now, like all structures, quite dead.

When people are comfortable in new local structures, it means the normal has changed; and, when local structures change, you can bet that big ones are also beginning to change. What Stacey found is that many practical people live on each day in the forward ranks of a new normal. Few are different from Pam and Dot in wanting to care for their children and themselves, in wanting to love and be loved, while also keeping a rewarding job in the world of work. When people carry on in some new local structure, reinvented as they go along, they may well have the ideals of the old family structure well in mind. The older structures still have a powerful impact, and not just by the slippery words of politicians who moralize about traditional family values without ever looking at their own divorces and abandonments, to say nothing of stooping to pick up the dirty laundry. The dreadful noises made by those who proclaim family values even they do not live could be the ghostly cries of people longing for families they wanted but never had. To say that structures are dead is not to say they are no longer real and powerful. In the case of the structure of modern or postmodern families, it is possible to see what the death of structures might mean. Pam and Dot, for example, did not run off to the desert to play their guitars and mumble mantras. They stayed and worked and took care as best they could, thus, with countless others in like circumstances, building up something new and different in the structures of kinship. Yet however different their actual families were, it would be hard to imagine that the ideal of *the* American family was not well lodged in their memories and impossible dreams. Structures, being long-enduring yet invisible social things, are always somewhat the same, and always changing—some more dramatically than others.

But do not forget the Frankies of the world. Though of a different, lower status in the class structure, Frankie and his Hangers cared no less about family and work than did Pam and Dot. He might have done more than he did to give himself a shot at the normal life modern society structured into him. But Frankie was far from being the only man to have failed in the world of work. Just as the world's expectations for caretaking come down on women differently than on men, so the world of work comes upon men in a particular way. And both women and men must come to grips with work and family from their different experiences of worldly pressures. These different effects are the fossils of the traditional structures of family and work—those that Talcott Parsons built into his sociology. Pam and Dot found new ways to be women, to take care of their beloveds, and to work within (and in spite of) the expectations tradition imposed on them. So too do many men, especially those of poorer station in the world, who struggle with the changing structures of work and family life. Imagine that Pam and

Dot were two women of lesser education, less well prepared to find a job in Silicon Valley. It would not then be wrong to imagine them as the abandoned or unconsummated partners of men without real work like Frankie.

Of the many ways the world of work is changing, the most striking is the disappearance of the kind of work traditionally performed by men. Right or wrong, in the past men were far more likely than women to work in the industrial sector of the economy, like steel manufacture, or its related occupations, like mining. Then, as now, when women worked outside the home, they more often worked in service jobs like teaching, the health professions, sales, or housekeeping. One need not be an economist to understand that today jobs of the former kind are disappearing, while those of the latter are increasing. In other words, jobs for women are still there as the world of well-paid work shrinks, but jobs traditionally for men, at least for the less skilled men, are going fast. Between 1989 and 1993, there were 1.3 million new jobs in sectors where women traditionally work and, by comparison, barely any in the industrial sector where men usually work.[52] Changes like these come down from the biggest social structures of all (where, even worse, the total number of jobs relative to willing workers is declining). As advanced technology eliminates the need for unskilled workers, economies have work only for the highly skilled or for those of meager skills willing to do the dreary labor of assembling electronic components while living in shanties along Mexico's border with the United States or, worse, willing to sew shoes and garments in sweatshops in Vietnam or New York's Lower East Side or Los Angeles. Just as the big corporations chase after the most skilled engineers and managers, they also run about the globe in search of workers who can be forced to take the lowest wages.

William Julius Wilson, whom I introduced earlier in connection with the Chicago tradition of urban sociology, is the author of three influential books on how the economic pressures changing the class structures have affected the work prospects of the mostly black urban underclass. *When Work Disappears* (1996), like his others books, is based largely on the evidence of these structural changes in Chicago's West and South Sides. As recently as the 1950s, when the old family values were felt to have been a reality, Chicago was one of the places where blacks as well as whites could reasonably aspire to the American dream of work and stable family life. Central Chicago in the 1950s was the home of large corporations like Western Electric, International Harvester, and Sears. But all these employers, and many more, have gone elsewhere, and with them have gone the hopes for well-paid work.[53] What remain today are poorly paid service jobs in garages, grocery markets, and fast-food joints scattered across an urban wasteland.

Just as the economically induced changes in the structure of work forced Pam, Dot, and other women of their higher social class into work careers they might never have dreamt of, so the disappearance of work in the deteriorated inner cities puts necessity before tradition. The neat line between men's and women's work has been erased. Wilson's book uses statistics and personal accounts to tell the stories of the poor in Chicago who struggle to earn their daily bread and to avoid a life in the same drug economy that so added to the despair of Frankie's Hallway Hangers. Wilson quotes one South Side Chicago woman:

> My husband, he's worked in the community. He's 33. He's worked at One Stop since he was 15. And right now, he's one of the highest paid—he's a butcher—he's one of the highest paid butchers in One Stop. For the 15—almost 18—years that he's been there, he's only making nine dollars an hour. And he's begged and fought and scrapped and sued and everything else for the low pay he gets. And he takes so much. Sometimes he'd come home and he'd sit home and he'd just cry. And he'd say, "If it weren't for my kids and my family, I'd quit." You know, it's bad, 'cuz he won't get into drugs, selling it, you know, he ain't into drug using. He's the kind of man he want to work hard and feel good about that he came home. He say that it feels bad sometime to see this 15-year-old boy drivin' down the street with a new car. He saying, "I can't even pay my car note. I worry about them comin' to get my car."
>
> —William Julius Wilson, *When Work Disappears* (1996)[64]

When the alternative to the job one has is selling drugs, it takes a man of personal courage to continue to suffer the indignities of real, but poorly paid, work.

As structures change, the ability of some to act may greatly expand, while the freedom of others to be agents of their children's daily bread shrinks. The same technology that allows the better-off to log on each morning to a world wide web of news, mail, and shopping arose from the dying structures of industrial work. *Deindustrialization*, as this process is so bloodlessly called, leads some to drugs and others to tears of frustration.

Those who enjoy the cheap thrill of e-mail and all the other entitlements of the globally well positioned might be inclined to think of the world as one big lively structure. But this is little more than an illusion conjured up by the instantaneous flash of electronic signals. The structures at work are doing what structures always do. The very instant structures present themselves as this or that effect in someone's life, they retreat into the past of the well-structured hard drives whence they came. Those structures that seem alive to those who tap away in the warm glow of brightly colored PC screens are just as often deadly to the butcher at One Stop. Arms and apron bloodied, from dawn to dusk he cuts away for his wife and children, so much more aware than others of the few choices he has for effective actions. He is, to be sure, the best agent of security for his family he can be, just as Pam and Dot are, endowed as they are with better, but still limited, rights of social movement.

Think of social structures as you will, but think of them you must when they come down upon you, not just to instruct and guide, but to close down the dreams of the good life all men and women, in their own ways, see somewhere on the all too often dimly illuminated screens of their sociological imaginations.

CHAPTER

NINE

~

WELL-MEASURED LIVES IN A WORLD OF DIFFERENCES

When W. E. B. Du Bois at a young age was rebuffed by a snotty white girl, or when Charlotte Gilman at a still youthful age was confined by her unconsciously arrogant male physician, they had each come up against social differences. Though poetic impulse inspires the dreamy ideal of society as one gloriously melted pot of human similarity, the practical truth is that people and groups are different.

More often than not, the differences, while cloaked in party manners or the best medical sympathies, are as tough and unyielding as rebuffs or confinements always are. Were it not for the anger and tears of the Frankies and One Stop butchers of the world, not to mention the Black Elks, those who rebuff, confine, and otherwise enforce the lines of difference might not always realize what they are doing. What the high and mighty are doing, whether they realize it or not, is sizing up, or measuring, the social distance between themselves and those to whom they condescend in their cold rejection of party cards or their handing down of warmed-over prescriptions for rest without work.

Just think of what we do when we measure in the mundane practice of daily life. Rice requires two cups water to one of grain; my Volvo requires a nearly, but not too, full level of oil; a school may require a specific score on admission tests. On it goes. In the course of cooking, driving, and schooling, one thinks of these ubiquitous deeds of measurement only at the moment of their application. For the longer course of life, we ignore the harsh reality that any and all measurements work by means of rules for assigning the mores or lesses of daily life. Too little water or oil, too low a score, and the rice, the engine, or the career will be scorched. You can count on it.

It is reasonable to suppose that rice and engines are insensitive to the scorchings they often get, but it is absolutely certain that the Hallway Hangers of the world feel the exact difference made by their lousy grades— just as the One Stop butcher felt the humiliation of a weekly paycheck always too little for the need, as Du Bois and Gilman felt, without at first fully comprehending, the measurements to which they were subjected by rebuff and confinement. Measurement can be, and often is, a sophisticated work of scientific sociologies. But before it occurs to the mind of science, measurement is the practical work by which people size themselves up against the greater or lesser power of others in and about their social worlds.

There are many occasions on which people rightfully celebrate their differences from others, even if the celebrations are sober, as were W. E. B. Du Bois's and Black Elk's very adult affirmations of the spiritual power of African and Lakota people against the force of American might. But celebrations of these kinds, whether festive or sober, must always be sung against the long history of pain and injury by which the lines of social differences are etched in the collective lives of a social world. When Du Bois wrote of the color line, he had in mind one of the more brutal lines of social difference in modern societies. But there are others. The line assigning women to the back rooms of modern society, of which Gilman wrote, is another, as is the line of class difference of which William Julius Wilson has more recently written.

Racial, gender, and class differences are among the more salient rulers used to measure the greater or lesser value attributed to people and groups. Professional sociologists study these markers of difference with fine mathematical care; practical sociologists attend to them with a lesser patience, excited by the trouble they can cause. Among other such lines just recently emerging from the closets of embarrassed silence is the one discriminating among people according to whether they are sexually oriented to lovers of a superficially same or different gender. Another, of course, is the difference between people according to whether their family stories tell of ancestors who were colonizers or colonized. It would not be wrong to think of these markers of social differences as the measuring lines whereby the structuring power of prestige, authority, and income come down upon practical people. That little white girl at a school party had the confidence to rebuff because of the prestige she had assumed from the power white people arbitrarily gain in their well-structured difference from people of color.

Charlotte's doctor presumed an authority set by no less arbitrary conventions assigning physicians the inexplicable right to instruct others well beyond the limits of their formal scientific preparation.

Among all the measures of difference, race, gender, and class have become, for the time being, the most oft-discussed. Others, like those that veil the realities of gay and lesbian society, are just as poignant in the practices of daily life. But a closer look at race, gender, and class allows at least a first glimpse at the nefarious manners by which the dominant enforce their codes of social differences.

In 1892, the same year in which Charlotte Perkins Gilman published *The Yellow Wallpaper*, another young woman published a book of a similar kind. She was Anna Julia Cooper, who probably had been born thirty-four years before, in 1858. The uncertainty of her birth date is a consequence of her mother's having been a slave to the white and wealthy Haywood family, one of whom is assumed to have been her father. Public records of children born of liaisons of this kind were not well kept. Later in her life, Anna herself did not hesitate to say what she felt of the conditions of her origin:

> I was born in Raleigh, North Carolina. My mother was a slave and the finest woman I have ever known. Tho untutored she could read her Bible and write a little. It is one of my happiest childhood memories explaining for her the subtle differences between q's and g's or between b's and l's. Presumably my father was her master, if so I owe him not a soul and she was always too modest and shamefaced ever to mention him.[55]

When she was, by best estimate, just shy of twenty years old, Anna Julia Haywood married George Cooper, an Episcopal clergyman, who died two years later from overwork. She never remarried. Anna Cooper went on to become a woman of power and authority in her community and the nation. Though, in her later years, she graduated from a prestigious program of graduate study, Cooper (unlike Charlotte Gilman) never became, or thought of becoming, a professional sociologist of any kind. Her life was devoted to teaching, writing, political organizing, and social settlement work among the poor in Washington, D.C. It would be difficult to come upon a better example of native social competence and practical sociology.

After her husband's death, Anna Cooper sought "an advanced course in some superior Northern college," as she put it in her letter of application to

Oberlin College.[56] She was admitted to the class of 1884 on terms we would today call financial aid. There she joined two other female students, Mary Eliza Church (Terrell) and Ida A. Gibbs (Hunt), who, like her, were destined to become leaders of their race. Cooper's path to that status was, however, the more difficult one because she lacked the advantage they enjoyed of coming from a family of financial means. Cooper, the daughter of a slave, bore the unique demands of her race and her gender with the added weight of her origins among the lower, indeed the lowest, classes. In more than one hundred years of life, she never acquired any substantial wealth. Just the same, Cooper saved what little she earned as a teacher to build a gracious home in Washington, D.C., where, after Oberlin, she took a position as teacher of classics, mathematics, and languages at the Colored (now Dunbar) High School.

Through a long life, Anna Julia Cooper (1858?–1964) enjoyed a great many triumphs. One of the grandest was having completed a doctoral degree at the Sorbonne in the University of Paris, where she commuted summers while teaching a full schedule in Washington and raising five orphaned children whom she had adopted when she was well into her fifties. This, like all of her successes, was won against the pointed prejudices that fell upon her because of her race or her gender. It was men of her race who had earlier fired her from her teaching position, and men again who tried to prevent her from completing her doctoral thesis; and it was, needless to say, whites who maintained the segregated, poorly endowed colored schools for which she worked. Yet, at every turn, Cooper seemed to know what to do or say to overcome as best anyone could. She was every bit the practical sociologist.

Just as Charlotte Perkins Gilman as a young woman simply understood what a woman needed to do for herself, so too did Anna Julia Cooper. But, even by comparison to Gilman, Anna Cooper's social circumstances were particularly fraught with troubles. Gilman, though she fought the odds of her gender, was white and of the modest, if not wealthy, middle class. Gilman savored a taste of advantage well beyond the social means of Cooper, whose race and class disadvantages very probably were more salient than those of her gender. It is one thing to be a woman struggling to define herself against what Gilman called the androcentric world, but another still more daunting to be a black woman contending as much with the racial barriers of society and those of her lowly class origins in slavery. Cooper was specifically aware that who she was, and how she lived, had to be fashioned against the pressures applied by the circumstances defined by her gender, her race, and her class. She could hardly have been unaware.

Power is not the sort of thing that descends upon all persons equally, as though they were all in the same social boat. This is the difficulty that socialization theorists like Talcott Parsons and his followers attempted to solve by the frail means of role theory. What socialization theory is meant to explain is two things at once: (1) how the powerfully structured contents of culture hold things together to create the common bonds that unite people in a single society; and (2) how, at the same time, culture allows for obvious differences like those between men *and* women.

The limit of this way of thinking is that, if one holds to the doctrine that roles are the inventions of a unified culture, then differences can arise only because the culture defining the roles must instruct the role players in many, diverse situations. Fathers play their roles one way when dealing with kids who won't eat broccoli, another in meetings with kindergarten teachers. Same father, same role; different situations. I once reached out to a teacher with stories of my troubles with one of my kids at the dinner table. The appeal was unconvincing. She knew I was there more to defend than to discipline—that while I presented myself to her in the role of a fellow adult, I was in fact playing the role of father. The difference is real and difficult to hide. Socialization theory's analytic solution to the problem of social differences falters on the appealing, but unfounded, belief that the differences are merely problems the wider society has *yet* to solve, illusions of the undeveloped short run.

Practical sociologists like Gilman and Cooper help us to see more honestly that the enduring social structures of the wider society only *appear* to be stable and uniform social things. In fact, the structures of power do their work in sharply different ways according to the many and various social circumstances in which people find themselves. Though some differences, such as those between Gilman and Cooper, are not great, others are located at many more degrees of social separation.

I never knew, for example, exactly why Gloria Quimby, my sixth-grade classmate, did not go on in math and science studies. She was white like me, and every bit as much of the secure middle classes. She was, in addition, smart as hell in math. It was only in recent years that it dawned on me that Gloria must have had a very clear understanding of the quiet discouragements that kept her from becoming a scientist. That an acutely self-occupied middle-class white boy, like myself, did not understand what Gloria must have felt about the rejections of her teachers and classmates, perhaps even of her family, is not surprising. In the 1940s, a brilliant white girl of good class position like Gloria usually had no one with whom to share her love of science or, even, the pain of her not being prized for her brilliance with numbers. She certainly did not then have the language feminism has given little girls today who encounter math and science teachers who call on the boys first and frequently, and the girls by whim. Gloria might today have known better what to say in retort when wise guys on the playground jeered the math wizards as the worst sort of sissies, thus to stigmatize fine intellectual accomplishment as girlish impotence.

It was not just Gloria who was unable to find the words to describe what went wrong with her love of numbers and science. It was I as well. I honestly do not recall if I ever teased her about her genius. I think not, because I do remember a brief two-week moment in the sixth grade when I let it be known that, as we said it then, I "liked" her—which state of faint love entailed little more than the passing of notes, chance meetings at lockers, and two very awkward phone calls. My insensitivity to Gloria and girls in general was so generic as to exceed even the consciousness required to jeer. I was seldom, if ever, called upon to reflect on the advantages I enjoyed as the white son of a doctor with good cash receipts. That I was a privileged white boy rarely entered my conscious thinking. Yet I now realize that this fact of my race, gender, and class privilege meant a lot to others who were well aware that important social things came to me and not to them. If I ever thought about who I was to enjoy this choice position, it was only on those occasions when I encountered surprises for which my innocence had not prepared me.

Strange as it may seem, one of the ways those of appreciably greater privilege and power carry around their advantages is through a well-practiced refusal to contemplate them—a practice permitted and encouraged by their being excused from being required to answer for themselves. When it comes to social structures, privilege is about possessing the power that accrues to those who possess the higher statuses, bigger offices, and deeper bank accounts. But when we are talking about individuals—the subjects of well-structured social positions—privilege very often takes the form of a greater innocence bred by an exemption from having to account for one's cushy place in the world. The privileged worry less than the rest about where their status, authority, or wealth comes from. Power may well be systematically structured across the wider society, but it comes down on individuals differently, as it did on Anna Cooper and Charlotte Gilman in the 1890s and on Gloria and little Charles in the 1940s, and on all of their brothers and sisters in the variety of positions individuals might occupy along the lines of race, gender, and class.

Here, again, a riddle: Why does it seem that Anna Cooper and Charlotte Gilman in the 1890s, like others in their circumstances, were so much more able to put their sociological competence into words than were Gloria and

Charles and those in their social positions in the 1940s? Why, in other words, would it be, as so it seems, that those who suffer the consequences of the disadvantaged are so often those who possess the more acute discursive sensibility—the finer and stronger ability to talk about the practical effects of their differences from others? Why are they the more thorough measurers of social differences?

To some, the answer is plain enough, though troubling, hence tough to swallow: Those who suffer the effects of power have the greater need to understand power because they must learn to deal with its effects if they are to survive. Though not obvious to everyone, this is a perfectly logical answer, one that has roots in the writings of Georg W. F. Hegel (1770–1831), the great German philosopher, and Marx, who took the clue from Hegel. The slave, said Hegel, like the working man, said Marx, understood the evils of a social system because those at the bottom *must* understand it. More recently, James Scott (b. 1936), a political theorist at Yale and part-time sheep farmer in Durham, Connecticut, has put an even more radical turn on the idea. In a 1990 book, *Domination and the Arts of Resistance: Hidden Transcripts*, Scott proposed that the scripts that govern public actions, including normal role behavior, are important instruments of power.

Scott, however, used the term *transcript*, instead of script. The difference between a script, such as those directing theatrical or real-life actions, and a transcript is that a script is the writing out of what *ought* to take place while a transcript is the writing up of what actually *did* take place. It is the difference between stage directions and court records. Transcript is an interesting term to use for the workings of power because, though there are scripts telling people with and without power what they may or must do, a great deal of power is acted out without people taking notice of it at the moment.

This idea will not shock anyone who has ever been humiliated in grade school, not for failing math, but for failing to toe the official code of good school manners. I was once paddled bent over, butt facing the class, by my math teacher for the crime of having spoken out of turn. I was hurt, emotionally more than physically, and my father was furious. But, in those days, even the rage of an angry parent made little difference to schoolteachers and principals. Physical punishment was normal role behavior. The scripts of that day gave teachers and other administrative fools every right to do as they pleased with the paddles. Today, however, you can bet that a kid thus punished would likely show up the next day with parent and lawyer, if not the cops as well. Today such an abuse of teacherly power would probably lead to an investigation. The teacher and witnesses would be interviewed.

Notes would be taken, and a record established. This transcript, like all written records, would likely include details that never occurred to the paddling teacher or the humiliated pupil and his frightened classmates. In my case, a good investigator might have established, for example, that this guy regularly paddled boys for talking out of turn, but never for failure to do homework. Written or otherwise recorded descriptions of past events may be imperfect, but they usually contain clues sufficient to indict the abusers of power—to show that, in addition to being bullies, they were doing their jobs badly. Lawyers, angry parents, sociologists, and other detectives of the hidden secrets of power are often quite expert at getting even the powerful to establish a public record of their abuses.

James Scott went on, however, to say that, against the public scripts for acceptably normal and well-controlled social action, the least powerful develop their own hidden transcripts of power, or, as he puts it, "critiques of power spoken behind the back of the dominant."[57] The sorrow songs of slaves or the sorrowful visions of Black Elk are transcripts of the horrors that went on in public view. Slaves sang those songs within earshot of the master's house, just as Native Americans danced openly with the ghosts of their dead. The privileged don't often understand what the dominated say behind the veil, in the hallways, around the mass graves, in the bathrooms, or wherever these hidden transcripts of rebellion are uttered. But this does not mean nothing is said. Social silence can be filled with the whispered noise of resistance.

If pushed far enough, this line of thought leads to the conclusion that the oppressed are the better practical sociologists and, possibly, the only ones truly wide awake to social life. Could it be that in this one respect the less powerful are the better endowed while the privileged are deprived? There is a lot to be said for the idea that the socially oppressed, while possessing no greater native competence, are the more disciplined at practical sociology. It would, in fact, appear to be that disadvantage requires a person to think and speak more frequently and carefully about what is going on in the world, if only to others similarly aggrieved. It is not, on the other hand, that the powerful are incompetent. They do, after all, run the world, for better or worse. Whatever one might think of the work the mighty do, there is enough good in the world to allow that, though some are downright evil, they are not exactly stupid about what they do in managing things.

Life is tough, but tougher on some than others. And, very often, the very toughness of life predisposes those who must endure against the odds to measure ever more precisely the unequal effects of power that create social differences. Behind the visible differences of race and gender, even of class styles, are told the stories and sung the songs in which the transcripts of resistance to power and good practical sociology are hidden.

How individuals and groups respond to the social pressures that come upon them by accident of their social conditions is a measure of who they are. Response to social pressure may be the measure of character, as it is often said, but it is also the way all social persons come to measure themselves against their worlds. Who we are is clearly bound up, in sociologically interesting ways, with what we think of ourselves. And what we think of ourselves is, in turn, the result of the stands we take, or are required to take, in the face of whatever society presents to us. It could well be said that who a person is proceeds from how she comes to measure herself in the social world.

Few practical sociologists illustrate better than Anna Julia Cooper the complexity of the social demands a person can face. And few were better than Cooper when it came to taking the measure of the socially powerful without ever denying the differences they make.

After graduating from Oberlin in 1884, Anna Cooper spent several years teaching college, first at Wilberforce in Ohio, and then at St. Augustine's in Raleigh, where her mother still lived. Then she returned to Oberlin for a graduate degree in mathematics in 1887, after which she accepted the position in Washington, D.C., teaching high-school classics. The remarkable breadth of her academic work was an early sign of the reserve of energy and intelligence that would drive a life of many involvements. As a young woman of not more than thirty years of age, Cooper was recognized for her qualities of mind and character. In 1886, the year before she began teaching in Washington, D.C., she was invited to address a national conference of black Protestant Episcopal clergy. Cooper's talk was delivered about the same time Charlotte Perkins Gilman fell ill and was confined to the room with the yellow wallpaper.

But Anna Cooper was not content merely to speak. She seized the occasion to discuss the subject "Womanhood: A Vital Element in the Regeneration and Progress of a Race." Although Gilman and Cooper were of about the same age, Gilman would require more time to formulate the criticism of the androcentric world that Cooper was ready to proclaim in this talk in 1886. The most memorable vehicle of Cooper's insistence on the importance of women to racial uplift was the twist she put on a famous expression of Dr. Martin R. Delany's (1812–1885). Delany, one of the first blacks to attend Harvard Medical School and in later life honored worldwide, was well known for the robust pride he took in being a black man. Hinting at what was to come, Cooper described Delany as "an unadulterated black man," who "used to say when honors of state fell upon him, that when he entered the council of kings the black race entered with him."[58] What Cooper said after this must have shocked the distinguished clergy:

> Only the BLACK WOMAN can say "when and where I enter, in the quiet, undisputed dignity of my womanhood, without violence and without suing or special patronage, then and there the whole *Negro race enters with me."*
>
> —*Anna Julia Cooper, Voice From the South* (1892)[59]

In claiming the moral leadership of her race for the black woman (it was she who emphasized the words), Cooper was directing attention to the social circumstances of the black woman in her community. She understood these circumstances exceedingly well from her mother's experience with slavery, from her own struggle to acquire an education, and, no doubt, from what she saw in the working lives of the women in her community.

Anna Cooper's announcement of the moral authority of the black woman became the first chapter, along with other talks and essays of her youth, in her famous book *A Voice from the South*. Today that book, published in 1892, the same year as "The Yellow Wallpaper," has become a classic of black feminist thought, just as Gilman's short fiction became a classic of what, by comparison, must be called white feminism. There is no evidence that Cooper ever met Gilman, though it is clear that she knew enough of Gilman to take sympathetic note of her death by suicide in 1935. Whatever Cooper knew of the particulars of Gilman's sociology of women, Cooper clearly measured her own understanding of herself as a black woman against the standards of white feminism just as exactly as she did against the black men whom she had gently rebuked in her talk in 1886.

Another chapter in Cooper's *Voice from the South* seems more to have been an essay than a talk, which is probable because the message was directed at white feminists. In the 1880s, a young black woman was still more likely to be invited to speak before men of her race than before whites of her gender. The essay, "Woman versus the Indian," is a gentle rebuke of the Reverend Anna Shaw (1847–1919), a leading white feminist of the day. In a widely circulated speech, Shaw had urged the rights of women with reference to their supposed superiority to the savage Indian; hence the title "Woman versus the Indian." Cooper, thereupon, challenged not the goodwill but the naïveté of the white feminist who had so thoughtlessly consigned the Indian to a social place outside the moral interests of white culture.

Cooper's reply to Shaw was to explain that, by considering the Indian or the Negro inferior, even the best-intentioned feminist was colluding in the workings of white power:

> Why should woman become plaintiff in a suit versus the Indian, or the Negro or any other race or class who have been crushed under the iron heel of Anglo-Saxon power and selfishness?
>
> —*Anna Julia Cooper, Voice From the South* (1892)[60]

Cooper went on to say that the interests of the white feminist could only be advanced by recognition of her alliances with those of different races and classes—those who had similarly suffered "under the iron heel of Anglo-Saxon power." Cooper, thus, was one of the few in her day to speak truthfully about the differences made by the convergences of lines of racial, gender, and class power. She was among the first to show how those abused by power possess the higher moral authority.

When these words were published in 1892, very few people, not even professionally trained sociologists, spoke, as we do today, of the vectors of social power: race, class, and gender. Yet Anna Julia Cooper, who was never a professional sociologist, brought these now-familiar categories to bear in a most delicate, but firm, criticism of the narrowness of social vision of a leading feminist of her day. Cooper's sociology was so rooted in practical experience that she had no need to speak in the formal language of a social science that, in any case, would have then had little to say about the problem she addressed.

What Cooper saw more clearly perhaps than anyone in her day is now better understood as one of the fundamentals of sociological thought. Like Du Bois and Gilman and many others, she told stories out of her experience. The most poignant of Cooper's descriptions of the multiple effects of race, gender, and class was offered in the form of a simple narrative set in a place no African American, then or now, would fail to recognize: the racially segregated, Jim Crow car of a railroad train. She described the rude treatment to which, as a matter of course, blacks were then openly subjected. Cooper then told of the train coming to a rest stop:

> And when farther on in the same section our train stops at a dilapidated station, rendered yet more unsightly by dozens of loafers with

their hands in their pockets while a productive soil and inviting climate beckon in vain to industry; and when, looking a little more closely, I see two dingy little rooms with "for ladies" swinging over one and "for colored people" over the other while wondering under which head I come.

—*Anna Julia Cooper, Voice From the South* (1892)[61]

To most of the readers of *A Voice from the South*, this story might have inspired indignation, or at least sympathy, for the insults to which Anna Cooper, and many others, were exposed. Yet, Cooper's purpose in telling the story was not to stir emotions so much as to clarify thought or, one might say, to promote a sociology of the situation represented by those signs—the transcripts of behavior within starkly ordered differences.

Anyone who, until not so long ago, traveled in the American South, as I did on family vacations about the time Gloria Quimby was being quietly discouraged in math classes, was accustomed to seeing such signs as these. Like most white people, I viewed them with indifference, though once near Chattanooga, Tennessee, I recall the excitement of local people when I innocently ventured to use the drinking fountain set aside for those of another color. Otherwise, these signs of social segregation were part of the landscape for whites, and something else for "colored people," to use Cooper's words. It never occurred to me to ask any of the black people in my life what they felt about these signs. I was, as I said, too foolishly engaged with the concerns of my own class, race, and gender advantage. Later in life, however, I finally thought to ask.

Mrs. Florence Brown Lyons (1915?–1995), until her death in 1995 at about eighty years of age, was a friend of many years. Though she was years older than I, we developed a friendship that overcame the prohibitions of the economic arrangements that brought us close, even though they were meant to keep us apart. Florence Brown Lyons understood firsthand the signs of which Anna Julia Cooper wrote.

Several years before her death, Mrs. Lyons offered to tell the story of her life, and I readily accepted. Over the years I had heard many stories, but few were as telling as those she told one long winter afternoon in the presence of a tape recorder. As a child, Florence Brown (later Lyons) had been left alone by the death of her mother and the abandonment of her father. She was reared near Plant City, Florida, by a white lady named Sarah. When

Sarah came to the end of her own life, she told Florence, then a teenager, it was time to return to her people, some of whom were still in Florida. Eventually, about 1938, Florence Brown traveled north to Cincinnati in a Jim Crow car not different from the one Cooper rode.

Shortly after settling with a brother, she took a job working long, hot hours in the old Ideal Laundry Company. There, as in many places even in the near south, the race lines were firmly drawn. The "colored" bathroom was located at great inconvenience to the workers, while the one for the whites was just off the shop floor. One day Florence Brown was too hot and tired to make the long walk. She approached the whites-only room, where-upon one of the meanest of the mean held the door tight against her. In the exact words she spoke into the tape recorder, Florence recalled saying in a firm voice: "Do y'u feel this door's goin' be tore down?" To which she added: "I'm goin' whip yuh 'til yuh git out of yur skin." She did just that. She won the fight. The white shop boss, Cain, declared the fight fair and fired the white girl who had tried to bar the door. When Mrs. Lyons told me this story, she used an expression that W. E. B. Du Bois had made famous in 1903. She said: "Other folks have broken other lines, that's when I broke the color line."

Mrs. Lyons was different from Mrs. Cooper in how she responded to the color line. But they both understood what the discriminating signs meant. The difference between them was a difference of class. In 1942, Florence Lyons had no education to speak of and was working for a dol-lar a day at hard labor. In 1891 or so, when she was riding a train, Anna Cooper had already been educated and had begun a middle-class job as a teacher. Yet both women understood the public script in the signs of racial segregation, and knew exactly what the bathroom signs were intended to accomplish. From the abstract distance of social structures, they were signs segregating the races and the genders. "I see two dingy little rooms with 'for ladies' swinging over one and 'for colored people' over the other while wondering under which head I come." But, from the concrete experience of a regular social encounter with signs of this sort, they represent the choices a person must make in order to decide who she is. Florence Brown Lyons had never heard of Anna Julia Cooper when she broke the color line at the Ideal Laundry Company in 1938 or so, but she understood, you can be sure of it, what Dr. Cooper meant. Mrs. Lyons's response as a young woman was appropriate to her character and class circumstances. She stood to fight. Mrs. Cooper's was different, as one notices in the conde-scension she quietly directed toward the sloth of the white men hanging about the train station.

Cooper's practical sociology turned on the conviction that the black woman, and she alone, was the central moral force, not just in the uplift of her race, but in the moral progress of the society as a whole. As Cooper said it:

> What a responsibility then to have the sole management of the primal lights and shadows! Such is the colored woman's office. She must stamp weal and woe on the coming history of this people.
>
> —*Anna Julia Cooper, Voice From the South* (1892)[62]

Cooper believed that, because of the crisis troubling American society, then, as now, only the individual who understood America in a thoroughly practical way could possibly mediate the tensions and overcome the differences. Only the black woman, who, over many years, had seen at first-hand the effects produced when power uses race, class, and gender to exclude some and advance others, could have the moral authority to overcome and to help others overcome.

Not only did Anna Julia Cooper exhibit the practical sociology of which I have spoken, but, more importantly, she was one of the first to exercise her sociological imagination in order to describe, well before the professional sociologists, the way power actually works on those subjected to it. It was not until the 1970s and 1980s, after professional sociology had adjusted to the effects of the 1960s, that professional sociologists began to think of social power as an effect produced, not from some magic place at the top of society, but from the people in more modest stations who do, or do not, acquiesce to its pressures.

Thus it is that the measuring of social differences by people of lesser power gives still another partial solution to the mystery of powerful structures. The idea that agency is not the opposite of structured power but one of the means of its working is most astonishingly evident in the hidden power of the less powerful. Far from being powerless, those who measure who they are in terms of the social differences assigned to them understand very well the power to be had in the basic knowledge of how power works. There is a distinction to be made between having the power to stigmatize or otherwise define the conditions of the less powerful and having the power to resist and thus to limit the force of power, sometimes even to change it.

Social power is created and sustained in the very specific differences people enjoy or suffer from each other. Social power always does its work *in* structures, like the schools or the shop floors or the systems of public transportation, but it does this work *through* the differences that separate people—differences such as those between the classes, the races, the genders, the sexualities. In a book that was published in 1990, nearly a century after Cooper's, a professional sociologist wrote of the same matters.

Patricia Hill Collins (b. 1948), who teaches African American studies and sociology at the University of Maryland and is a president of the American Sociological Association, drew heavily upon the practical experience of black women in the United States for her book *Black Feminist Thought*. The largest section of the book describes the most important themes in black feminism through the years since (and before) Cooper. What distinguishes Collins's idea of "theory" is that the theories to which she refers are all rooted in the social experience of black women in communities. She writes, for example, of the unique relationship black women have to work. Because they are often the heads of their households, they are not in the same situation as the white women Charlotte Gilman had in mind. For years, most black women were limited to domestic service, restaurant or occasionally factory work (which was Mrs. Lyons's experience), or, at best, service as teachers or social settlement workers (Mrs. Cooper's experience). When black women measure their place in society, they very often must do so against the limited opportunities provided by the wider society, which for centuries relegated them to a low status. At the same time, in their own communities, black women are often breadwinners and community leaders in positions of high status. This, in turn, causes them to be treated by the men of their communities as though they are too domineering. Thus, Collins, like Cooper before her, understands what hardly needs understanding as far as most black women in America are concerned. A black woman of modest or poor income is measured by the numerous and complicated ways the powers of society come upon her, and she responds to the combined effects of her racial, gender, and class positions.

Collins, borrowing from the writer bell hooks (b. 1955) and other black feminists, describes these forces as a *matrix of domination*. A matrix is, in effect, a web of social forces in which an individual lives, and to which she must respond if she is to be socially alive. Those who are sociologically alert to the ways power acts upon them understand that it is in the coming together of the well-drawn lines of their race, gender, and class situations that they are made vulnerable, yes. But the matrix also invites a response.

> In addition to being structured along axes such as race, gender, and social class, the matrix of domination is structured on several levels. People experience and resist oppression on three levels: the level of

personal biography; the group or community level of the cultural context created by race, class, and gender; and the systemic level of social institutions.

—Patricia Hill Collins, *Black Feminist Thought* (1990)[63]

Both Florence Lyons and Anna Cooper endured the common effects of their racial situation. But their gender experiences were different because of the effects of class power by which educated black women, like Dr. Cooper, were able to attain a higher status by teaching in the schools, while others, like Mrs. Lyons, were confined to domestic labor of various kinds. Meanwhile, in the 1940s, Gloria Quimby, being white and middle class, though discouraged from the pursuit of science, was able to go on to many things that few of her black classmates could aspire to. Meanwhile, too, skinny Charles Lemert, being a white boy in good standing with his class, could imagine a greater number of things, including medicine and science for a while, then preaching and political work, before he settled into that which he has become. It is true, of course, that Gloria and Charles had the freer range of social choices. But Patricia Hill Collins's theory implies that even they became who they became by measuring themselves against the advantages of their race and class, and gender (in my case).

Power does its work differentially. It gives more to some than to others. In the process of creating differences, power requires that all people must measure who they are according to just how much power comes to them as it rushes up and down through the matrix of domination. Today, the idea of social power as creating a matrix, or web, is widely accepted, though the terms used to describe it may vary. The idea has been expanded, in recent years, to include, as well it should, other elements in the matrix of domination, such as the ways in which power works to abuse persons whose sexualities are gay, lesbian, or otherwise outside the heterosexual norm. And the matrix of domination also reaches to entrap those born into the former colonies of the world-system, such as women in Afghanistan or India who are traditionally subjected, not just to the agents of foreign colonial power, but also to dominant men in the colonized villages and cities who seize the power to limit women's legal rights, even to sell them for profit into the sex industry.

A professional sociologist is trained to measure the effects of differences created by power. Doris Wilkinson (b. 1936), a sociologist at the University of Kentucky, has shown by precise statistical evidence that what Anna Cooper and Florence Lyons experienced and responded to was not by any means their private and local experiences. In the years between 1890, roughly the year of Anna Cooper's train trip, and 1930, when Florence Lyons was growing up in the care of Sarah, the percentage of working black women engaged in poorly paid domestic labor increased from a low of 42 percent to a high of 64 percent. In the same period, the percentage of working white women in higher-status public service or professional work increased (and get this) from 10 percent to a high of 50 percent. In the same period, black women in the professions remained constant at about 2 percent. Dr. Anna Julia Cooper was in this fortunate 2 percent. In 1925, near the end of this statistical period, Cooper completed her doctoral studies in France. In other words, during the years when Charlotte Gilman's sociological writings were written and read, the white women for whom she wrote did indeed enter into more prestigious work, while at the same time the black women for whom Cooper wrote became more and more dependent on domestic service.[64]

Professional sociologists thus measure the external effects of the larger structural forces. In the case of Wilkinson's report, between 1890 and 1930, race oppressed black women more or less evenly, even though those, like Florence Lyons, who migrated north were able to find steady, if demeaning, work in the homes and enterprises of white people. At the same time, the structures affecting gender freedom for white women opened somewhat as more of those women entered the better-paid professions, and all of them won the right to vote. These were among the important structural shifts that took place. Uncannily, if you compare the scientific evidence in the graphic with the realities of black women's experience in America, they tell the same story of being measured for so many years out of the world of real economic opportunity. All that is changing now, but, sadly, like all deadly structures the measures they impose recur both in the statistical tables and on the kitchen tables of homes with hungry children.

What the professionals measure are the effects that play out in the greater and lesser statuses within the matrices of domination. At the beginning of the period, in 1890, Cooper had already become a woman of character and force because of how she had responded to the experience of being the child of a slave and her master. Florence Lyons, at the end of the period, was, in her way, a clear-headed and strong woman as she took her measure against the color line in Cincinnati, thus taking up her position in the matrix of race, gender, and class. Shortly after the period ended, in 1937, little Gloria and Charles were born to play out different lives in response to the advantages they enjoyed from their higher statuses within the web of power.

A Matrix of Domination: Occupation of Employed Black and White Females 10 Years Old and Over: 1890, 1910, and 1930.

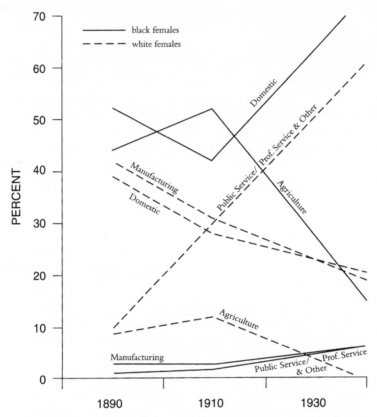

Adapted, by permission of the publisher, from Doris Wilkinson, "The Segmented Labor Market and African American Women," in *Research in Race and Ethnic Relations*, ed. Dennis Rutledge (Jai Press, 1991).

Before it is the serious work of professional sociologists, measurement is the ordinary work of practical sociologists, who become who they become according to how they contend with the local, not at all abstract, effects of social structures when and where any one of us enters the world of the socially living.

GLOBAL THINGS

TEN

❧

GLOBAL METHODS

Imagine this story, if you can:

A young man of twenty-nine grew up in a small town in the country-side. For generations his fathers before him had been engaged in min-ing or agriculture. His family never had money, but they were not exactly poor. There was always something to eat. Because his native region enjoyed a mild climate, the family's land produced, much of the year, at least enough to feed a few sheep and cows for meat and milk. Even with all its security, this was not the life the young man wanted.

Things were changing all around. When his parents were his age, his country won its independence, after which it prospered. When he came of age, the young man moved to his country's largest city—a cos-mopolitan center teeming with international trade. He was the first in his family ever to move to his country's center of learning and cul-ture. At the university, other students admired his literary gifts. He learned all the latest methods and did exceptionally well in English. He began, after a while, to work in a small inn that catered to travel-ers from other countries. Its owner was a much older, more traditional man. Still, the young man persuaded him to modernize the inn, after which it flourished.

The young man dreamt of a still-better life. He hoped to start a business selling craft and other products from near his native village on the international market. At first his enterprising spirit led to contacts and the promise of success. Just as quickly his hopes were dashed. Foreign clients seldom paid a fair return. Though he worked hard, he had little to show for it—few prospects, not even of better pay in the job he had. He gave up his studies. He wasn't sure that further learning would help. Many of his friends studied longer than he, to little benefit. Few used their education in what work they could find. Some had no work. His ventures into business eventually failed. But every day he heard tell of people his age already enjoying the life he dreamt of. As he approached the age of thirty, he began to wonder sadly about his dreams. He sometimes stayed up too late and drank too much. More and more he was late for work.

When I say, "Imagine this story, if you can," I mean no insult. Of course, few could not imagine this young man's story, which in a local sort of way is nearly universal. His could be a life story from almost any time in the last few centuries, nearly any place in the world—wherever young people migrate for a better life. Some succeed. Most do not. To imagine oneself in this story is to imagine a life in the modern world, where migration has always been a common method for making a better life. Somewhere in the near or far past of almost every family there is a story of someone who moved for the good life, as this man did. The good life always requires a good place.

This is a story so deep in world culture as to be, as it is said, a grand narrative—a story recognized by many as big enough to give meaning to their different lives. Even by the measures of the 1940s in racially well-segregated Cincinnati, Ohio, Florence Lyons and Charles Lemert were as different as people could be. Still, she and I did not grow close because we understood each other. I couldn't believe the things she'd eat. She couldn't believe the things I'd say. But what we could figure out were the stories I would bring home from school on Tuesdays and the ones she told me as I sat in the front pew of her ironing-board ministry. In hundreds and hundreds of these occasional tellings, over more than fifty years, we figured out (she before I) that each had traveled on different trains to find a better life. Where we ended up, and how we got there, were different social places, to be sure; but the stories of the journeys were familiar enough to seal our bond. People who cannot begin to understand each other's social differences can, nevertheless, imagine each other's stories across their differences. Within limits, that is; and the limit is not where it is supposed to be.

Where there is a limit to our ability to measure the differences in our worlds is not with our ability to understand the strange and different we encounter here and there. Strictly speaking, to understand is to stand under (or in) another's position in the world. To understand, thus, is to move close to others to explore the familiar in the stories and practices.

This, after a fashion, is what professional sociologists do when they practice ethnography—the method of visiting another culture to experience it firsthand, thus to write the stories of those people. Understanding trades on recognition of the familiar—getting close enough to measure whatever is different against whatever is familiar. But this kind of ethnographic realism, whether practical or professional, falters at the outer range of what we already know, if only because what we already know can be a most unreliable way to measure the different. Thus, to be a sociologist of any kind is to try to figure out how the stories we hear from others have come to pass in the complicated array of social things that made them and the storytellers possible.

To know what's truly going on in a world of real, unabridged social differences we need a global method—one able to respect, but get beyond, what we hear in the course of living in, or on official ethnographic visits to, Casablanca or Brooklyn or wherever people tell their tales. The very fact that stories of young men in strange new places—stories like those of Frankie from Clarendon Heights or the One Stop butcher from Chicago—do not always come true means that behind the local stories there is something more to tell. This is where measured differences come in. This, therefore, is where the sociological imagination must leap beyond the familiar to those enduring, organizing, salient social things that are so nastily invisible to the naked eye. How does the imagination reach for the most powerful of social structures? It is never enough merely to measure where one is in the matrix of domination—even to have a good story that describes tolerably well where one is, higher or lower, in the scheme of power relations. Global methods are unforgivingly about the most distant structures.

Reaching for the structured social things is never easy, as is plain to see when the real and very sympathetic man in the story is introduced. Though the details are different, as is the name, the story might as well be of a twenty-nine-year-old Moroccan man—Abdelkrim. His native language would likely be Arabic. Since several dialectics of Arabic as well as French and Spanish are the principal languages of Morocco, Abdelkrim's brilliance in English shows how exceptional he is, making his failure all the more sad.

The first people of today's Morocco were the Berbers, who were given their name by the Roman colonizers. Berbers remain today the majority in this country along the Barbary Coast of North Africa—a name derived from them, as their name was given from the Latin for "barbarians." Morocco is home to descendents of the Berbers and other North African Arabs who, over the centuries, migrated to this beautiful land bordered by the Atlas mountains to the east, the Sahara desert to the south, and the Atlantic Ocean to the west. To the north lie the Mediterranean Sea, the Straits of Gibraltar, Spain, and the rest of Europe.

Until 1956, when Abdelkrim's parents were young, Morocco was a French colony. After independence, unlike many newly independent states in Africa, Morocco did reasonably well economically. Though not fabulously wealthy, Morocco has managed its national debt well enough to gain credit from the World Bank and to attract investment capital from abroad. This advantage meant that Morocco, like other countries in its position, found it necessary to encourage its young people toward more, better, and higher educational achievement. Abdelkrim's hope of a new life in Casablanca, like the hopes of thousands his age, was founded on Morocco's economic success relative to most so-called developing nations. Developing nations need an elite of new business and professional leaders who know the world's languages and understand its sciences and technologies. Abdelkrim was thus able, as the young often are, to introduce the global world's tools of the trade, like the fax machine and electronic mail, that were mysteries to the traditional, much older owner of the hotel but in the new world tools without which no modern business can survive.

Abdelkrim's talents and ambitions are many. From all appearances, he is the right man in the right place for the dream he is so sadly far from realizing. What is going wrong? He has the right idea. He has done the hard work. He made the right moves. He got the education. Yet, he is going nowhere. Why? What structures are coming down on him and others like him in today's world? What kinds of structures are these that give hope to the young with one hand while the other takes it back?

This is the kind of question asked more and more today by professional sociologists like Shana Cohen (b. 1966 in Texas), who did her graduate work in sociology at the University of California at Berkeley which led to a remarkable book, *Searching for a Different Future: The Rise of a Global Middle-Class in Morocco* (2004).[65] Her research took her to Europe and North Africa, where she put her mastery of French and of the several Arabic dialects spoken in Morocco to good use. She is one of a new breed of twenty-first century sociologists who travel the world and speak its languages in order to figure out the practical sociologies of people outside the dominant European and North American societies. Cohen's work in Morocco led her into one of the newest, and most important, areas of social studies today—the cultures and social lives of postcolonial people.

To be *postcolonial* is to live in a society or region that was once controlled by a world colonial power—usually, but not always, European or North American. The postcolonial subject is one who, having been freed legally from the degradations of colonial life, often remains dependent on the former colonizers for economic and sometimes military aid. Morocco is an independent nation-state today, but it relies on its cultural and economic ties to France. In this sense, the Lakota of Pine Ridge (not entirely free of control by the U.S. government) are also postcolonials, as are indigenous peoples in the Canadian north—as are Abdelkrim and others like him in Casablanca. What they all have in common with millions of men and women in the Caribbean, Asia, the Middle East, and Africa is the experience of living today with the stories of a former colonial existence. Black Elk was a sacred man because he kept alive the tales of the Lakota tragedy in 1890 at Wounded Knee. Somewhere among Abdelkrim's generation there may arise such a one who will tell the stories of brave men and women who prepared themselves for a new Morocco that, in the end, had no place for them. Postcolonial people are often more determined to keep these stories alive, if only to use them to measure their progress against the modern ones.

What Shana Cohen found in her research is that those who filled the positions the new Morocco offered are doing very well. They are proud to be Moroccan in times like these. But change is never precisely calibrated, and in this case, as often happens, more young people were trained than there were positions to fill or market opportunities to capitalize. Many others are in Abdelkrim's position. They suffer the melancholia, or sadness, that comes from having dreamed and done well, then failed—having, that is, to find yet another way or give it up. After many months of weekly meetings with Shana Cohen, Abdelkrim told her just how he felt (a feeling many others like him shared).

> Everybody is looking for something to make them okay with their life. Happiness, no, satisfaction, is always inside. We can find it. It is just a question of time. Sometimes, it can come late. It has come late for me. I am like in prison or something. A lot of people dream to have my job. But not a lot of people dream to have my salary. I could go outside Morocco and have more materials, but that may not do it. . . . The problem is time. After thirty, everything goes so quickly.

Youth passes quickly—sucked away by things we seldom see; and when it goes, it leaves behind the measured failures.

Cohen explains that Abdelkrim is typical of many young men and women—many highly trained professionals without a job suitable to their qualifications. Though they feel otherwise, this is not so much their fault as it is what comes down when the social structures of one's world are changing. When, in the course of a generation, a country frees itself from a colonial system and begins the long road toward what some economists call economic maturity, the lives of individuals will be affected in different ways. Some, the fewer, will be carried along as social things develop for the better. Others, like Abdelkrim, will be carried only part of the way; others fall away, or back to the villages they had fled.

When structures turn deadly on us, as they may have for Abdelkrim, we are taken by surprise. This is the way it works with enduring, organizing, salient, but invisible social things. We can never see them at work. They are hard to imagine. Then, all of a sudden they sneak up on us.

When I first wrote this book—now more than five years ago—I had two children, two boys I loved dearly. Today, I have two children, but a different two. Noah is still very wonderfully with us, working as an outdoor educator after graduate studies at Harvard. Anna Julia Lemert was born in 1998. She came to us after a long search. We knew we would find a child to love. Among delights and surprises too many to count, Annie came out to us from her very white birth mother as black as Muhammad Ali. She is not as dark as Florence, her adoptive grandmother of whom she'll hear the stories, but dark enough to compound the mystery of social things. Annie at age three with no discursive awareness of the concept race, ran about the house with next to nothing on, as boxers do, shouting, "I . . . Hammad Ali." Annie was to us like those surprises of the social life that bring zest to living—strange to the understanding, but completely wonderful, structured by events over which we have no control. Some structures work thus to the good. Others do not—tragically not.

Matthew, Annie's and Noah's older brother, committed suicide early in 2000. He was a brilliant, brave, honorable, and exciting man—an officer in the Marine Corps. Then one night, out of the blue, we came home to find the Marines at our door bringing the terrible news. You can imagine that I don't tell this story easily or lightly. But the telling helps soothe for a while the chronic pain—and the worst is that we didn't see it coming any more than we saw Annie coming just as she was and is. The one a tragedy, the other a blessing; and both came down without warning.

We think of suicide and sex as among the very most private of actions—more private even that Abdelkrim's move to a new place for a better life. Those who commit suicide and we who enjoy our sex seldom think at the time that the action is a social thing. Suicide and lovemaking, even more than lonely migrations to strange cities, are the more solitary events of the private life. Their privacy, however, is more apparent than real. They thus pose the sociological question all the more acutely.

Are we, even when acting alone, connected in some way or another to all other individuals in the mystery of social things—even perhaps to the rest of the world? When I say "connected" I mean something social, along the lines of what Durkheim must have had in mind when he wrote of social facts as very real things in themselves. The trouble is that neither Durkheim nor many other professional sociologists ever really took seriously what practical sociologists know very well. When it is said that we are connected in practical social life something more telling is meant. What we do or don't do, what we might one day do or may never be able to—these actual and possible actions are not entirely of our own private making. Abdelkrim, filled with hope, did what he did because of his connections to those about him—his family and friends back home, his new friends in Casablanca (against whom he measured himself), the global market of possibilities that dealt out promises (not all of them kept). Social things are like that. They tie us as much to the past behind and the future to be as to the present at hand.

So, too, when Annie's dear birth-mom made tender love one night in Florida, and when my very dear boy hanged himself one morning in Texas—they were doing what they did as individuals. But neither was entirely alone. When we make love or suffer impossible nightmares of the soul, there are always others lurking in the shadows. We may think that our sexual experiences are with a single other (if they are), but even then there are numerous others in attendance. Our lovers never come alone. They come to us as they are—some are kind, or lonely; others are rough and angry; some are there for the night, others for breakfast, some for the duration. When we give ourselves to these comings and goings of various men or women we often feel still others watching over the scene, even when we don't really know why they are there or where they've come from. These others, like those who hover about us in the long nights of despair, are a chorus of ghosts, shuffling along as we move about. This is how the dead structures that endure from the past come down on the most lively of subjects, as on the most sad.

Do not take lightly the ghosts in your closet. Their hauntings are, in fact, one of the more important new contributions to a critique of global methods, of which the classic work is *Ghostly Matters: Haunting and the Sociological Imagination* (1997), by Avery Gordon (b. 1958)—a cultural and literary critic and political activist who teaches sociology at the University of California in Santa Barbara. Some lively subjects, like Florence, live very well with the evil that haunts them; some, like Matthew, struggle bravely with their ghosts for a good while and then, for more reasons than the living can imagine, shuffle off to be with them. And others, like Abdelkrim, have yet to figure it all out. Just because we cannot say exactly how structures work, it doesn't mean they don't exist. That is the way it is with ghostly structures. They determine how we measure the worth of others or our own self-worth. Unfortunately, or fortunately (it is hard to say), we don't attend to our ghosts most of the time. But they are there, waiting at the ready, doing whatever they are doing.

The bigger and more mysterious the structures, the harder it is to figure out how and why they come down as they do. Abkelkrim is no different from anyone else. He, like the rest, must be able and willing to figure out the worldly structures close at hand but out of sight. Figuring them out, and being able eventually to talk about the figurings out, are what may be called *methods*.

The methods we use depend, to a great extent, on the kind of a world we live in—specifically, our positions in that world.

The very simple word *position* has taken on a special meaning to many sociologists. Dorothy Smith, the Canadian feminist who now lives in British Columbia after retiring from teaching at the Ontario Institute for Studies in Education, was among the first to explain the importance of one's position (or standpoint) as a resource for figuring things out. Many feminists and sociologists speak today of a woman's subject *position*—and mean by it the methodological benefits gained from starting the study of social things with one simple question: How might a woman's position in the world affect what she knows? Is it possible that knowledge is, as it is said, situated in these subject positions? Of course the question applies equally well to the longer list of possible positions, including those of men—especially men and women who are in Abdelkrim's postcolonial position.

Taking subject positions seriously is a double-edged sword. So seemingly slight and sensible a move actually cuts apart some long-cherished assumptions about the sociologies. Dorothy Smith was also one of the first to undress professional sociology's fascination with objectivity. When *objectivity* serves as a standard for getting social things right, it serves a good purpose. But when it becomes a standard for limiting the sociological imagination, it does not. "Objectivity" is a particularly loaded word. Smith, for example, writes of what she calls simply the *relations of ruling*—the actual social connections by which social things like businesses, governments, schools, even professional sociologies administer the social worlds.[66] In the modern world, ruling is more often than not the harsh work of administration; and, through the years, ruling has been administered mostly by men who, in effect, believed what their ghosts whispered in their ears. When the dead structures your fathers invented tell you to rule the world, you tend to believe this is the world's objective truth. Even today, when fewer men in domestic partnerships are the only ones bringing home the bacon, men will drive themselves crazy measuring their success or failure as breadwinners.

On the other hand, it may or may not be true that women, by their natures, are better able to see the world. But it probably is true that women, like others who have been measured less worthy by the man-made world, see the world differently. What they see and say, as James Scott and many others going back to Hegel said, may be the better, if hidden, transcript of social things. The method by which social things are figured out determines how those things will be understood—and positions are where understanding begins.

But what becomes of these positions—all the positions and standpoints comprising the worlds of practical life—when the worlds themselves change in ways that may render the familiar measures and the well-known stories a bit out of joint? Is this perhaps what Abdelkrim came up against while playing his hand in Casablanca?

When the world—and people's positions in it—change, everyone has to figure out new methods. Once, years ago when Matthew was a kid, we took a thrill ride at an amusement park. After paying the price of admission, we entered into a large cylinder. There were, I think, twenty or so other people in there. We were told to stand against the wall in a circle. Then, after all were ready, the thing started to spin around and around. After a short while the bottom fell out—that is, the floor just dropped away and there we were hanging on to nothing but the wall. The centrifugal speed of the rotation forced everyone against the wall. No one was at particular risk. But everyone was terrified (or tried to act as though they weren't). That whole world, little and silly as it was, was changed and none of the methods we knew about were worth a damn. We wanted to grab for something, but nothing was there. We had only to relax (nearly impossible) and let the spinning cylinder take care of things. The thrill, if that is what it was, was in learning for a few minutes to trust forces we had never really figured out, forces for which we had no method to determine whether they should be trusted or not. That's the way the world is today. Nearly everyone needs a new method.

One of the most interesting things about today's spinning, bottomless world is that everyone agrees that the thrill ride is called *globalization*—a worldwide process of change in the structure of global things. The term and its meaning (often implied) are themselves tricky. For one thing (and this is what is seldom said), it is not clear whether *global things* are still social things in the sense of people being connected—that is, truly connected, across the world. It is one thing to imagine the connections in a smallish social world (as in a town, some cities or regions), or even in the larger ones (a society such as the Canadian or Moroccan or Chinese ones). But the larger the worlds get, the harder it becomes to think of them as social, with real people actually connected. They all seem so very different. The differences make the world as a whole appear even larger than it is. Globalization, by calling us out into this enormous and different place, invites the impression that people will lose what some call their "human nature." Though almost no one can say what this "human nature" really is, there is widespread belief that it is important and can be lost when social things get too big. It is possible that one element of human nature is somewhat like agoraphobia—an unfounded fear of open and very big places. In any case, this fear of global things is experienced as the bottom dropping out—or, as not knowing what will happen when the spinning stops.

There are at least two schools of thought on globalization. The first might be called the *transformationalists*—those who accept that the globalizing world is significantly changed but, at its core, remains much the same. For reasons unclear, many transformationalists are British, perhaps because their ghosts had experience running a colonial empire, the remains of which are still in evidence. Anthony Giddens, the Giddens who made the distinction between practical and discursive consciousness, is the most famous transformationalist. But, close after, is David Held (b. 1951), who holds the Graham Wallas Professorship in Political Science at the London School of Economics. In *Global Transformations* (1999), Held and his coauthors give as much evidence as one could need to show that something in the world began to change just after World War II, has been speeding up ever since, and seems to have become the dominant reality of the world order at the turn of the century.

Sooner or later, everyone who has something to say about globalization gets around to the *nation-state*—by which is meant, as you would expect, the political order identified by a national name and culture, as in the United States of America or the Republic of Congo. The nation-state was always considered the important political form of modern societies. The American Revolution of 1776, for example, was fought in the name of the American colonies in order to form a new nation out of cultural and political principles thought to be special to the "American people." The point is that nation-states are the political homes of national values or, as sociologists are likely to say, "societies." Being a member in good standing of the "American people" involves more than being a citizen of the United States of America—obeying the laws and reciting the pledges. Members of the society in a nation-state expect each other to share, at least to some degree, whatever values and habits are currently in practice. This, of course, is an improbable scheme, as anyone knows at election time when neighbors stop talking to each other until it's all over. The idea that legal members of a state would also share a commitment to that state's national culture—or society—is, in a word, absurd.

Americans, it happens, are very big on their nation-state. Few other people talk on as tirelessly about their way of life. Still, just like Morocco and almost every other nation-state—with some exceptions, perhaps Iceland or Nunavut—the U.S.A. is made up of very different groups of people who share almost nothing in common except an occasional willingness to fight wars with outsiders or discriminate against select insiders they would prefer were outsiders. Still, politicians will talk about the *American way of life* just as many sociologists will talk about the American society.

Globalization, it is agreed, has somewhat devalued the nation-state as the structural coin of the global realm. Transformationalists like David Held and his colleagues give some startling numbers to prove it.[67] Over the course of the last half of the twentieth century the number of nation-states on the planet doubled from 81 to 167 (in 1991). That is a lot by twice. But it is nothing compared to the increase in the number of diplomatic relations among all the nation-states—from 2,140 (1950) to 7,762 (1991), or nearly four times greater. A lot more, but still nothing compared to other ways in which nation-states are now connected, namely: by intergovernmental organizations (like, famously, the United Nations or the World Trade Organization) and international nongovernmental agencies (like, for example, Doctors without Frontiers or the Red Cross). In 1900, when there were fewer than 50 nations, there were fewer still of these governmental and nongovernmental ties between nation-states. But at the end of the twentieth century, with about 200 nation states, there were nearly 8,000 of these connecting organizations, and the greatest number of them (by far) were international nongovernment organizations (or INGOs). And this does not begin to count the number of business and informal ties. In other words, the number of these organizations is a good measure of global connectedness. It means that if you give blood to the American Red Cross, you are linked, even if your blood stays near home, to a brother or sister giving blood in Turkey or Chile; and the nation-states have little to do with the organization that helps you save lives (except perhaps to provide legal and sometimes military protection for the INGOs your nation-state happens to approve of).

Yet, when it comes to globalization and the nation-state, the transformationalists are cautious. The world has changed in the direction of its parts being more variously and deeply connected. But they are just as inclined to point out, quite sensibly, that connections of this kind have been around since around 1500, when Europeans first set out to colonize the world. A half millennium later, connectedness may even have gotten the upper hand in world affairs. Certainly the nation-state, so important to the modern world, is now less salient in the run of global things. Still, when the last word is said, David Held says that there remain good reasons to be optimistic about the nation-state and its political and social communities, if (perhaps a big if) the nation-states adjust to the New World Order. In other words, the transformationalists stop short of giving up on the modern order, including the nation-state, by using a gently nuanced locution. Globalization has *reshaped* the modern world—a difference in degree but not in kind. This is a sensible point of view, especially when early in the twenty-first century it seems evident that the American nation-state, still the most powerful, gets its way most but not all the time.

Still, there is room for disagreement. There are of course those (Held calls them skeptics) who believe that nothing important has changed. But the more interesting alternative to the transformationalists we might call the *globalists*. A globalist is one who believes that global things are more than reshaped. She would more likely believe, much like the feminists and others who write about the methods of subject positions, that the very change in the relations of the members (whether individuals or nation-states) to each other is a change in the world as such.

One of the more interesting globalists is Manuel Castells (b. 1942), currently a professor of sociology, urban planning, and European studies at the University of California in Berkeley. Castells is himself interesting because, though older than Shana Cohen by more than a generation, he was one of the first of the new breed of global sociologists. Born in Spain, he lived in Paris before moving to the United States. For years he has traveled the globe to lecture and teach in Caracas, Hong Kong, Taiwan, Amsterdam, Moscow, Mexico, Montreal, even Boston, among other exotic places. He knows the world, and not just from its hotels and tourist venues. In *The Network Society* (1996), one of his four books on global things, Castells describes many of the same facts that appeal to the transformationalists. But Castells is a globalist in the sense that, in his words, "the network society represents a qualitative change in the human experience."[68] There you have it—"the human experience," a cousin to "essential human nature." To say that "the" human experience is changed qualitatively is to say that when people change their positions in relation to each other, they also change *who* they are. This, you see, is more than reshaping. But, if different, in what way and why?

Whether one is a transformationalist or a globalist, practical life today is affected by global things in two virtually inescapable ways. For one, most people are indeed connected to global things, most importantly by whatever job they have or hope to have. Global labor markets, among all the other ties and connects, make individuals global creatures in the sense that they are vulnerable to the biggest of social things. For another, people are *personally* drawn into the wider world, often against their wills, by virtue of their being logged on to one or another network—hence, Castells's phrase: the *network society*.

Globalization certainly involves information networks, of which, it goes without saying, the Internet is the most notorious. But even if you don't email or surf the Net, you probably watch television, which is another network, of course, and one that is changing just as rapidly as the rest of the networked world of high-speed telecommunications. And even those few (if any) who don't watch television at least use the phone system, which today is cheaper, easier to use, and available for all kinds of purposes from faxing to banking to phone sex, not to mention the strange things one can do with mobile phones, which are, of course, still another network. There are more. It is nearly impossible not to live with, even in, some or several global networks. This can get both interesting and confusing.

A globalist would find it obvious that when people live in networks of these kinds, their positions relative to each other, as to the global network as a whole, are more than just transformed. Relations in an electronic network are, for better or worse, fundamentally different from face-to-face relations (which, we should hasten to say, are not always that great themselves). This is what globalists have in mind when they speak of the network making a change in *the* human experience that goes beyond being connected. Connections are between still-independent parties. Networks are parties unto themselves. To know your position in the matrix of domination is to know your place; to be drawn into these networks is to have your position sent out to a place that may be no place at all. It may be, globalists say, that those who use and live in these networks are becoming a different kind of being.

Certainly, the globalist point of view calls into question most parts and positions in the world as it was. Castells, thus, is much more likely to say that such staples of the older modern world as the nation-state are not just "reshaped" but "threatened." One of his most interesting examples, and one easily imagined, is crime. The economics of crime are global. The connectedness of illegal trade in drugs with the global sex trade with markets for illegal weapons with all the other smugglings that thrive on poverty and other social miseries is probably spinning as wildly out of control as are the number of INGOs. We'll never know, of course, because there's no way to count the darker parts of the global underground. What is clear is that, try as they might, the nation-states have one hell of a time doing anything about the illegal black markets that constitute some impossible-to-calculate but very real proportion of the global economic product. If you doubt this, just ask your One Stop butcher who sees it every day in the darkened windows of BMWs passing him by as he waits for the bus.

So, between the transformationalists and the globalists there is a small, but important difference. From the point of view of professional sociology, it is impossible today to have any more than a well-informed opinion on the dispute. When global things change, it takes time for people to see how big and, as Castells says, "qualitative" the change is or whether the change is but a transformation. Still, as usual, what a professional sociologist knows, and how he knows it, is another thing from what the practical sociologist can know, if she will.

Remember Mr. Alsahybi, who was murdered in the deli he ran to make a world in Brooklyn for his kids brought over from Yemen? The last I heard (from his oldest son, who took over the deli), no one knows for certain who killed him or why. Still, everyone—the cops, the neighbors, the newspapers, probably the family for all I know—assume he was killed for drug money. This terrible little story changed and charged the little worlds in and around DeGraw and Henry Streets in Cobble Hill of Brooklyn of New York of the many, many wider and other worlds that come together on that corner as they do on most. We who lived there thought the murderer just had to have been an invader from the outer worlds. One reason we thought that way is that everyone who lived there, especially the Italian Americans, knew that several of the families lived nearby. No one of right mind would dare commit a crime in our neighborhood. Screw around with one of the families and, as Annie puts it, you'll be a goner. Little did we—we WASPs, that is, or the African Americans, or the people from Yemen who lived a few blocks up and over, much less the Italians—little did anyone suppose the global trade in drugs would send its evil down so close to home. But we supposed it very well after this lovely man on whom we all counted was murdered. It makes you think.

It also puts you in the world, and makes you wonder where in the world you are living. There was Mr. Alsahybi who came to Brooklyn from Yemen. Unlike its oil-rich neighbors, Yemen is very poor. And so those who can, come to places like Brooklyn. Like Abdelkrim (whose Morocco is better off than Yemen), they want a better world, even when there are risks. Did Abdul Kareem Alsahybi realize that the risks would include some shadowy guy? Probably not. That, again, is one of the ways worldly structures sneak up on you in the dark. They never stop.

Actually we left the corner soon after Annie sneaked up on us. We decided to make our home in what New Yorkers call the country. We did-n't have to leave when we did, but we chose that time because Mrs. Lee, who owned our building, sold it. She was moving back to California to spend her last years in a Chinese American community. She made a killing on the sale. She did because in the happy 1990s, people were making a killing in the stock market. They were because the American economy was the pow-erhouse of the global economy. The new rich wanted more and more expen-sive houses. They moved in. Rents went up. We moved out. We saw the first signs when a new restaurant opened—the Bouillabaisse! I know bouil-labaisse because I once lived in France. It is Mediterranean, but hardly a Middle Eastern dish. Soon after, that part of Brooklyn came to be a really hot place for fine restaurants, none Middle Eastern—or so I read in the papers. We haven't been back since we moved after Mr. Alsahybi from Yemen was killed, when Annie came to us from a night in Florida, when Mrs. Lee went back to a home on the Pacific Rim.

That is the way global things work. It is a little bit too easy to say that globalization is about information networks, or about the rapid flow of money in capital networks and the rise and fall of fast money. Globalization is these things, of course. But it comes down to us on the corners where we live. More true perhaps in some than others, but true enough in all. Pine Ridge is a remote place, but people there are wired and wronged by the global things.

On and on these global things spin. They take the bottoms out of our corners where, sometimes tragically, they demand of us some greater, often reluctant, sense of the wider worlds on the globe. Global things are different—from each other and from us who are already there when they move in. They are, thus, different from other social things.

Because global things are different, they make a difference in everyone's position—in at least the degree and possibly the kind of our connections with others in the global scheme of things. When global things get the upper hand some social things may be reshaped or threatened. Either way, they can't any longer be taken for granted.

Thus, again, among other examples, the nation-state is no longer as salient an enduring, organizing social thing as it once was because—connections and networks being what they are—fewer people limit their social homes to what shelter their nations offer. Sooner or later, for more and more, the information highway paves the way for the now well-beaten pathways of the seekers after a better life. The story is different today if only because so many more can and do set out for someplace new.

Consider the migrations of Florence Lyons alone in the 1930s to Cincinnati from Florida, of Abdul Kareem Alsahybi and his family from Yemen to Brooklyn sometime in the 1980s, and of Abdelkrim to a new life in Casablanca in the 1990s. Each sought a better life. Each left a difficult place for one they hoped would be better. Florence and Abdul Kareem got someplace—though neither made the best life possible, both made good enough lives in their new worlds. That Abdul Kareem was gunned down mid-dream does not mean he failed. The deli he established remains to feed his children. Still, there is a difference. Florence did not feel she had to leave the nation-state of her birth and citizenship.

One of the practical and down-to-earth benefits of a nation-state is that it provides a kind of home for most, if not all, of its citizens. To be a citizen in the heyday of nation-states was to be a member of a social thing that at least served to protect people from invaders, if it could, and at the most to bestow on them an *identity*. To have an identity, strictly speaking, is to be able to recognize yourself in some other socially enduring thing, however grand or small—to be, that is, "identical with" some social thing not exclusively or privately yours. That other may be as elemental as people's ideas of who they happen to think they are. Florence Lyons thought herself to be a tough, inventive, funny, hardworking, well-dressed, Christian lady—and she was. But she had this personal identity because, as Erving Goffman would say, she also had a *social identity*—that is, certain social things of which she was recognizably a member. When, in my day, and hers, white people would refer to one of her groups as "those people," they meant nothing kind, but they said something specific. Florence was not, for example, just any kind of Christian woman. She belonged to the Zion Baptist Church, which everyone thereabouts knew was a leading African American church. Those people were in fact "her people" in another, more affectionate sense. And so it is that who a person is as an individual is certified by her recognizable social memberships. Identity is, therefore, membership. It may be experienced as very personal, but identity is a thoroughly social thing—one of the more intimate ways the structures come down to haunt. Had she wanted to, which she never did, Florence could have changed church memberships, but in the community she would have still been known as the one who sang for years in the Zion choir.

Nation-states still inspire societal canopies that shelter a strong sense of social identity. It may be that Americans are more comforted by their national identities than, say, people from Yemen who have had to flee for the better life. But, around the world, global things have come to sap the identity-bestowing force of, at least, those nations lacking the power to certify whatever promises of the good life they may have made. The structural power of the nation-states, enduring and organizing that it may be, is less able to assure the comforts of practical life on which the ideals of a social identity depend. Identities travel the networks from and to the far corners of the globe, just as do the goods on our shelves and jobs we hold for the time being.

What is one to do when the goods and jobs disappear all of a sudden—or when the dream of being the one who has the good life turns cloudy as it did for Abelkrim? It is then that one must have a method—a global method that draws the social imagination into the connections and networks of global things. What is the method available to those who move out to move up only to find themselves stalled? Those trapped with no place to go, or no thought of going anywhere else, have only to get by as best they can. Some, like Frankie, turn angry and resort to the false hope of a futile self-assertion. More often than not, they fall away. Some, like the One Stop butcher, keep on cutting away for the paycheck that cuts too short. They have no choice, at least none they can imagine, and so they heroically resist the code of the street and, tears in the eyes, work at what they have.

But what about Abdelkrim and those all around the world who share his melancholia? Abdelkrim, as Shana Cohen tells his story up to the early years of the 2000s, has come up against the limit of those she calls the *unplaced*—that is, those who make all the moves called for, yet were excluded from the social position they believed would be theirs. Still, having done relatively better than either Frankie or the One Stop butcher, Abdelkrim stills looks for a method that might work against the odds. Not ready to rebel, not sure how to innovate, not yet willing to resign himself, Abdelkrim continues to look. Cohen found that many of the unplaced are gradually giving up on Morocco, becoming members of the *detached middle class*—that is, those sadly giving up on their society's promise of the material substance of a better life. Remember Abdelkrim's words, "A lot of people dream to have my job. But not a lot dream to have my salary." He, and many others, have middle-class jobs, or middle-class qualifications, but little or no hope of a middle-class income. And many detach themselves not so much from the middle class but from the nation-state that promised them a place if they worked hard enough. They begin to turn away from Morocco or Yemen and to think of their identities in global terms.

Global methods are those by which one finds a home, not so much in a society as in the world of global things. They move away from whatever shelter they find in being Moroccan or Yemeni, in order to move again, possibly to some other place in the world. A home sufficient to provide a social identity requires a good enough place, and very often the place in which one is trapped is not place enough. Those fortunate enough, as Mr. Alsahybi was, to be able to move to Brooklyn, or some such global corner, move themselves at a cost to their self-understanding. I don't know if Mr. Alsahybi had become an American citizen, or whether he particularly thought of himself as an American. And it may have been that back home in Yemen he was still known as the one who went to America to find a better life. Though perhaps not middle class in the usual sense, Mr. Alsahybi was not unplaced. But neither was he any longer from Yemen, in the sense of being Yemeni. If he did not consider himself yet from America, it may have been because for the time being at least he was from the world itself. Those who live still in their national societies and thus consider themselves French or Canadian may find this a peculiar way to think of oneself. But the truth is that there are millions of people who may still call themselves by the name of their native society but who are in fact global people. Yasir Apiu Ugila is a friend I met in our church in New Haven. He says he is from the Sudan. But he lives in America, works for a technology company, attends a very English church, and visits what remains of his family in Uganda where they fled the ravages of civil strife "at home." What then is his home?

What is the method available for finding a home in the world of global things? What method is there for Abdelkrim? Was it the one Yasir used? Whatever it is, it is different from the one Florence used in 1938. As big as the change was for her she did not have to stop calling America home, even when America was yet to make a home for her. She found a place in the national home she already had. What do those who travel the more worldly paths do?

To speak of global methods is, in part at least, to speak of new uses for the older methods. Florence's method, for one, was well known to migrating people since forever. She used those connections she had in 1938. She came to Cincinnati because she had family already settled there. She had a place to stay until the laundry job paid enough to settle herself. It is entirely likely that Mr. Alsahybi relied on the same kind of connections to family or friends. Though there were fewer global connections in Florence's day, the transformationalists are right to say that globalization is about their multiplication around the world—connections that tie people in knots more complex than ever before.

Years ago, in Illinois, I met the Korean man to whom this book is dedicated. Years later, I saw him once in New York, again in Los Angeles, and another time in Seoul. Years later still, I had a Korean American student whose father and I knew each other in Harvard thirty years before. When Matthew died, he helped me make contact with Professor Han who, twenty years before, delighted Mattie the day he made kimchi in our Illinois kitchen. The ties that bind the global net. When today people use their connections to travel in real space to a new social place, they are using an old practical method that, by its degree of transformation, is just shy of being an entirely different method. Even those who do not travel in physical fact can and do live in the global network of places they would never dream of going.

But what kind of a home does the network of global connections allow? How might it come down even on the world's homebodies? This is where the practical sociologists can learn from the professional ones.

Since the days of Durkheim and Weber, professional sociologies have hovered back and forth between two different but mutually necessary methods. One type includes all the *universalizing methods*—that is, those methods that aim to tell the whole story all at once. These are the methods that rely usually (but not always) on statistical summaries of what truths can be told. When, for example, Doris Wilkinson carefully studied the available data on occupational positions for black and white women, she used the numbers to draw the graph (on page 163) of their relative positions over the course of nearly a half century. The bare lines of a shifting web tell a universal story of women who lived lives as similar yet different as those of Anna Julia Cooper's in the 1890s and Florence Lyons's in the 1940s. No sociologist, practical or professional, can live without the numbers. It is surely the case that unplaced friends of Abdelkrim in Casablanca must use the numbers they can find at the click of a mouse to estimate their chances in Melbourne or Paris or New York. Still, the universalizing methods may not be enough.

Practically speaking, if you want to move to Australia, you need to know more than the bare fact that there are openings for people with experience in hotel work. It helps to have the connections with people of a familiar kind—whether real or virtual. No less in fact, though much more in technique, getting close enough to people to have a sense of the familiar in a strange place is the other method used by professional sociologists, as well as practical ones. This method might be called, as Max Weber put it, the *method of understanding*—that is, all those methods by which sociologists try to figure out what homes in strange places are like by moving in—literally or imaginatively. Of these, the most famous are ethnographic methods. When Herbert Gans moved into the Urban Village, or Jay MacLeod got close to Frankie and his gang in Clarendon Heights, or Susan Krieger danced with a lesbian community in Iowa, they went to hear the stories. None could say that the stories they heard were universally true of all Italian Americans or working-class boys or gay women. Like all tales of differences, many sound fantastic. Is it really true that the Urban Villagers had no self with which to see the destructive force of the structures that took their homes? Still, a good many people trust stories of this kind because they seem so real—that is, they tell a realistic story of what they might understand were they to visit the home places of these people. Ethnographies, as they are traditionally practiced by professional sociologists, are usually (not always) more sophisticated versions of the practical studies people like Florence use to determine whether Cincinnati would offer a better place than Plant City, Florida. She had ways to know what stories there were of the strange place— from kin who lived there, from friends who visited, from even the Cincinnati Reds baseball team that practiced in Florida, and much more. From these, she figured out that the different place was familiar enough to be worth the trip—and so it was.

But the problem with methods of understanding is that they may not be general enough, just as the universalizing methods may be too general. Those who move want to know what the odds are, but even if the odds are good, they want to hear someone they know tell them a story or two. Likewise, an ethnographer wants to collect her stories, but when she writes them up she needs to tell them in a way that those who know the numbers and graphs will recognize something familiar.

The trouble today with the usual methods is that, when people are connected in networks, they can never get enough of the familiar to overcome the strangeness of others in global things. Mr. Alsahybi had no way of imagining that Brooklyn was a place where the cost of his gain would be so mortal. What he knew from what stories he may have heard, or from what numbers he could get, is that Brooklyn was familiar enough to be worth the trip. But global methods are necessarily different from those that worked reasonably well when social things were more simply protected by the nation-states. When people change homes for another world, neither numbers nor understandings may be sufficient.

The strangest thing about global things is that they require a method for *getting close at a distance*—that is, for figuring out the stories told by people in places so different as to be always at a distance. In this sense, global realities bring home the truth of social structures of all kinds. The invisibility of social structures, especially global ones, results from their ghostly origins—alive in the moment they come down to kiss or maim, but in themselves strangely far away. Those who live more or less agreeably in a nation-state, and choose to let it be a home for whoever they think they are, enter thereby into an agreement to fool themselves. This is the strict meaning of the overused expression "to identify with." They agree to be the ones who are known to believe in and live by the stories of their societal home. But when, like those in Abdelkrim's unplaced place, people can no longer believe the home stories, they begin to look to the wider world for a home.

To find yourself amid global things is to identify with social things that, far more than being big and strange, are always wildly and irreconcilably different. The nature of the global world is unremitting social differences. One may search for the familiar in such places and find its shadow here and there, where kith or kin have sent you, but all about on the streets everything else is strange to the tongue and soul. This is when and where global things show up the limits of traditional methods. In the world as it really is, as distinct from the televised one, one cannot possibly control all the social differences, nor measure precisely their central tendencies. Such a social thing has no standard deviations. How does one universalize the truth of a neighborhood like that around Mr. Alsahybi's deli? Many tongues were spoken. Skins were variously colored. Habits were oddly at odds. Summer holidays the Italians sat out on their stoops to sing and shout far into the night and do whatever they were doing. It irritated the hell out of me. I could not understand any more than the obvious and superficial—that whatever they were doing down there, it was their way of doing it. And this had to be respected. Anyhow, the cops would never have made them go inside just so I could get my sleep.

When people move down and in with each other, it is nearly impossible to understand the global differences, which, of course, are the very same differences that make it impossible to universalize. It makes you wonder about your own social identity. It means you have to make a home always at the risk of being overheard or, worse yet, overseen by those who may have more influence with the cops than you do.

The sociological imagination must reach beyond all understanding, even beyond all the best facts to be had, to a social thing that is always there at hand—to stories told of those who journey for the good life, of those who wish they could but cannot, of those who no longer wish and thus no longer dream. In the never-ending day trading between the practical and professional, the practical gives understanding to universalizing as the professionals give a bold vision to the practical. But, in the world of global things, the method required is one that respects both of these, while letting the imagination settle at a distance from the stories told by those so different from us that we would never think of calling the cops to break up their party. You might as well try to figure this out as they keep you up with their shouts and songs far into the summer night.

CHAPTER

ELEVEN

~

GLOBAL THINGS
QUEER THE SOCIAL

One school year (I forget which one) when I was, perhaps, thirteen years old, I began to measure myself with particular attention to what others close by thought of me. Why is it that when children become teenagers they suddenly begin to take closer account of how they are viewed by others is a question better answered by the psychologists. For me, it had something to do with the surprising juices that had begun to boil in my blood. It was not just any of my schoolmates I was worrying about so much as the girls. Much later in life, I was able to determine that, for better or worse, I was a boy who, when it came to romance, liked girls more than I liked other boys. But in the heat of early teenage life, this was a difference I could not think, as indeed I was unable to think clearly about much else other than how, or even if, I would ever get laid.

This much of the story may be psychological, but in my state of rabid emotional excitation, I was also aware, if unable to talk much about it, that my circumstances were very much sociological. At the least, like most of my friends, my ability to think about who I thought I was or wanted to be turned acutely on the subject of what other kids thought of me. So intense was the dilemma of these social things that, of course, it never occurred to me that they weren't thinking of me at all—only about how I and the others thought about them. We were all in the same little social boat, cut adrift from the anchorage of childhood pleasures, longing for the shores of what would turn out to be the exaggerated bliss of adult freedom. Worse yet, the pathetic little boat we were in was precariously balanced on a sea of adult authorities whose sole purpose, we felt, was not to get us to a safe harbor but to torment us with rules and restrictions. Still, we carried on, sleeplessly ignorant of what we were doing. Each had his or her own way of dealing. Mine was to be the class clown, a choice determined as much by my lack of self-confidence as by the slim pickings my little acts brought in.

One day that year, all these social things came crashing in on me—all too literally. The occasion was a history class lorded over by a particularly nasty teacher of uncertain qualification in his subject. The class was forever in an uproar due to the gathering force of the itch in our butts and the bee in his. The circumstances were ripe for my trickster act. I was, I supposed, hilarious—funny enough in my own head to incite me to cross the line. On this day, in a year I forget, I executed a perfectly brilliant verbal joke, the details of which I have also forgotten. What I know for certain is that that day's joke brought a flood of wicked laughter from my classmates who, I did not then realize, were excited less by the genius of my fun than by its daring.

Clearly, I had ridiculed the teacher. He, in turn, demanded my immediate presence at the front of the classroom, whereupon he ordered me down on my hands and knees with the seat of my pants facing the class. That I obeyed so passively is itself interesting but not nearly so as what followed. Trembling with rage, the teacher came from behind the desk, his hand holding something behind his back. He forced my head between his legs then exposed the object he held—a paddle we had heard of but never seen. He then told me off in a teacherly way, while paddling my rear end to the point of tears. After, I returned to my seat humiliated, as he took his satisfied. The event was never spoken of again. It never occurred to me to tell my parents of it, perhaps because then, unlike now, such things did not cause a public stir.

Early in the 2000s, in those parts of the planet where people think of themselves as more advanced, a public beating of the neighborhood doctor's boy would stir up quite a bit of public bother. It was not that, in the 1950s, my father the doctor, had I told him, would have done nothing. He could be a wild man in his own way. But his rage never, so far as I knew, led to the police, much less to the lawyers and the courts, as today it might. In the 2000s, parents and kids routinely demand severe justice for such actions—suspension or dismissal of the offending adult, even criminal charges of abuse to a minor. Of all the possible charges that today might be brought is one that, in the 1950s in Cincinnati, Ohio, simply did not exist—that is, abuse of a sexual kind.

In those days, in the blush of a world changing after a long war, we were mindlessly focused on something that came to be called "the good life." Except for a few professional sociologists and most people on the economic margins who had no reason to call this life good, well-fed white people of my kind gave little thought to whatever was going on below the surface of social things. We, kids and parents alike, had been through a long depression of our economic prospects and then a war that put political hope in doubt. In periods of scarcity or war, there is little time for pondering the deeper meaning of social things. The attention is focused on survival—looking for work and food, looking out for snipers. When relative peace returned in 1945, the Depression of the 1930s was over; in the peace, there was work for Americans. But, after years of training the eye on the visible surface of want and fear, we were ill-prepared to examine what lay below and behind.

Among the facts of life that lay below and behind was sex. In the 1950s, sex was not a subject of public discussion as it is today. Then a condom was, so far as we knew, not a sheath for saving lives but a prophylactic against the spoiling of reputations. Then teenage pregnancy was high on the list of subjects not to be openly discussed; and so we said little about the long and mysterious absences of an occasional girl who had suffered an accident on one of our rare adventures with actual, as opposed to fantasized, sex. All things being equal, which they never were, rubbers (the only word we then knew for them) were about sex—plain but hardly simple. But for good boys and girls in the 1950s, rubbers arose mostly on the hush of our talk stimulated by the near perfect absence of occasions for their intended use. A few years after my humiliation in history class, having grown up a bit more, I made friends with a girl down the street. In the years we were friends we never once had sex—by which we meant, in a word few of us knew and none could pronounce, coitus or, in the word we all knew but would seldom utter in mixed company, fucking. The code of silence did not of course quiet our raging desires, but it did put the brakes on how far we were willing to follow them. What we did, my girlfriend and I, was to masturbate each other, several times a week, in the spirit of friendly respect for our technical virginities. Sex education was nearly as useless as rubbers and was, therefore, unheard of. In its place, in the schools there were absurd films about bodily grooming—combing the hair, brushing the teeth, washing the face, avoiding the evil substances. The only one of these that came anywhere close to interesting was a now famous film called "Reefer Madness." But in my crowd, we had even less access to reefers than to sexual intercourse. In such a world, it is no surprise that the public abuse of my rear and nether end would have been taken as a normal, if upsetting, social intercourse between a nasty teacher and an ill-mannered boy. That the intercourse might at some later time be thought of as not only abusive but sexual was as remote as the real thing that kept us up at night.

Even now, one might wonder how the paddling was sexual. Certainly, it was not sexual in the sense that we now know Catholic boys were being sexually abused under the priestly gowns of a refusal to speak of sex as a fact of social life. Of course, then as now, everyone above a certain age was either having it or wishing they could—a fact well documented by the Kinsey reports on sex in America that began to appear from Indiana University in 1948. Even in a conservative Ohio town, there were some who had heard of Sigmund Freud's theories of the deep and universal importance of sexual desire in the human animal. Still, evidence aside, in the little world of my incompletely spent youth, sex was everywhere and nowhere. We thought about it constantly. We talked about it rarely.

Much later, when it had become more acceptable to talk more openly about sex, I was better able to appreciate the sexual undertow of what in my teenage years was considered no more than a routine cruelty of school life. For one, the paddling could have been performed in the privacy of a cloak-room or the principal's office (as they often were). For another, the punishment did not require the exposure of my nether parts to girls and boys alike. Though fully clothed, there was no mistaking the teacher's half-witting intent to attack where I was most vulnerable. A thirteen-year-old boy's fragile hold on self-esteem tends to collapse before the shame arising from even a veiled exposure of his skinny butt and tiny penis. Though the truth of the latter's physical dimensions was not widely known, an ill-formed member was chief among the bodily facts upon which we fixed our dread that we would never come in the embrace of a girl, much less a woman. To force a boy to display that region of his immature body, even if fully clothed, could not have undressed him more. Then too, there was the odd positioning of the punishment. My head was thrust between his legs, ever so close to the teacher's own sexual apparatus. That nasty man knew on some level of his dim wit that the best way to silence a sex-starved adolescent was to expose him as a sissy—which then meant, precisely, a boy of scant potency who, unable to get it on with girls, might as well be queer!

In those days, there was no mistaking the effect the slur queer could achieve. To call a boy queer or a fairy (faggot was far beyond us) was to call into question his very being. Then the word queer and its cognates meant two damning things at once. It called out for public scrutiny the fact that, like everyone else, this one is sexual, yes, but sexual in a perverse hence socially stigmatizing way. To know what a hard-on longed for, but with little hope of properly servicing the need, was for us about as queer an experience as could be. A queer was then, for me and my hetero pals, a terrifying category of sexual limbo the force of which lay in the fear that it applied to us. As for direct knowledge of homosexual boys, we had none. This acute aspect of our innocence was aggravated by a wider culture that silenced public talk of the sexual in its rich array of pleasures and possibilities. We heteros wanted to fuck girls and could not begin to imagine intercourses involving anything but erect penises and juicy vaginas. We knew of course what a blow-job was, but for most this was knowledge decoded from what we overheard from the older boys, for whom, it seemed, the experience was no more than a daring step beyond third base that could be enjoyed without violating the technical limits of virginity. Virginity was defined by a prohibition on the most scarce, hence sacred, of physical intimacies—insertion and ejaculation, which we who took ourselves necessarily to be obligatory heterosexuals thought was the sum and substance of the matter. Sex was *hetero*; *homo* was a queering of the real thing, hence a perversion. What others knew of butt-fucking I cannot say. So much a hetero boy was I that I could not imagine it.

The silent fog hovering over our necessary heterosexuality served, we now know, to protect reputations of far greater global importance than those of nice girls. Today, the sexual code of silence is an element in the enforcement of *heteronormativity*—the cultural norm whereby heterosexual practices are considered not just "normal" but essential to the moral health of society. Now, when I try to explain this idea in the vulgar language of my youth, it seems opaque and absurd. The logic (if that is the word) is, roughly, that homosexual practices pose a threat to the heterosexual family which, in turn, would collapse under the moral gravity of the alleged perversion; which collapse would lead in short order to a decline in the moral culture that made America great—great enough to defend the world from communism. As ludicrous as this line of thought may appear on the surface, one must respect its staying power. Astonishingly, globalizing heteronormativity is still widely held as truth, long after the communists have more or less disappeared, after even America has risen to unparalleled global power, even after the heterosexual family of two parents living together with two kids in a suburban house has itself nearly disappeared from the surface of the earth, save as a dream of what once was.

When people think this way they are involved in something vastly more serious than a mere prejudice. They are thinking in truly global terms.

Globalization is about many, many things, as anyone alert to the news these days realizes. But even about sex? One might suppose the proposal of a connection of this kind is just another sociological extravaganza—a wild scheme for pulling anything and everything under the tent of social things.

Yet, there is a connection that bears investigation because, among the social things it ties together, is the surprising way that global realities led not so long ago to a transformation in the use of the notorious slur. Relatively early in the 1980s, a series of events were set in motion that, by the end of that decade, would cause the word *queer* to become a banner of defiance. But this move was far more than a taking back of the power to tell the world who and what queers were. Pride was cut by fear and anger—outrage at what was evidently a new and extremely dangerous development in the heteronormative silence. Queer politics began in 1990 as a deadly serious assault on the silence then surrounding a discovery that would change the course of global history.

The event was the discovery that a virus, previously limited to animal populations, had crossed over into the human. In 1982, after several cases had been diagnosed the year before, the disease was named Acquired Immune Deficiency Syndrome—AIDS. Two years later, the virus itself was named HIV, for Human Immunodeficiency Virus. In time, it was discovered that the crossover into human populations occurred first in Haiti, Africa, and the United States sometime in the 1970s. In the years since, the rate of infection and the number of deaths worldwide have grown exponentially. By 2004, the number of cases worldwide had reached more than 40 million. In that year alone, there were 5 million new cases and 3 million deaths, many of them children—a rate that represents an increase over the already high levels in the previous years.

Before advances were made in the knowledge of this global epidemic, the causes of its spread, and the treatments that allow those suffering the infection to live longer and productive lives, those at risk began to develop political strategies. From the early 1980s, gay-health groups, particularly in San Francisco and New York, began to press for governmental funding for research, education, and care for those infected. By 1990, AIDS activism, fighting an uphill struggle against leaders who wanted nothing to do with what they narrow-mindedly considered a moral failure of gay sex,[69] came out in the open as a radical social movement, of which the most striking umbrella term was Queer Nation. At that point, the one-time slur became a rallying cry in a global assault on repressive heteronormativity. Worse even than the prolonged sexual silence of earlier generations, the new movement took aim on the particular prejudice of the culture against other-than-straight sexual practices. This was crucial because the refusal to acknowledge the global AIDS epidemic was, more then than now, meant to maintain the cloak of sexual silence by defining it ignorantly as a disease of gay sexual practices—thus a disease of the morally deficient. The ignorance of the heteronormal culture was killing millions. The response to the crisis was *queer politics*—a more general name for the many expressions of radical politics of the kind associated with Queer Nation. Queer politics soon became a prominent part of a global movement.

It may seem too improbable to be true but the apparent historical facts are that a disease, AIDS, that was (and to some still is) thought to be a gay man's disease is, in fact, a global epidemic of many causes—one that has spread unabated since its beginnings among humans around 1980. Queer politics, it might be said, began in earnest out of concern for gay men who were exposed to the virus, but its global power derived from the gradual dawning of the reality that all men and women, whatever their sexual practices, were at risk. Not coincidentally, the dawning of the AIDS threat came to be an accepted fact of global life in the 1990s—when, just precisely, globalization came into its own as a way of thinking about the oddity of postmodern times. Globalization theorists do not normally consider AIDS a major factor among the changes in the global situation. Still, the striking fact is that globalization became a buzzword at almost exactly the same time when queer politics, joining with (and in many ways challenging) world health officials, forced acceptance of the harsh reality of AIDS. The epidemic lent gravity to the single most unsettling fact of the new global realities—that social differences among the peoples of the world are, at one and the same time, both more familiar and more threatening.

These, then, were among the first indications of the extent to which globalization queers social things. For most of its history since the last decades of the nineteenth century, sociology thought of social things as organized by the salient and enduring structures of a given society. Though it was not always stated in so many words, American sociologists would speak of "society" with American social structures in mind—with, that is, the cultural and social things that were to be found in a specific territory in North America defined by the political terms set down by the United States of America. A society was understood as the social things of a nation-state. For most of their histories modern cultures developed primarily within the confines of the nation-states—or, more simply, within the national cultures unique to various states. Sociologists for the longest while spoke of "society" as an obviously very large social thing of general and indefinite effect. When pressed to say where this society was they were forced to give the example of one or another national society. Even then, this was an odd thing to do because all national societies have always been dependent on an international system of states constituting the modern world system. Sociologists were willing to pretend that the world system was somehow less important than the national society in which social things take place—and to an extent, this was a reasonable way to think. Until, that is, global things began to intrude on the national societies. America is still a salient and enduring national society, but today it is impossible to think of it without thinking of its odd position in the global system—as the world's most powerful military power that is nevertheless unable to keep itself safe from attack at home or wars abroad. Among other ways that global things queer the social things of national societies is that, just as the nations cannot keep the terrorists from blowing up their towers or trains, nor can they keep out a virus that kills without prejudice or the carbon residues that choke the air. The AIDS virus carries no passport.

Put differently, *globalization* is a name for the experience that all persons on earth are related to each other in any number of ways without being able to imagine themselves as the family of a global sort they are. While it is usually thought that televisual media—including film, television itself, and the Internet—are chiefly responsible for this bizarre uncertainty of a certain human bond, it is just as likely that the media are no more than the messengers of the bad news. Whatever else media do, they make it impossible for anyone, wherever they are, to remain ignorant of the risks abroad on the planet. Starvation, global warming, joblessness, and poverty are surely among the more evident, but so too is the global disease of the twenty-first century—AIDS. Anyone making a global map in the early 2000s could plot the global spread of poverty and HIV in virtually the same social places—Africa, Haiti, the poorest parts of Asia, the poorest cities in the first world, the poorest quarters of the best cities.

Whatever good may come from globalization, the one hard-to-get-around fact is that it puts us all in the same boat—a boat vastly more significant than the little and silly one of my sexually charged teenage group. The human boat may not include everyone—and it is not safe from those who would sink it, any more than it is assured of finding anywhere in the world a safe harbor—but it has at least the wonder of confronting the variety of human beings with the facts of their shared risks. This is something importantly new, which may be why so many refuse to climb on board.

⟨∞⟩

On average, what people want to do when faced with a risk like AIDS is to hide from it. Avoiding the facts of AIDS was, in large part, what queer politics and world health officials had to fight in the 1980s and 1990s. Their work was, however, made all the more difficult because the threat from which people sought to run was not at all what they believed. People who are HIV-positive, thus at risk of dying from AIDS, are infected in many ways other than gay sex.

By the 2000s, it had become clear that, worldwide, heterosexual women are most likely to be infected. Whenever sexually active people fail to practice safe sex they are at risk, no matter how or with whom they seek their pleasures. This now is a day when those rubbers of my youth came out from under the hush. Condoms are now a matter of life and death. For the first time, perhaps, in the history of prudery in the modern world, homo- and heterosexual people are, if not exactly joined as one, forced to think of themselves as in the same boat. This, in itself, has not put an end to the global wish to hide from the facts of life. Not only do millions, in most and various cultures, still refuse to practice safe sex, many refuse to accept the hard truth that AIDS is not a disease of the morally deficient. The fearful are inventive as they look for reasons to hide. In this case, they still believe that gay men get sick because of the perversion of their sexual practices, which the ignorant have been taught to think of as a result of promiscuity. Never mind that there is no evidence that gay and lesbian people are any more inclined toward promiscuity than are the straight and narrow, the ill-informed theory is readily available for application to heterosexuals. They too, goes the prejudice, are sick because they mis-behave sexually. A variant to the false theory of moral deficiency is attributed to those infected by the sharing of drug needles. There is little to be done when people insist on their moral superiority. Yet, even many of those people are forced to pause before the fact that anyone in contact with infected blood can be exposed. Early in 1992 the predominantly heteronormal world of sports was shocked to learn that Arthur Ashe, one of the world's most admired athletes, was HIV-positive. The one-time tennis champion had been infected from a blood transfusion during surgery several years before. He died in 1993, still a young man. No one ever thought of Arthur Ashe as sexually promiscuous. His infection was an accident of the modern world. Though advances have been made in preventing infections like Ashe's, and in protecting and keeping alive babies and others who are HIV-positive, the risk remains. Still, even when the risks are global there will always be those who run and hide.

Hide and seek is a near-universal game among children at an early stage in their emotional development. But children who play at hiding understand that they will be sought out, and some even enjoy the thrill of being outed from their hiding places. Why is it then that so many grown-ups make of their lives a continuous game of hiding in which they do *not* want to be found? As it happens, queer politics has begun to help us understand this most remarkable fact of the human condition—that false consciousness, whatever its cause, is common and dangerous. Among the aspects of the homosexual life that queer politics began to transform is the tactic of hiding as a way of avoiding the violence with which heteronormals discredit and attack gay people—hiding, that is, by *passing* as if one were straight. The term associated with this, sometimes realistic hiding, is the *closet*—one of those political and cultural expressions where the "the" is important. *The closet* is of course not really a closet so much as a figure of speech that points to the harsh reality that when people are at risk of abuse, one of the necessary responses may be to hide themselves—to pretend that they are "perfectly normal" to representatives of the world who put them at risk. And this is a very different kind of hiding from the smug superiority of those who pretend they know better and are better.

As Steven Seidman (b. 1947), author of *Beyond the Closet: The Transformation of Gay and Lesbian Life* (2002)[70] and one of America's most important sociologists in the queer theory tradition has shown, the closet, apart from being necessary, can also necessarily be a place of productivity—one hides to gather the creative and political energy to come out to engage, sometimes to change, the world. This is an indication of the newfound honesty about the facts of social and sexual life that queer politics has brought into the open—or *outed*.

Queer theory is the cultural movement, largely (but not exclusively) engaged in by academic social theorists, that is devoted to thinking through the intellectual implications of queer politics. Many queer theorists might not see their work as having a political origin (theorists, whether queer or not, tend to be cautious about politics), but queer theory has shattering implications for the way academics conduct their scholarly work. Ironically, one of the key terms in queer theory is, again, the closet. Even when the expression is not used, queer theory is concerned with uncovering the hidden in the way people and their cultures operate. And this striking fact of queer theory is, as we shall see, one of the ways globalization can be interpreted as itself a queer thing. As is often the case, the words used to describe social things come into play rather late in the history of the actual social things. Queer theory and globalization both came into use at about the same time—during and just after 1990, even though a growing awareness of the events that came to be described by these terms had been around for a good while, back at least to the 1960s.

Today, it is very often said that the founder of queer theory was Michel Foucault (1926–1984), a French social historian who died of AIDS in 1984. Foucault, though openly gay, was not originally interested in studying topics that could be labeled gay, queer, or even sexual. Yet, throughout his short life, Foucault's thinking was, in effect (if not self-consciously), queer—that is, queer in the original use of the word: the act of *queering* established assumptions. *To queer*, as many have recently noted, is, simply put, to upset the apple cart of normal expectations. This meaning of the word fell away in time, especially after the 1920s when homosexuality was defined as a sickness or a moral lapse. It was then that queer came into use as a slur for those who did not enjoy heteronormal lives—queer in the sense of abnormal or perverse. In effect, Foucault's many books used historical evidence to queer prevailing assumptions as to the nature of the modern world's most respected institutions—the hospital, the mental health system, criminal justice system, and, even, the social sciences were chief among his subjects. Foucault did this work before *queer* reverted to its original sense as a queering of the normal. Still, few did more than he to demonstrate the importance of queer theory as a queering of modernity's false promises.

Foucault did not take modern society at face value. He studied the hidden causes of what appeared obvious to normals. In this respect, his method was similar to those of Marx and Freud. Marx said that modern capitalism, far from improving the economic and social prospects of the poor, was just as exploitative as the feudalism it replaced. Freud, likewise, was famous for saying that modern people were no more reasonable than any others because all humans were driven as much by their unconscious desires as by their conscious decisions. In a similar way, Foucault argued that modern culture, in spite of its boast that it is a culture of reason and knowledge, was no less interested in power and domination than any other culture. That is quite a claim, especially when one compares modern societies to the overt cruelty of slave societies and the misery of peasants under feudal ones. For Foucault the only difference between the traditional and the modern is that the modern world uses culture and knowledge to exercise power to control people. For example, hospitals and prisons when they were organized in the eighteenth century were thought of as institutions that could bring people back into bodily and social health. Today, we in America know better, certainly with respect to prisons and mental hospitals, which are so evidently lock-ups with few rehabilitative programs. What Foucault showed was that from their beginnings the modern hospital, the rehabilitative prison, the mental health system, even the public education system were in fact organized to instill in patients, the incarcerated, and the general public a sense of themselves as members of a gentle and progressive society. Prisons have long since given up the promise of remaking inmates into moral citizens. But the so-called health care system and the educational system linger on to sort the ill and the poor out as inferior members of the social community. It is not so much that the poor are forced to attend lousy public schools as that, whatever schools they go to, they are taught to think of themselves as good but unfortunate citizens, which means learning to behave in ways that led them to be excluded.

As class clowns go, I was the lucky one. I got my ass kicked more than a few times, but I was the doctor's boy, which I now know gave me a pass from the most severe punishment—assignment to the workshop classes and exclusion from the college prep courses. I had average grades but still I went to college. Others of my pals, like the one with whom I first discussed the meaning of rubbers, were unlucky. He was no more a clown than I. I was no more intelligent than he. But Stevie was from the other side of an already unimpressive town. His father ran the gas station. Stevie worked there on weekends and nights and had little time for schoolwork. He did poorly in school. His clown act was meant to hide his sense of failure, as mine was to cover my embarrassment at who I was. Stevie and I both started our little circus acts in class for much the same emotional reasons. But the social consequences were as different as could be. He dropped out of school when he turned sixteen. I saw him but once after that when he checked the oil and filled my gas tank of the new Ford my father gave me when I turned sixteen. I never went to his station again. It was too awkward. He had no time to joke around about getting laid. Years later, I heard that his father had died, the station closed, and Stevie had moved on. No one knew where, or cared. This is how culture does its dirty work. Somehow Stevie, like all the Frankies and Hallway Hangers of the world, got the idea that he was destined for a life of hard work, fated to come home with hands dirty from the grease of his social exclusion.

Foucault's most famous concept was *power/knowledge*—a concept formed by the putting together of two words "power" and "knowledge"—usually considered separate and opposing social forces. In this modern world, power is in knowledge and culture. Thus all of the modern world's proclamations of social progress based on ever-expanding knowledge applied as social technology to solve social and economic problems is, according to Foucault, no more than a subtle ruse masking the underlying fact that in the modern world there are just as many poor and miserable human beings as ever before. And nowhere is this shocking fact more evident than in the numbers of children who are not educated and the number of AIDS patients who are not cared for. We know how to teach children, as we know how to prevent infection or to slow the effects of HIV, but we teach and treat mostly, if not quite only, those in the more comfortable and familiar classes. You do not have to study the statistics to know that the average schoolgirl who attends, say, an elite university is going to have a better chance in life than one who attends beautician school nights while clerking at the drugstore during the days. The two end up differently but the remarkable fact is that the girls with the lesser lives seldom rebel as one might expect them to. This obvious fact of the world can only mean that the way power works is by getting into the thinking of moderns to cause them to believe that their new world is very much better and more "humane" than in fact it is. The result is that people are subjected to the authority of ruthless leaders dressed up in fine costumes. Whether they are Nazi enforcers or nasty teachers or greedy corporate executives, what remains is that the masses of people follow the orders that lead them to death or economic misery, rebelling seldom against the unfairness in plain sight. Some, like Frankie and Stevie or the One Stop butcher, even learn to blame themselves for their failure when it is really the fault of the society.

As you can see, especially if you were to compare the outlines of Foucault's thinking to the ideas of C. Wright Mills (who died before Foucault came to prominence), Foucault was at least a practical sociologist and very plausibly a professional one without the name. His work was to reveal the hidden structures of modern society; and, though the word had not come into use by the time he died in 1984, Foucault's unnamed sociology of modern life queered the false claims of modern culture. Foucault, thus, advanced the insights of Freud and Marx and others, who, in effect if not in name, were engaged in the work of outing modernity's claims to superiority over other cultures. Nowhere was Foucault's queer theory more in evidence than in the project to which he devoted the last years of his life, a history of modern sexuality. Foucault's *History of Sexuality, An Introduction* (1976), the first of several books on the subject, opens with a revealing statement:

> For a long time, the story goes, we supported a Victorian regime, and
> we continue to be dominated by it, even today. Thus the image of the

imperial prude is emblazoned on our restrained, mute, and hypocritical sexuality.

—Michel Foucault, *History of Sexuality* (1976)[71]

You would have thought he was talking about me and my teenager friends and the foolish contradictions of our sexual practices. And, in a sense, he was. Foucault's social history of sex was, like his other works, an outing, or queering, of the hypocrisy of modern sexual attitudes (of which none is more dishonest than the American ones).

Foucault, in addition to his brilliant writings and public lectures, was involved in political work on behalf of gay and lesbian rights. The pressures of being a celebrity in Paris were so great that he took to trips abroad, particularly to California. He sought relief in the sexual freedoms of pre-AIDS San Francisco and these encounters may have led to his infection and his death by AIDS in 1984. This was still well before queer theory came into its own, even before it was known just how global the threat of AIDS was. Still, it is clear that, like the kind of sociological imagination C. Wright Mills proposed, Foucault meant to describe the social structures that caused the personal troubles of homosexuals in a hypocritical heteronormal culture. His work told a story that queers the powerful myth of Victorian prudery. Foucault's study of modernity's code of sexual silence is, in fact, the story of the underbelly of the official Victorian one. The silence and caution imposed on public talk about sex was actually a cover for the countless occasions in modern life in which men and women, boys and girls, are actively encouraged to talk and think about sex.

When I was a schoolboy, those irritating and silly health class films about good grooming and brushing one's teeth were, it turns out, not prudish at all. Though they did not use the word sex, they were all about controlling our sexual behaviors. We were being taught, in the most subtle of ways, that we must keep our clothes clean, our hair tidy, and our breathe fresh because only in this way could we hope to be "popular." Teachers may not have all been as evil as the one who paddled me, but they could not have missed our sexual itch. They knew, I am certain, that you need only get a teenager interested in being popular and sex will come to his mind. The power was in the unstated but transparent practical knowledge—*If you want to have sex, better keep clean. Good girls don't go with dirty boys.* Not able to "have it," we dressed up, washed up, and paraded about as if we had. Conversely, since having it could make us "dirty," we in fact didn't have what little we could. All this prudery is changed today. Or is it? If when an urge meets an opportunity, all you can think about is condoms, it may not call the passion to a halt, but it does affect the desire. Some don't; some do. But the method of control is the same. Those who don't, don't. Those who do—do so much of it that they are inclined to rebel less against the authorities, which leads them, like Stevie, to hopeless lives of economic failure, which, according to Foucault, is where the powers want the social cast-offs to end up.

It is not difficult to see now that the *kind* of sex "the other Victorians," as Foucault put it, are encouraged to talk about is hetero-sex. And this, in a nutshell, is how heteronormativity was encouraged and built up and how it maintains itself in our time. On the surface, the silence (never total) was meant to define normal sex as hetero-sex in the marital bed—a sex that needed no further explanation because all of the romance stories of classic literature were hetero-stories: of "normal" boys and girls like Romeo and Juliet who would never think of making love (much less sex) with their own sexual kind. We were encouraged to think about heterosexual popularity, even when we could not speak of it. Nothing was ever—even remotely—said of the fact that most of us, when we thought of getting laid, could only think of a hetero-lay. The silence spoke volumes.

Sex is everywhere, constantly coming to mind. Because of this, our silence on the subject may serve somebody's idea of a Good Society. Michel Foucault was one of the first to expose the powerful and terrible effects of a cultural system that teaches kids to hate their sexual desires. In this respect, at least in my day, those who grew up to discover their gay identities were in the same boat. In a weird way, they may have been, as kids, better off. We heteros were taught that sex was, well, okay, but we were not to have any of it. Boys my age who would come to discover their homosexuality must have been doubly confounded by these well-coded instructions in hetero-culture. At least they didn't have to worry about the girls. But then they must have worried about why they weren't worried about getting girls.

Then, after 1982, all this changed. Heteros and homos soon enough found themselves in same boat, one drifting toward the dangerous waters of infection and death.

Michel Foucault was not the first to queer the modern code of silence, nor was he the last. As is often the case, Foucault and those of his day and since who took up the practice of outing the myths of modern culture were at least as much responding to changes in the world as they were giving vent to their individual genius. No social thinker, whether practical or professional, will have anything to think if she is not somehow responding to what is going on in the world that always comes to her through the encounters of daily life. Someone refuses our party card, another touches us tenderly on the leg, another cuts our pay or paddles our butts, and so on. In these encounters, the structure of social things comes in our faces. We are not taught so much as twisted and torn, stimulated and pleased, by them. And so it happened that in the years between the discovery of AIDS in 1982 and the coming out of queer politics in 1990, there was a gradual evolution of many different social and cultural movements under many different names—movements that, in time, had the similar effect of calling into doubt the ideals defining allegedly normal social behavior.

In 1990, for example, there appeared a book that quickly became one of the most influential academic books of its time. Its title is *Gender Trouble: Feminism and the Subversion of Identity*.[72] Its author, Judith Butler (b. 1957), currently is a professor of rhetoric at the University of California at Berkeley. As Foucault was, Butler is openly gay. Like him, her many books are often unsettling for their reach into areas from which many would rather hide. Like Foucault, the question of sexuality (as distinct from sex plain and simple) is a theme in Butler's work. Also, like Foucault's, Butler's work has a powerful sociological effect, whether or not she is considered a sociologist. But the differences are important. In many ways, Butler and many other feminist and queer theorists of the 1990s and since have developed many of the finer points that were just coming into their own in Foucault's time. For example, in the 1970s, when Foucault was beginning his research on sexuality, many feminists like Dorothy Smith were developing the concept of the *feminist standpoint*, which is another way of pointing to the importance of a person's *subject position* in influencing both *how* and *what* she knows.

Feminists in the 1970s explored the reality of women's experience as different, yes, but also as a powerful source of social knowledge. Man knows things one way, woman another. The difference is the experience. One may not be better than the other; but a woman's subject position allows her to know the world in important ways that men, who are more often trained to look down on the world from their higher and mightier social positions, cannot conceive. Men tend to think of social things as objects; women tend to think of them as practical experiences. To be sure, there are some men who think the other way sometimes—and women who think as men, though this is most often because they feel they must pass as men-thinkers in a man's world in order to survive, even when they know better. The differences are less striking today, but in the 1970s they were still rather stark, which is why earlier feminists made quite a splash when they wrote from and about their experiences as women. Yet, even these earlier feminists ran aground of their own insights. Some, if not Dorothy Smith, tended to forget that a woman's standpoint, while different, may not always be superior. This was a thought that first occurred when they encountered lesbian feminists whose experiences were, of course, different in one way and, a little later, when they encountered feminists who were anything but white who most certainly had experiences of still another kind.

One of the more famous other-than-white-or-straight feminists of the 1980s was Gloria Anzaldúa (1942–2004) who, in addition to being a poet, described herself according to her several social experiences—as Chicana, Tejana Indian, lesbian, *and* feminist. Her best-known book, *Borderlands/La Frontera: The New Mestiza* (1987), is a poetic exploration of the social experiences of those from the American Southwest who cannot and choose not to think of themselves as any one thing. They may not be lesbian, or feminist, but at the least many of them are today descendants of the indigenous people who were conquered by the Spanish, who knew Mexico as their cultural home but whose ancestors were stranded in the United States after 1848 when Mexico was forced by the Americans to give up its northernmost territory—including New Mexico and Texas, where Anzaldúa spent a good bit of her life. These were the geographic borderlands that cut and divided her interior sense of who she was. Anzaldúa wrote as a poet but thought, again, as a practical sociologist when she told personal stories to call attention to her experiences shared with others, most especially the experience of living with and between borders. One of the more amusing stories in that book is of her encounter as a lesbian with naive heteronormals:

> In a New England college where I taught the presence of a few lesbians threw the more conservative heterosexual students and faculty into a panic. The two lesbian students and we two lesbian instructors met with them to discuss their fears. One of the students said, "I thought homophobia meant fear of going home."
>
> —Gloria Anzaldúa, *Borderlands/La Frontera* (1987)[73]

Instead of laughing at the girl who mistook the fear of homosexuals for the fear of going home, Anzaldúa embraced this queer interpretation of homophobia. As a woman of many identities—as many ways of thinking of herself as there are experiences that shaped her—Anzaldúa understood the fear of going home. Any individual who takes seriously her experiences—all of them—will, if she is honest, be led to explore more than, even, her experiences as a woman or a lesbian. She will have to take them all in, which will have the effect of experiencing of herself as a coming together of social differences that meet at artificial borders. All women experience their worlds, but a Chicana lesbian will experience hers very much differently from, say, hetero and white Darlene Loving of Cincinnati in the 1950s, with whom I never really got to first base. And if one embraces all the experiences that make her who she is and can be, where is home? How do you go home? And what becomes of home when those who you thought were keeping a room for you won't let you in because you are queer, or radical, or too educated for a woman, or too gringo, or too Indian, and so on?

Judith Butler went beyond even Anzaldúa. One difference is that Butler writes unashamedly as an academic. Some may find *Gender Trouble* a difficult read, but no one could mistake its main point as in tune with the experiences of many feminists who in the 1980s attempted to come to terms with a woman's standpoint and found that it was not one thing but many. Butler's idea is well introduced by a story with which she began an essay written about the time *Gender Trouble* was published:

> When I spoke at a conference in 1989 I found myself telling my friends beforehand that I was off to Yale to be a lesbian, which of course didn't mean that I wasn't one before, but that somehow, then, as I spoke in this context, I was one in some more thorough and totalizing way, at least for the time being.

> —Judith Butler, "Imitation and Gender Insubordination" (1991)[74]

It is one thing to chose to speak about one's identity; it is quite another to be asked to speak about *one* dimension of one's experience. In a way, this is the other side of the coin of Anzaldúa's experience at some other New England college. If one is honest with herself, then to be, say, a "professional" lesbian is not to be a real person. In the same way she makes a joke of the people who want her to be a lesbian, Butler describes gender itself as trouble of a broader and more significant kind.

Butler begins *Gender Trouble* with a recollection from her childhood days of the irony I too experienced. Making trouble, like insulting a teacher, got one in trouble. But then Butler, being a troublemaker of a special kind, adds, "I concluded that trouble is inevitable and the task [is] how best to make it, what best way to be in it."[75] This was a clever way of introducing her queer theory of gender, which is that gender is trouble because it is not so much a given natural state of sexual being as a continuous performance of gender possibilities. If a lesbian can go to Yale to play the lesbian, so too a straight boy can go to high school to play the boy, which is exactly what

we one-dimensional white boys did in my youth. There is, she says, no original and fixed gender or sexuality—only the ways we perform ourselves when
in the presence of others, sometimes stripped naked for sex, more often
dressed up in the search for it. You may not fear going home, but you know
that when one goes off to be a lesbian or a feminist or a white guy or whatever one might be going off to be, there is no home there. The trouble with
home is that we are led to believe we will always have one, and thus to ignore
the incredible fact that only the lucky ones have a home and then only for
the early years of life. After that they join the mass of those who never do
have a home. As Canadian sociologist and cultural critic Audrey Sprenger
(b. 1969) says in her new book *Home Goings*,[76] home is the stories we tell of
a place in the world. Thus, the trouble gender and sex make are nothing
more than a queering of the hope of finding ourselves cuddled before the
maternal fireplace, the fire of which had actually gone out even before we
began to worry about our hetero or homo ways.

Butler's gender trouble is the trouble of taking seriously the experience
of being whichever identities may come together after the home fires have
died out. Hence the irony of taking experiences with others for what they
are—one is no longer able to be completely confident of who she is exactly.
The self has no single home, which is not the same thing as being homeless. Gender, Butler says, when it is understood as a series of performances,
is itself an unsettling thing. Whether a practical or professional sociologist,
one cannot help but think about the differences between himself when he
is, say, dressed up for work first thing Monday morning and, perhaps, when
dressed up in drag for a Halloween ball. Which is the original me? Are not
both? And if both, then neither?

Butler goes on to point out that the gay practice of dressing up as the
other is, in sexual practice if not in the bodily detail, a kind of reversal of
the closet—*drag* is the performance whereby an individual who is gay queers
the heteronormal expectation that, lacking a desire for vaginas, his desire
to dress as a woman is not at all a betrayal of the man he is expected to be as
a statement that we are what we are as we encounter the troubles of life
without a home and of a life without a fixed and single identity. To make
oneself up or over sexually is to perform the most human of roles—that of
one who is not limited by sex or gender or any other of the attributes by
which the cultured powers divide and conquer us. To be queer is vastly more
than to be sexual in a certain way; nor is it, when being sexual, to pass as
though one were pretending to be heterosexual by being, say, butch or the
dominant sexual partner. There are no originals, says Butler. There is no
necessary normal when it comes to sex or gender. Life, like sex and gender,

is necessarily a performance. To be gay is to be in drag; but then, so too is being straight. To be a social being is necessary drag. If true to our selves (plural) then to live with them is to be queer because, in their comings and goings, our many selves queer each other.

It may seem that queer theory has nothing whatsoever to do with globalization—except when you consider that global experience is a migratory one. It is living according to global methods that take one away from a native home to others that never truly become home. And the migration can happen without going anywhere at all except into the worlds within. Anzaldúa's formative experiences were shaped by social structures long dead in the time of history but very much alive in her day-to-day life. Global struggles between the English and Spanish in the seventeenth and eighteenth centuries for control of North America and America's drive to become a global power in the nineteenth century were among the, to her, invisible structural forces that shaped the conflict between Mexico and the U.S. Southwest in 1848 that took away the home of her great grandparents. These invisible struggles may be present to people in Gloria Anzaldúa's subject position in no more than a ghostly way—in the architecture of the Southwest, in the languages she and others speak (English, Mexican, and various native dialectics), in the shared awareness of the barbed wire border between Mexico and the Southwest, in the foods and music, in the stories of a past none experienced but all can remember. This is what it means to be a new mestiza—a person of the mixed cultural and personal borderlands whose identities are more a coming and going than a sure thing. This is exactly what Judith Butler means by the subtitle of her book *Gender Trouble: Feminism and the Subversion of Identity*. When one takes hard account of her identity in this world, she finds not a fixed core of a singular self but an interesting if hard-to-manage instability of unsettling borders. And this precisely is where the queer theory and politics are part and parcel of globalization—and why the queer awareness of AIDS in 1990 is so closely linked to the first uses of the word globalization.

We sometimes think that words are no more than signs for naming real things. When it comes to social things, however, worlds are often the things that give rise to their names, or to words. The term *queer* came into a new and powerful use because the worlds in which people lived were themselves queer. AIDS was an important factor in the queering of social things but it was far from the only one. The mysterious role of the media, televisual, and personal telecommunications systems may not in fact be the technological miracles they are often said to be. They are wonders, to be sure; but they are wonders that broadcast realities. The complaint often heard of local evening news is that it is all about murder and crime, never about the good people do. True; but in this world (perhaps in most worlds, but certainly in this one) ordinary goodness is boring. Violence, sex, war, and poverty are news because, in a literal sense, they are usually new to the local eye and ear.

Imagine Abdelkrim's grandparents in the foothills of the Atlas mountains in Morocco. Their lives were not comfortable, and this is why Abdelkrim and others like him left home to search for a better home. But, however boring, even painful, may be the lives of people in small rural villages swept by sand in the summers and snows in the winters, they are at least places they can think of as home. When the children leave they do not necessarily fear going home—unless, that is, they take upon themselves the honest differences they usually discover while living in a worldly city. Still, even a home place in this idealized sense of "back there where I came from" is an illusion arising on the wish that life could be simpler.

Homophobia, in the sense Anzaldúa's student mistook it, is in fact a common experience when people like Abdelkrim must make their homes in one or another of the global cities that, even more than Casablanca, welcome the pilgrims who have used global methods to look for a home to replace the one they left. Abdelkrim, so far as I know, has yet to leave his native Morocco as Mr. Alsahybi left Yemen. One wonders which home may have gone through Mr. Alsahybi's mind as he lay dying in his shop in Brooklyn. This I cannot know. I do know what home Florence Lyons thought of before she slipped into a terminal coma. I was there. She was thinking of Plant City, Florida, where a few cousins still lived as she had for a short while. She was also thinking of Cincinnati—of the members of her Zion Baptist Church, which had been a home of sorts for most of her adult life (and whose members and ministers she found, on margin, irritating). She thought also of the home she had made with me off and on over the same span, of the houses she had owned in the West End. In one sense, the stories of Florence's homes were more like Gloria Anzaldúa's. Both had migrated more or less within the same national space, always with access to a familiar set of normal expectations. Florence was hetero, Gloria was proudly homo—but it was not their sexual practices that might have joined them, nor was it any single shared experience. They shared no experiences directly, save for one. They were both—like Mr. Alsahybi, and millions of others today the world over—people who found homes not in a single place but in their ability to travel the interior microworlds within—the worlds within where all of us, whether we like it or not, are necessary pilgrims, crisscrossing the borders of our minds.

The reason that I, as a thirteen-year-old boy of unrelenting erections, knew very little beyond my small white and suburbanly adolescent world was not because of my gender. Rather it was because, unlike Florence and these others, I was not required to have a global method. Kids of my day knew little because, having grown up in wartime, we learned to look only at the surface of social things, never below. Had we, it might have occurred to us that queer was a word describing an experience of the worlds—an experience vastly more human and full of life than even the experiences that might have come from inserting erections in some other cavity than the ones we heteros craved.

To be able, today, to enter and live in the many different social experiences that are all about requires a global method indeed. Today, even the preciously privileged must interpret the stories of the far places others can only dream of. And they, too, like anyone looking for a better deal in the world must calculate the odds of getting there solvent and alive. Few are those who are not forced to give up the thought of having a single home. Even if, as rarely happens anymore, we die at the same address we are born to, globalization is the queering of home by the way it makes us travel, in our heads if not with our feet. We must, thus, become homophobic in this other nonsexual sense, which may be why the other homophobes are afraid of people who are not heteronormative.

Globalization is queer because it queers the longing for a settled home. *Globalization*, the word, came into use at about the same time the word *queer* assumed another identity because globalization queered deep parts of the hitherto normal social things. Social things are, as we now know, the factual things proper to societies or social worlds. But, as we now know too, this is at best a rough way of speaking the truth. Global things do not erase the social ones, but they do upset the way one thinks of them. AIDS may not be the only global thing to force people to think about just how insignificant their social differences are. Certainly AIDS is but one of many global events brought home with blinding speed to our local televisual worlds—wars (now almost always world wars), or the changing in global climates (less striking unless you live in Mexico City or Shanghai or any of the global cities where the air is clogged by the fumes of progress), or hunger and poverty (even the well-fed and wealthy cannot ignore the homeless who press them for coins), or others. But the thing about AIDS is that nearly everyone knows that anyone can die from it and that the virus can come to us in the most intimate of social things—the mere act of seeking pleasure or comfort, or whatever we seek on the bad days, in the giving and taking of bodily fluids.

Globalization queers the code of silence that closets sex. It requires us to think differently and to consider that how we think may be different, if not necessarily worse, than how the girl next door thinks. Globalization requires global methods because to live in the sphere of global things is to face the necessity of sizing up who we are as we come up against astonishing others—many of whom, like the gays I unconsciously closeted myself from in 1950, we never knew existed. To know the global others is to make them all, by the sheer multitude of the differences, normal—thus to queer the malicious idea of the abnormal. If nearly everyone is different, then differences are normal and hardly anyone is abnormal. In global times, the so-called abnormals are constantly in our faces and we must face the reality that what we considered normal in 1950 (or whenever it was for you) turns out to be quite hetero. To thus face realities as they are is certainly more than a sexual experience. It comes in our faces from many different sources. The thing about sex, though, is it is one of those social things that exposes us for what we are.

We get naked, the juices flow, parts grow hard, and, like it or not, we are who and what we are, warts and all, with all the whomevers who see us. There is, in that moment, no other home. We are, in that instant, never just one, always many, whatever we suck and whichever cavities we explore for their dollops of pleasure. When it is over, we fall back exhausted as from a long journey to an unknown land where we seek homes better than the ones we left, but never better enough to be the perfect final resting place.

TWELVE

~

LIVING AGAINST
THE CONCLUSION

We all die one day. Some, like my son Matthew and Mr. Alsahybi, will go suddenly and before those who love them are ready. Others will die quietly after long lives, as did Anna Julia Cooper and Florence Brown Lyons. Death may come as we are still hard at life's work, as it did for W. E. B. Du Bois, or after we have left the scene forgotten, as it did for Charlotte Perkins Gilman. Only the very few will choose the precise moment, and then only when some unbearable and useless pain has all but taken the freedom from life. Death comes when it chooses.

The lives we live are lived against that unknowable moment of passing. No one—not even the most privileged—can truly control the final moment, much less the countless ones that reach from the first screech for breath to the final gasp. For the young, these concluding facts of life are absurd, irrational—unless, perhaps, they are long acquainted with grief, as was Matthew. The modern culture of the West is infatuated with youth and scornful of aging because it considers the passing of youth time's harshest measure. If, as Weber taught, the modern West was founded on a social ethic of rational control as the force of human progress, then it is obvious that death, being beyond control, will be feared as the ultimate irrationality. This may be why our culture provides such meager instruction as to the comforting necessity in the promise of dying. Not all cultures hold death at such an anxious distance from daily life. Were death not so terrifying to ours, we might more warmly embrace life itself. I have the idea that Matthew knew death long before he took it on, and that this is what accounted for his robust living.

Life must be lived at the outer envelope, where we are most out of control. This is another of the lessons the Frankies and Black Elks have to teach. The differences between bitter white boys in urban projects and spiritual princes weeping tears of human understanding are superficial at best. Every day and everywhere men and women rage or weep for losses they are powerless to control. It is true, to be sure, that some hold reins to powers that control others. But even the powerful come upon uncertainties of the same kind, if not in the same degree, as those Abdelkrim and others face. It is hard enough to manage the local destinies. The global ones are harder still. Still, this little book of mystery stories has told of men and women, boys and girls, who lived well and did good in the face of events they could not control. No one lives perfectly because no one is given control over the social things that come down from the structured worlds. The most fundamental lesson of the sociological life is that the individual who intends to live well must begin not with grand accomplishment but with the simple acceptance of what comes across the path. Acceptance of the unyielding realities is not passive self-effacement. Rather, it is the personal courage that gives us a chance to imagine the world as it is and might be—to change what we can. Social things are perfectly able to crush the human spirit. But, more often than not, the living are able to take on whatever comes down, resisting or weeping as may be necessary, to fashion lives with others, even on the meager wages of failed dreams. We get on with life, when we do, because personal courage is among the competencies given us. But it is up to us to exercise it—to face the unacceptable realities, to imagine the better possibilities, then to live with those we hate no less than those we love. Such living is not very often neat and pretty.

Truth be told, the sociological life is not a party to which we come scrubbed down and polished up, a proper invitation well in hand, expecting to be received with grace for the little cards we worked so hard to color bright. Most parties have some weird, rough edge; and many turn nasty when the edge of social things cuts too deep. When others have the power—real power, this is—there will be trouble, and someone will get hurt. Do not suppose that imagining and living a world different from the one currently in fashion is a prize easily won.

Thus it is, more times than not, that living the sociological life makes you a rude, improper guest who crashes someone else's well-planned party. When a fully alive sociological imagination enters polite company, it often shocks the established habit or spoils the traditional idea. In a world of global things where good neighbors are murdered for small change, sociological rudeness is far from the worst that could present itself at the doors of the genteel.

The challenge of the sociological life calls from beyond the differences that separate. We live according to local customs, but we live with the structured social things that fence us in with each other. To live in the world, as it is, one must live with others who disturb our peace by their strange songs, or others still who humiliate us with their dirty jokes based upon our differences, who trash our offices or party cards, who ignore our eager hands in math class, who frighten our children in the night, or worse. We are all fellow travelers along the global pathways that require us to speak and act in the unsentimental plural.

In the end, life is always life together. To live is to accept life as it comes with all the bumps and bruises of social differences—the hard realities without which we would cease to be whoever we happen to think we are. The sociological life is a practical work filled with disappointments and surprises. Social living is the courage to accept what we cannot change in order to do what can be done about the rest—thus to enjoy as best we can whatever thrill ride we might be on.

ACKNOWLEDGMENTS
~

Many, many people have helped with this book. I have tried to thank them in the previous editions and will not here repeat the words that remain insufficient, save for several whose special contributions continue. Dean Birkenkamp signed the book and brought it into being. His influence on my work is enormous. Alan McClare, who moved in when Dean left for Paradigm, took up where Dean left off, reading the manuscript closely while tolerating my ways graciously.

Audrey Sprenger came into the mix after the first edition. She has since influenced, if not always changed, my thinking about many aspects of the book. Everything I say here about home stories is from her work that will soon be published in *Home Goings*. Again, I thank Shana Cohen for help with the story of Abdelkrim in chapter 10. She went over every word I wrote of her then not-yet-published book to assure its accuracy—even to the extent of discussing it with Abdelkrim himself. Though I have yet to meet him, I was able to send him a signed copy of the second edition. Shana's work on Morocco appears in *Searching for a Different Future* (2004).

Also, thanks to Doris Wilkinson and her publisher for permission to use the table in chapter 9. It was my pleasure to have visited with her during a time at the University of Kentucky. And to Chet Meeks, in whose memory this edition is dedicated, who died after a long fight with cancer—leaving us all with the benefits of his wisdom and an aching sense of loss. Also, thanks are especially due to Anthony Elliott, Audrey Sprenger, Sam Han, David Stein, Daniel Chaffee, Dan Reif—to mention but a few of the friends who in many ways over a number of years have lent me their thoughts on the several editions of this book. Also I thank individuals whose names I can only guess at who offer the publisher excellent comments for this new edition. I have used nearly all of them and would have used more were I smart enough to figure out how to fit it all into a book that, for good reasons, must remain relatively short. And to Victoria Stahl (again) thanks for advice on the new chapter and other forms of support. Several of them tried to talk me down from some of the sex-talk. None is responsible for what remains.

Every day, in all ways, I give thanks for Geri, Annie, and Noah. We hold each other in the hard times when the poetry fails—and dream the dreams of what might have been and still could be. And Matthew is never far away, his mischievous beauty still glowing on the dawn of times to come.

Charles Lemert
New Haven, Connecticut

NOTES

1. Ryszard Kapuściński, *Imperium* (Random House, 1994), pp. 11–12.

2. See Emile Durkheim, *The Rules of Sociological Method* (1894; reprint, Free Press, 1982), chapter 1. The words given are Durkheim's but they are rephrased for simplicity's sake. They are nearly the same as those used in the preface to his later book, *Suicide* (1897).

3. C. Wright Mills, *The Sociological Imagination* (Oxford University Press, 1959), especially chapter 1.

4. Charlotte Perkins Gilman, *The Yellow Wallpaper and Other Writings* (1892; reprint, Bantam, 1989), p. 4.

5. Charlotte Stetson was born Charlotte Perkins. After divorcing Walter Stetson, she was single for a number of years before marrying George Houghton Gilman, from whom she took the name by which she is best known today (and with whom she enjoyed a long marriage of thirty-four years). I use the first name Charlotte, not out of disrespect, but as a way to refer to those earlier years without having repeatedly to introduce the two other names (Perkins and Stetson) of her young life.

6. Gilman, *Women and Economics: A Study of the Economic Relation between Men and Women* (1898; reprint, Source Book Press, 1970), p. 5.

7. Gilman, *The Yellow Wallpaper and Other Writings*, p. 20.

8. Erving Goffman, *Interaction Ritual* (Doubleday, 1967), p. 45.

9. Anthony Giddens, *The Constitution of Society* (University of California Press, 1984), pp. 41ff.

10. Among other places, see Erving Goffman, *Relations in Public* (Harper Torchbooks, 1971).

11. Pierre Bourdieu, *Outline of a Theory of Practice* (Cambridge University Press, 1977), chapter 2.

12. Ibid., p. 72.

13. Marianne Weber, *Max Weber: A Biography* (Transaction Books, 1988), p. 105. (I have changed the order of the phrase about dueling, but not the words themselves.)

14. Max Weber, "Science as a Vocation," in *From Max Weber*, ed. Hans Gerth and C. Wright Mills (Oxford University Press, 1946), p. 135.

15. On the use of the name Willie, see David Levering Lewis, *W. E. B. Du Bois: Biography of a Race* (Henry Holt, 1993), chapter 3.

16. W. E. B. Du Bois, *The Souls of Black Folk* (1903; reprint, Bantam Books, 1989), p. 2.

17. Ibid., p. 3.

18. Immanuel Wallerstein, *The Modern World System* (Academic Press, 1974).

19. Robert Park quoted in Lewis Coser, *Masters of Sociology Thought* (Harcourt, Brace and Jovanovich, 1977), p. 368.

20. William I. Thomas and Florian Znaniecki, *The Polish Peasant in Europe and America* (1918–19; reprint, The University of Illinois Press, 1984); quoted from a selection in *Social Theory*, ed. Charles Lemert (Westview/HarperCollins, 1993), p. 274.

21. Max Weber, *The Protestant Ethic and the Spirit of Capitalism* (1904–1905; reprint, Scribner's, 1958).

22. Ibid., p. 182.

23. Karl Marx and Friedrich Engels, *Manifesto of the Communist Party* (1948), in *The Marx-Engels Reader*, ed. Robert Tucker (W. W. Norton, 1978), p. 476.

24. Georg Lukács, *History and Class Consciousness*; quoted from a selection in *Social Theory*, ed. Charles Lemert (Westview/HarperCollins, 1993), p. 225.

25. Walter Benjamin, "The Work of Art in the Age of Mechanical Reproduction"; quoted from Lemert, *Social Theory*, p. 277.

26. Karl Mannheim, *Ideology and Utopia*; quoted from Lemert, *Social Theory*, p. 238.

27. For example, Talcott Parsons, *The Social System* (Free Press, 1951).

28. Robert K. Merton, *Social Theory and Social Structure* (Free Press, 1949; revised and enlarged, 1957).

29. Ibid., chapter 4.

30. Facts were provided by Red Cloud Indian School, Pine Ridge, South Dakota, 14 August 1996.

31. *Lakota Times*, 14 September 1995, section B, p. 1.

32. Frantz Fanon, *Black Skin, White Masks* (1952; reprint, Grove Press, 1967), p. 140.

33. Fanon, *The Wretched of the Earth* (1961; reprint, Grove Press, 1968); quoted from a selection in *Social Theory*, ed. Charles Lemert (Westview/HarperCollins, 1993), p. 391.

34. Alvin Gouldner, *The Coming Crisis of Western Sociology* (Basic Books, 1970).

35. Dorothy Smith, "Women's Experience as a Radical Critique of Sociology," reprinted in Dorothy Smith, *The Conceptual Practices of Power* (Northeastern University Press, 1990), p. 21.

36. Nancy Chodorow, *The Reproduction of Mothering* (University of California Press, 1978).

37. Judith Stacey, *Brave New Families* (Basic Books, 1991).

38. Susan Krieger, *The Mirror Dance* (Temple University Press, 1983), p. 169.

39. Charles Tilly, *From Mobilization to Revolution* (Addison-Wesley, 1978).

40. Jay MacLeod, *Ain't No Makin' It: Leveled Aspirations in a Low-Income Neighborhood* (Westview Press, 1987), p. 68.

41. Source of the income figures is the United States Bureau of the Census, Historical Statistics of the United States, and a number of the bureau's Current Population Reports, as reported in *USA by Numbers: A Statistical Portrait of the United States*, ed. Susan Weber (Zero Population Growth, 1988). The figures are based on U.S. Bureau of Census data for 1986 and 1994; and the 1999 United Nations Development Programme, cited in David Held and Anthony McGrew, eds., *The Global Transformations Reader* (Polity Press, 2000), p. 343. The 2002 numbers owe to a widely cited study by Branko Milanovic, who was (and may still be) affiliated with the World Bank.

42. *Black Elk Speaks: Being the Life Story of a Holy Man of the Oglala Sious As Told through John G. Neihardt* (Flaming Arrow) (1932; reprint, University of Nebraska Press, 1979), p. 270.

43. Erving Goffman, *Relations in Public* (Harper Torchbooks, 1971), p. 288 n. 44.

44. Max Weber, "Politics as a Vocation," in *From Max Weber*, ed. Hans Gerth and C. Wright Mills (Oxford University Press, 1946), p. 78.

45. The [Archibald] Cox Commission, *Crisis at Columbia* (Vintage, 1968).

46. Elijah Anderson, "The Code of the Streets," *Atlantic Monthly* 273 (May 1994), pp. 80--83.

47. For example, Jeremy Rifkin, *The End of Work* (G. P. Putnam, 1995).

48. William Julius Wilson, *When Work Disappears* (Knopf, 1996), chapter 2.

49. Herbert Gans, *The Urban Villagers* (Free Press, 1962).

50. Theda Skocpol, *States and Social Revolutions* (Cambridge University Press, 1979), p. 4.

51. Talcott Parsons, "The Kinship System of the Contemporary United States," in *Essays in Sociological Theory* (Free Press, 1954), chapter 9.

52. These and other figures on the world of work are from William Julius Wilson, *When Work Disappears* (Knopf, 1996), chapter 2. The number of new industrial jobs is 100,000, small by contrast, but ever smaller against the need.

53. Ibid., especially pp. 34--35.

54. Ibid., p. 69.

55. The passage quoted appears in a hand note of Cooper's held today in the archives of the Moorland-Spingarn Research Center, Howard University, a facsimile of which appears in Louise Daniel Hutchinson, *Anna J. Cooper: A Voice from the South* (Smithsonian Institution Press, 1982), p. 4. In the passage, the word "sou" is the old French colloquial equivalent for "penny."

56. The letter quoted in Hutchinson, p. 34.

57. James Scott, *Domination and the Arts of Resistance: Hidden Transcripts* (Yale University Press, 1990), p. xii.

58. *Anna Julia Cooper, A Voice from the South* (1982; reprint, Oxford University Press, 1988), p. 30.

59. Ibid., p. 31 (emphasis Cooper's).

60. Ibid., p. 123.

61. Ibid., p. 96.

62. Ibid., p. 145.

63. Patricia Hill Collins, *Black Feminist Thought* (Unwin Hyman, 1990), p. 227.

64. Doris Wilkinson, "The Segmented Labor Market and African American Women from 1890--1960," in *Research in Race and Ethnic Relations*, ed. Rutledge M. Dennis (Jai Press, 1991), p. 6:92.

65. Shana Cohen, *Searching for a Different Future: The Rise of a Global Middle-Class in Morocco* (Duke University Press, 2004). The passage quoted on the next page is from Cohen's 2000 University of California doctoral thesis from which grew the book.

66. In *Texts, Facts, and Femininity: Exploring the Relations of Ruling* (Routledge, 1990), among other places.

67. David Held, Anthony McGrew, David Goldblatt, Jonathan Perraton, *Global Transformations* (Polity Press, 1999), chapter 1.

68. Manuel Castells, *The Rise of the Network Society* (Blackwell Publishers, 1996), p. 477.

69. Special thanks to Chet Meeks for reminding that in the early months of the AIDS panic the then-puzzling infection was temporarily labeled GRID for Gay-Related Immune Deficiency, thus indicating as well the homophobic panic to which it gave rise.

70. Steven Seidman, *Beyond the Closet: The Transformation of Gay and Lesbian Identity* (Routledge/USA, 2002).

71. Michel Foucault, *History of Sexuality, An Introduction* (Random House, 1976), p. 3.

72. Judith Butler, *Gender Trouble: Feminism and the Subversion of Identity* (Routledge/USA, 1990).

73. Gloria Anzaldúa, *Borderlands/La Frontera: The New Mestiza* (spinsters/aunt lute, 1987), pp. 19–20.

74. Judith Butler, "Imitation and Gender Insubordination," in Diana Fuss, ed., *Inside/Out: Lesbian Theories, Gay Theories* (Routledge/USA, 1991), p. 13.

75. Butler, *Gender Trouble*, p. vii.

76. Audrey Sprenger's forthcoming book by Penguin Books, *Home Goings*, is a completely rewritten version of her 2000 University of Wisconsin doctoral thesis, *Place Maps the Sociology of Home*.

INDEX

~

About the Author

~

CHARLES LEMERT (b. 1937) is the John C. Andrus Professor of Sociology at Wesleyan University in Connecticut. He is the author of many books, including *Muhammad Ali: Trickster in the Culture of Irony*; *Postmodernism Is Not What You Think: Why Globalization Threatens Modernity*; *Dark Thoughts: Race and the Eclipse of Society*; *Durkheim's Ghosts*; and *Thinking the Unthinkable*. His most recent book is *Deadly Worlds: The Emotional Costs of Globalization*, with Anthony Elliott.